The
Grief
of God

The
Grief
of God

IMAGES OF THE SUFFERING JESUS
IN LATE MEDIEVAL ENGLAND

ELLEN M. ROSS

New York   Oxford • Oxford University Press 1997

Oxford University Press

Oxford   New York

Athens   Auckland   Bangkok   Bogota   Bombay   Buenos Aires
Calcutta   Cape Town   Dar es Salaam   Delhi   Florence   Hong Kong
Istanbul   Karachi   Kuala Lumpur   Madras   Madrid   Melbourne
Mexico City   Nairobi   Paris   Singapore   Taipei   Tokyo   Toronto

and associated companies in
Berlin   Ibadan

Published by Oxford University Press, Inc.
198 Madison Avenue, New York, New York 10016

Oxford is a registered trademark of Oxford University Press

Library of Congress Cataloging-in-Publication Data
Ross, Ellen M., 1959–
The grief of God: images of the suffering Jesus in
late medieval England / Ellen M. Ross.
p.   cm.
Includes bibliographical references and index.
ISBN 0-19-510451-X
1. Suffering of God—History of doctrines—Middle Ages, 600–1500.
2. God—Mercy—History of doctrines—Middle Ages, 600–1500.
3. Jesus Christ—Crucifixion—Art.   4. Christian art and symbolism—
Medieval, 500–1500—England.   5. Christian literature, English
(Middle)—History and criticism.   6. England—Church
history—1066–1485.   I. Title.
BT153.S8R67   1997
232.96—dc20   96-5502

1 3 5 7 9 8 6 4 2

Printed in the United States of America
on acid-free paper

To Mark

Preface

For the medieval Christians considered in this book, the blood flowing from the wounds of Jesus Christ is the love of God literally poured out onto all humankind. Divine compassion rains down upon humanity in the shedding of Jesus Christ's blood, and viewers are invited, as *The Prickynge of Love* expresses it, to enter into the joy of the Godhead through the bloody wounds of Jesus' flesh. Drawing on artistic, literary, and devotional sources in late medieval England, I explore the transformative power of Jesus' wounded body as it manifests divine presence and love in the world.

The Crucifixion was not an event of the past for the authors and artists considered here; rather, it was a living sign of God's merciful love for humanity. I analyze how medieval persons were brought to new understandings of their relationship to God and to neighbor by encountering the bleeding flesh of the wounded Jesus. I further examine the lived, performative spiritualities by which believers imitated the suffering of Jesus. The spiritual authority gained by imitating the enfleshed God—through sacramental life, prayers for the dead, liturgical role-playing, and even christological self-wounding—enabled medieval Christians to function as powerful advocates for those who were seeking divine mercy.

My study explores the theological complexity and emotional sophistication of medieval piety. My concern is not with medieval theology per se but with analyzing the religious and cultural dimensions of medieval portrayals of the suffering Jesus. The christological images under review here make up a "rhetoric of appeal and response" by which viewers and readers were encouraged affectively to experience the full meaning of God's love definitively demonstrated through the Passion of Jesus.

As the Abingdon Missal's depiction of the Crucifixion (see fig. 2.9) demonstrates, the suffering of Jesus Christ was an act of a trinitarian God's love for humanity. In the Abingdon image, the dying Jesus hangs on the cross, and the dove (the Holy Spirit) hovers above, looking up toward the First Person of the Trinity, the Father. The First Person reaches out his hands, both offering Jesus to the world and receiving Jesus to himself, saying, as *The Mirror of the Blessed Life of Jesus Christ* puts it, "Come my sweet son. . . . I shall embrace you in my arms and take you into my bosom." It was not Jesus Christ's rising from the dead that captivated the imagination of medieval Christians but rather the miracle that God became enfleshed in order to suffer on behalf of humanity. My thesis is that it is the Crucifixion of Jesus that is the focus, one might say the obsession, of late medieval culture: God bled and wept and suffered on the cross to manifest the full mercy of divine compassion.

I thank Syracuse University Press for permission to republish as part of chapter 1 my article, "Suffering, the Spiritual Journey, and Women's Experience in Late Medieval Mysticism," in *Maps of Flesh and Light*, edited by Ulrike Wiethaus (Syracuse, N.Y.: Syracuse University Press, 1993), 45–59, and I thank the American Academy of Religion for permission to republish in chapter 4 part of my article, "Spiritual Experience and Women's Autobiography: The Rhetoric of Selfhood in 'The Book of Margery Kempe,'" *Journal of the American Academy of Religion* 59 (1991): 527–44. I express my gratitude to those whose work and lives have inspired me: Geri and Donald Duclow, Richard Kieckhefer, Ann Matter, Bernard McGinn, Barbara Newman, Virginia Reinburg, and Darice Wallace. I am grateful to my research assistants, Wendy Cadge, Paul Crego, Rachel Graham, Jennifer Lyders, Karina Martin, Elsie Pan, and Cornelia Schütz, and to my many students and friends who have participated in the conversations which engendered this book. I thank the National Endowment for the Humanities, the American Academy of Religion, Boston College, and Swarthmore College for funding travel and leave time to conduct the research that led to the writing of this volume. I am grateful to my friends and colleagues at Boston College and Swarthmore College for their support. I thank Minda Hart at the Interlibrary Loan Office at Swarthmore College and librarians Libby Amann, Nancy Bech, Alison Masterpasqua, Julie Miran, and Steven Sowards for their patience and expertise in processing my book requests. I thank Cynthia Read, Peter Ohlin, and Paula Wald of Oxford University Press for shepherding my work through the publication process, and I thank Natalie Goldstein for her care in copyediting. I am grateful to my siblings—Seamus, for ideas and constant support; Richard, for inspiring creative endeavors; and Therese, for companionship on life's journey—to my parents, Kathleen and Jim, for ongoing encouragement, and to my aunt and uncle, Eleanor and Manny Bairos, for their celebration of life. I thank my children, Katie and Christopher, for the wonder and delight they bring me each day. I dedicate this book to Mark Wallace with appreciation for his painstaking attention to my work and for our ongoing conversations about the Middle Ages; with warm memories of our adventures seeking keys to small parish churches in the English countryside and studying in libraries, well-known and obscure; and with deepest thanks for his poetic and enthusiastic gesture toward life—all of which have made this book possible and have brought joy to the time spent writing it.

Swarthmore, Pennsylvania   E. M. R.
August 1996

Contents

A section of illustrations follows p. 54.

The
Grief
of God

Introduction

The gaze of late medieval England was fixed on the broken body of a wounded and bloody Jesus surrounded by weeping bystanders. Church wall paintings, manuscript illuminations, rood screens, roof bosses, reliquaries, and carvings graphically depict the anguish and pain of the tortured Christ. Sermons recount the agony, dramas reenact it, and spiritual guides counsel their disciples to meditate on the torments of the dying Jesus. In this book, I investigate the graphic Passion images that pervade late medieval English sermons, drama, art, and devotional literature. Two questions orient this study of religion and culture. First, what is the nature of this christological portraiture which shaped the ethos of late medieval England? Second, what lived responses did this portraiture seek to engender? That is, what is the connection in medieval religious life between the wounded Savior and personal transformation, public works of compassion, and even bodily imitation of Jesus' suffering?

From the time of Jesus Christ's own life, and most visibly in the Crucifixion, suffering has been a major theme within the Christian tradition. But attitudes toward suffering and the functions of suffering in the Christian life have changed over time. Contemporary scholarly analyses of the forms of twelfth-century English religious devotion reveal an increasing focus on the humanity of Jesus; by the fourteenth century, depictions of the suffering Jesus were predominant.[1] From the twelfth century to the fourteenth century, a growing number of theological texts pondered the nature and effects of Christ's Crucifixion; in painting and sculpture, depictions of the suffering Christ in agony began to outnumber representations of the majestic Christ of Resurrection and judgment; liturgical dramas reenacted the circumstances of Jesus' Passion and death; and poets lamented the anguish of the suffering Savior and his bereaved followers.[2]

Medieval sermons also became more focused on the theme of the Passion. Preachers, speaking more and more often on this topic in the vernacular, preached not only in churches on Sundays but also on feast days, at festivals, and on other special occasions. They spoke not only from pulpits in churches and cathedrals but also from movable pulpits carried out to churchyards and into town centers or at the site of preaching crosses outside church buildings or at town and city gathering places. Indeed, the preachers themselves often held wooden crucifixes as they preached.[3] Medieval sermonizers were the popular media of their day, and the Passion of Christ was one of their dominant theological themes.

Churchgoers were further surrounded by vivid depictions of Jesus' life, death, and resurrection in the art and architecture of medieval churches.[4] The image-rich environment in which preaching about the suffering Jesus occurred reinforced the christological subject matter of the sermons; even the smallest parish churches in England were often embellished with graphic floor-to-ceiling wall paintings and colorful tapestries chronicling the Passion of Christ. In many churches, huge crucifixes hung on the wall above the pulpit. Preaching crosses were decorated with scenes from Jesus' Passion, and tapestries and painted cloths adorned the movable pulpits. Norwich Cathedral, for example, housed a spectacular fourteenth-century artistic rendering of Christ's Passion.[5] Also, around the turn of the fourteenth century, the pietà, a new form of religious portrayal of the suffering Savior, emerged. Fascination with the relics of Jesus' suffering increased, and artistic representations of the instruments of Christ's Crucifixion multiplied—all indicative of increasing attention to the humanity of Jesus and, even more specifically, to the Passion and death of Jesus Christ.[6] Blood drips from this Savior's gaping wounds—torment and anguish abound—and yet all of this, in literature and art, claimed to nourish the spiritual life and to stir people to worship God: "And so when we come into [a] church . . . and when you see a cross, think with great sorrow and compunction of heart of the death Christ suffered for humankind; and so before the cross that moves you to devotion, worship Christ with all your might."[7]

Still, modern historians of religion are often suspicious of so-called spiritual suffering and devotion to a wounded God. Is not the suffering Jesus image really about a tyrannical God of judgment who cruelly demands the torture of the "Beloved Son" as satisfaction for humanity's wrongs? Is not the visage of Christ in agony in fact a reflection of a religious world of gloom and fear, a sign of the "dark ages," of an angst-ridden society terrified by death and mesmerized by a bloody and tormented figure who is a constant reminder of the fate that awaits unrepentant sinners?[8] Or, alternatively, from an equally critical perspective, is this fascination with the suffering Jesus not attributable to excesses in devotional practice which manifest the decline of medieval culture? Is this devotion to a wounded God not excessive and even maudlin? And is the piety of the wounded Jesus not theologically naive and so enamored of Jesus' humanity as to have lost sight of his divinity?[9]

Two Themes: Jesus as Agent of Divine Love and Power of Human Transformation

In response to questions like these, I explore the religious integrity of the cultural environment behind this "gospel of gore" as a world where many medieval believers could experience authentic spiritual transformation and renewal. The first of the overarching claims informing my work, then, is that far from being the creation of excessive outpourings of untempered spirituality, the image of the suffering Jesus, present in the concrete, physical events from arrest to Crucifixion, functions as the primary scriptural symbol for conveying the depth of a merciful God's love for humankind. Jesus Christ's endurance of agony and death reveals a God of boundless love seeking to heal the breach between humanity and God. The Passion of the Christ who is willing to suffer on humanity's behalf offers a vivid narrative of divine mercy, a startling portrayal of God's love for humanity. To the medieval viewer and reader, the pathos of the First Person and the willingness of the Second Person of the Trinity to endure anguish, torture, and death testify to the immensity of divine love for humankind.

Two central claims about the significance of the suffering Jesus have emerged from my research. First, in response to historians like Jean Delumeau who focus on the late medieval depiction of a wrathful and judgmental God, I articulate how images that at first appear to be incongruent—the fear- and guilt-provoking God of justice, on the one hand, and the merciful and compassionate God of love, on the other—are, in fact, inseparably related to one another in medieval religious life and, even more important, are linked in a critical way in the figure of the suffering Jesus.[10] To the medieval mind reflected in the texts discussed in this book, the search for the meaning of piety was an attempt to comprehend the mercy of the Divine manifest in the suffering of Jesus Christ. Why would a God of unsurpassable might, the source of all justice, become human in order to die on humanity's behalf? The dialectic of the mercy and justice of God has been a feature of Western religious thought and a topic of some controversy since soon after Jesus' death. The question of the nature of divine justice was critical in leading the twelfth-century Anselm of Canterbury to articulate the "satisfaction theory" of the Atonement as an alternative to the traditional theological view which suggested that the tricking of the devil was at the center of Christ's work.[11] The late medieval English public theology of sermons, art, and drama was not overly concerned with exploring the justice of God (a variety of views about divine justice are reflected in the art and literature of late medieval England); rather, the authors and artists considered here are characterized by their desire to name, depict, and experience the awesome character of the Passion as an act of divine mercy directed toward humans.

Second, in contrast to historians like Johan Huizinga whose analyses of the *passio Christi* phenomena suggest that medieval piety centered almost exclusively (and even "excessively") on the humanity of Jesus, I argue that consideration of medieval sources suggests that the concentration on Jesus' suffering was consistently directed toward and complemented by an understanding of the divinity of Christ.[12] Far from signaling mere humanity, as it does for many contemporary viewers, the physicality of the wounded Jesus, presented with shocking palpability in medieval art and narratives, manifested the reality of divine presence in Jesus Christ and made tangible the doctrinal claim that the Divine became human. In this vein, I illustrate how some of the common iconographic details of late medieval Crucifixion scenes (the depiction of the chalice beneath Jesus' feet into which his blood pours or the cross as the tree of life) manifest an integral focus on the divinity of Jesus in depictions of his suffering and death. I demonstrate the theological sophistication of the God of medieval popular culture and counter the claims of historians like Aron Gurevich who point to the "qualitative distinction" between the "bread of theologians" and the "crumbs of folk Christianity"in medieval literature and spirituality.[13]

The polymorphous evocation of the divine compassion manifested in the suffering Christ goes beyond a demonstration of God's love, however. This leads to the second overarching theme in this book: the flooding of viewers' senses with extravagant depictions of pain and anguish comprises an urgent appeal to the audience to respond to Jesus Christ's expression of love. The significance of the suffering Jesus tradition in medieval piety is not its testimony to a declining culture but rather its dramatic witness to the depth of divine love for humanity and, inseparable from this, its significant role in evoking a *response* of love on the part of humans.

Two themes emerge in my analysis of the medieval response to the suffering Jesus. First, in the dynamics of appeal, the physicality of Christ is central to the rhetoric of transformation generated by the bleeding figure of Christ. Christ's wounds and anguish are magnified in order to evoke the believer's compassionate response to the agonies he endures. Empathetic reflection was a cornerstone of medieval religious life: in sermons, drama, art, and literature, the suffering Jesus invited medieval Christians to remember actively the events of his death, to enter into the events, and to weep and mourn at his suffering along with and in imitation of his first-century followers. While historians like Thomas Tentler have recognized the importance of the believer's sorrow in the process of healing in the late medieval sacramental system, I call attention to the integral place of the suffering Christ in *evoking* that curative sorrow.[14] So, for example, recollections of Jesus' Passion highlight his suffering and indicate that he suffered not only because he was in physical pain but also because he grieved when he saw Mary's sorrow as she witnessed his agony. Authentic and Christ-inspired sorrow thus functions in medieval texts to betoken the believers' acceptance of the divine offer of mercy; the insincere or misdirected expression of sorrow, as depicted by the antagonists in the martyrs' narratives discussed in chapter 4, marks their refusal to respond to divine mercy and signals their subsequent condemnation by God.

Sorrowful compassion awakens believers to their own complicity in the sins for which Christ suffers; encountering the bodily presence of the bleeding and tormented Savior jars believers into attending to this relationship. In the personal encounter with the Divine Other, bleeding wounds make tangible the sin-based alienation of the human from the Divine. In one narrative, which I consider in chapter 1, Mary appears to sinners who have sworn oaths by Christ's Passion, arms, side, and bleeding wounds. She holds the bloody Christ child in her lap and accuses the oath-takers of "dismembering" her son. Recognizing and acknowledging their own implication in the sin for which Christ suffers leads believers to confession. Through confession, humans are reconciled with the Divine and, as some texts suggest, become even closer to God than they would have been had they not sinned.

This leads to the second theme. In the late medieval English context, devotion to the suffering Jesus did not inculcate an individualistic private piety; rather, love of God and love of neighbor were understood as being intimately related. The believers' alliance of compassion with Jesus enabled them to perceive Jesus in other humans. Christ-identified compassion thus becomes the basis for the transformation of the social world into one in which believers, in imitation of the merciful Jesus, learn to extend Christ's mercy to their neighbors. Alliance with Jesus refigured the world as a cosmos infused with the presence of the suffering Jesus, so that, modeling themselves upon Jesus, believers acted with mercy to alleviate the suffering in their own communities. The suffering Jesus functioned to inculcate common social practices such as confession and works of mercy (feeding the hungry and providing shelter for the poor), practices which contributed to the cohesion of medieval society. Thus in construals of the Last Judgment, persons are judged according to whether they saw Christ in their needy neighbors and responded with the compassion evoked by meditation on the suffering Christ.

In late medieval English Christianity, the figure of the suffering Jesus functioned to promote a conservative and ecclesiastically based social cohesion (in part through the association of Christ with the sacramental system and with the wider social system of good works). In the materials considered in this book, for the most part, the figure of the suffering Jesus is not allied with any widespread movements to subvert the medieval social order; yet, within an ecclesiastical setting, and especially in the narratives of holy people, including holy women, the figure of the suffering Christ does function to empower individuals to stand over and against society, both as God's representatives to others and as advocates for humans before God.[15] My findings, then, corroborate and advance the work of medievalists such as Caroline Walker Bynum and Richard Kieckhefer who have noted the prevalence of suffering in medieval texts but have not always been explicit in developing the theological and social implications of this theme.[16]

This project is an exercise in cultural and religious history. By systematically analyzing the now disparate but plentiful data that sheds light on the theme, in England, of the suffering Jesus, this project contributes to the history of medieval religion, which has long noted the dramatic presence of the wounded Christ in the late medieval world but has not satisfactorily accounted for the religious meaning and function of this phenomenon. Since this christological focus of piety is not unique to England, my exploration of its significance in the geographically and chronologically unified England of 1250–1450 will contribute methodology, data, and theory to the study of the suffering Christ theme in other areas of medieval Europe. This project also contributes to the work of historians and scholars of religion who maintain that in order to understand the religious sensibilities of a historical era, we must find ways of gaining access to the lived religion of the people.[17] My method in approaching the suffering Christ theme through sermons, drama, church decorations, hagiographic narratives, and spiritual treatises calls attention to the resources that illuminate medieval practice and belief and contributes to our understanding of the intersections between medieval theology and medieval piety.

The questions of the provenance and secondary interpretations of these narratives and works of art in the history of Western culture are important questions, but they are not the questions addressed in this book. I am interested, rather, in the study of these media from the perspective of a late medieval "aesthetics of response," so to speak. That is, I am interested in interrogating the literary and religious *meaning* and *function* of these texts within the popular culture of fourteenth- and fifteenth-century England—whatever might be the historical origins before or the readings of these texts after my frame of reference in the late Middle Ages. To study the function of these texts and artifacts in their late medieval contexts is not the same, however, as arguing that we can re-create the inner thoughts and consciousness of medieval readers and viewers. Instead, it suggests that we can roughly interpret the mediated sensibilities of an age in which gory figurations of the suffering Jesus—refracted through the media of sermons, drama, spiritual guidance literature, and art—commanded the hearts and minds of an entire culture. I do not think that it is possible to excavate an author's or creator's original intentions in producing a particular work. I do think, however, that the historian can make informed judgments about the meaning of particular images and themes by studying the culturally embedded significations projected by the works in question. In other words, I focus on how this material functioned in late medieval culture by interpreting the meaning of the available artifacts in light of my own methodological questions and presuppositions. When one looks at a culture like that of late medieval England, one can identify, almost like a gestalt, certain "patterns" or "configurations" in which particular images meaningfully appear and reappear. In analyzing these patterns of appearance, the historian can make fundamental claims about how these configurations of meaning functioned to shape and define the spiritual ethos of a culture.

Overview of the Project

In chapters 1 through 4, I provide a general analysis of the religious meaning of the suffering Jesus in English narrative and artistic depictions. The first section of chapter 1 considers the meaning of the Passion of Christ conveyed to medieval audiences through popular spiritual guides and a variety of homily collections designed for preaching to lay audiences. I explore the manner in which the wounded Jesus advocated on behalf of humans to the Divine and also sought to evoke a spiritual transformation in the witnesses to his life and Passion. I draw on medieval exempla, the tales preachers used to illustrate their sermons. Although these are stock tales, centuries old in some cases, my concern is not with their origins but with how they function in fourteenth- and fifteenth-century sermons to concretize the relationship between the medieval Christian and the suffering Savior. I ask how they portray the Divine and the divine offer of mercy and how they seek to stir a response on the part of the audience. Sermons and spiritual guidance texts portray the suffering Christ as God's loving offer of mercy to a fallen and sinful humankind. Christ appeals to people to respond to the divine offer of mercy.

In keeping with the observations of the first section, the second section of chapter 1 is a theological exploration of how medieval Christians' own identification with the suffering Christ functioned to transform and deepen believers' relationships to God and to the world. I consider the works of two spiritual guides, Margery Kempe and Julian of Norwich, and consider three common types of Christ-identified suffering which emerge in the lives of individual believers: suffering borne of contrition, compassion, and longing. Reflection on the Passion of Jesus does not lead to the pursuit of suffering for its own sake, but rather it is a medium for experiencing the presence of suffering in the lives of Christ's disciples during the believer's spiritual journey toward love of God. Julian and Margery depict a Christian life-journey directed toward an experiential love and knowledge of God. Pain functions in these texts as a part of the process of identification with Christ as the person advances in relationship to the Divine and learns to perceive God as Love.

Why did religious figures like Margery Kempe and Julian of Norwich seek to imitate the suffering of Jesus? The answer lies in one of the underlying tenets of fourteenth- and fifteenth-century spirituality: namely, that one understands through experience. Comprehension at an intellectual level is superseded by a deeper level of affective understanding through experiencing or feeling. Along with this notion went the conviction that the praxis of imitation provided one of the best ways to understand the world through experience. Many medieval religious figures, both men and women, set out to refigure mimetically in their own lives the Christ who redeemed them from sin and made God present to them. The life of imitation took many forms, from the Dominicans' and Franciscans' imitation of Christ's peripatetic life; to the ethical imitation of Christ characteristic of spiritual leaders like the fourteenth-century Walter Hilton, who taught his readers to model their religious lives on Christ's example of charity; to the more dramatic imitative actions of religious figures such as Mary of Oignies and Heinrich Suso, who marked their own bodies with the stigmata and signs of Christ's suffering. In the fourteenth and fifteenth centuries, writers often expressed a strong desire (some might say obsession) to share in the sufferings of Christ. Through christological role-playing, histrionic displays of grief, and even self-mutilation, medieval imitators of the Passion reenacted the events surrounding Jesus' suffering and explicitly linked themselves with Christ's salvific work. In a worldview that connected the suffering Jesus with the work of Christ in the world, modeling themselves after Christ provided a way for believers to change their own, and others', spiritual demeanor. The imitators of Christ could learn to act in the world as Christ did. I will suggest that by imitating Christ believers could understand something of who Jesus Christ was as both human and divine. I take this view to be at the heart of the pervasive references to Jesus' Passion in the late Middle Ages: identification through suffering with Jesus' humanity leads to an experiential understanding of his divinity.

Although this book is primarily a study of written texts, chapter 2, in keeping with Barbara Raw's recent work on Anglo-Saxon Crucifixion iconography, demonstrates the significant connections between artistic and literary sources in medieval culture.[18] Arguing that a successful analysis of Middle English piety must also be attentive to the visual arts (certainly one of the most powerful conveyers of medieval religious belief), I analyze illuminations in Psalters and Books of Hours as well as selected wall paintings to explore the meanings and contexts of representative examples of artistic depictions of the suffering Jesus.

Artistic depictions of the Passion of Jesus in Psalters and Books of Hours visually refigure the world so that time reveals its "truest" meaning as an ongoing commemoration of the merciful work of Jesus Christ on behalf of humanity. This liturgical transformation of temporality links the present with the past by naming the present as the time for recollecting the events of Jesus' life and death; it also links the present and past with the future as the time of the coming to fruition of the Passion of Christ. Contemporary temporal existence, therefore, is charged with sacred purpose because it has the potential for serving as a living reenactment of the "hours" of Christ's Passion and death and of their ongoing meaning. Consideration of church wall paintings further illustrates how the recollection of the Passion of Christ also transformed space by consecrating churches into places of remembrance of the suffering and death of Jesus. Transformed by art, space and time bring salvation history into the present, and viewers are invited to participate in the events depicted in the paintings and illuminations.

Among the many meanings of the Crucifixion, I highlight three aspects of Crucifixion iconography. First, I consider the link between the Crucifixion and the Hebrew Scripture tradition of sacrifice to explain the work of Christ on behalf of humanity and the association of the crucified Christ with the Eucharist. I draw attention to a sample of artistic renderings of the Crucifixion, the wounds of Jesus, and the instruments of torture to exemplify the iconographic details that demonstrate the understanding of the divinity of Jesus Christ which is at the heart of the meaning of Jesus' death for medieval Christians. Second, I consider the role of the suffering Jesus as the divine source of spiritual food for humanity. Images in which disciples such as Mary Magdalene and Joseph of Arimethea drink the blood of the crucified Christ depict the life-giving power of Christ feeding his followers and make visible the nurturing transformation of humanity by the suffering divine body. The cross-gendering of Jesus so prevalent in medieval literature—Jesus as Mother who feeds the world with his/her body— is also reflected in medieval art in which the Jesus whose blood nourishes the world has clear iconographic parallels with the nursing Mary whose milk feeds Jesus.[19] The third category I discuss is central to medieval English literature and art: Jesus as healer. As explained by the fourteenth-century Augustinian canon, Walter Hilton, among others, the name "Jesus" means "healer" in Middle English.[20] The healing of the blind Longinus who spears Jesus in the chest and then is cured as Christ's blood falls into his eyes parallels the allegorical healing which reflection on the suffering Jesus affords to Christian believers. In reading and praying, believers were taught by the christological art that surrounded them to recognize Jesus as divine sacrifice, as nurturer, and as healer.

Chapter 3 considers liturgical drama, including the York and N-Town mystery plays, and demonstrates that in liturgical drama the words and actions of the suffering Jesus, literally and typologically portrayed, constitute a rhetoric of persuasion, appealing to the audience to respond with repentance and gratitude for Christ's reconciliation of God's justice with God's mercy. Through an elaborate interweaving of scenes prefiguring Christ's Passion—in which religious figures prophesy it, events record it, and characters recollect it—the audience's attention is focused on the suffering Jesus. Thus, viewers are taught the "spiritual grammar," as it were, fundamental to the teachings of English religious leaders of the fourteenth and fifteenth centuries. In the social context of ritual celebration in which the performers enter into and are transformed by the world they depict, the audience is invited to inhabit the cosmos created by the plays. In compassionate response to the agony of the suffering Jesus to which all the dramas point, the audience becomes part of the transformation enacted therein. The performances engender the very spiritual world they depict by providing living models for how the audience is to respond to the christological actions they reenact.

In particular, the plays promote the sacraments of baptism, Eucharist, and confession as critical to the spiritual health of Christians. The words and actions of the medieval plays are not solely etiological stories; they also teach audiences how to comport themselves in the present to prepare for receiving the sacraments. For the most part, I understand the mystery plays as extensions of the educational mission of the more progressive clerics of late medieval England.[21] The plays are not primarily subversions of spiritual practices and goals of the church hierarchy. On the contrary, the plays promote the sacramental system that in turn guaranteed the place of the priestly class in medieval society. The sacrament of confession was, in the words of Thomas Tentler, "a comprehensive and organized system of social control" whose goal was to "make people obey not only men, but morality and law."[22] The religiosity reflected in liturgical drama is a social phenomenon in which society is refigured as a manifestation of divine presence, and individuals are invited to be part of the orderly transformation of place and time into a sacred world. Throughout the book, I will note that the same vision of reality unfolds again and again in art, drama, and sermons and that viewers are invited to inhabit the sacred cosmos created by the ways of living described in these different media.

Chapter 4 develops my analysis of the "literature of response" to the Passion of Christ by examining the gender-identified public responses of female spiritual leaders to the suffering Jesus. In considering the Middle English versions of the lives of four holy women—St. Katherine of Alexandria, St. Margaret of Antioch, Elizabeth of Spalbeek, and Margery Kempe—I explore the ways in which the female body becomes a literary figure for mediating Christ to the world in medieval spiritual literature. These women carry on the work of Christ by graphically imprinting Christ's pain on their own flesh through the willing endurance of torture (as in the cases of Margaret of Antioch and Katherine of Alexandria), through self-beating and self-mutilation (as in the narrative of Elizabeth of Spalbeek), and through weeping and shouting as they take Christ's suffering into themselves (as in the life of Margery Kempe). These mimetic exercises link the female body with the Divine so intimately that these women become conduits of divine power and advocates on behalf of humans to the Divine. The stories of Katherine, Margaret, Elizabeth, and Margery testify to these holy women's tenacious physical identification with the suffering Christ; in and through their suffering in solidarity with Christ, medieval holy women become identified with him so closely that they become brokers of the spiritual power that inheres in

Jesus himself. Through their suffering, holy women become like Jesus: purveyors of divine power who act on humanity's behalf.

In connection with this, the concluding section of chapter 4 considers the public work of Margery Kempe as a way to explore how she "becomes" Christ to the world. I point in particular to the vast power wielded by figures like Margery Kempe who claim to influence the status of hundreds of thousands of souls in purgatory. Lest this sound excessive, I suggest that this extravagance is not uncommon in texts about women and reveals something of the public domain of women's spiritual power. While the saying of masses was a common priestly and thus male practice, weeping and praying on behalf of the world in association with the suffering Jesus constitute an analogous and largely female form of spiritual influence. Like the Margaret and Katherine of the martyr narratives, and like Philip of Clairvaux's Elizabeth of Spalbeek, Margery Kempe is both an agent of spiritual transformation for the faithful in this life and an advocate for divine mercy for souls in the next.

A Christ-Centered Culture?

In words which apply to art, drama, and devotional literature, the fourteenth-century English preacher John Waldeby described the goal of preaching as "not only to stir the intelligence towards what is true by means of the inevitable conclusions of arguments but also, by means of narrative and likely persuasion, to stir the emotions to piety."[23] This study of the Passion of Christ, one of the most emotional and theological of focal concerns within medieval piety and preaching, opens a window onto the religious sensibilities of late medieval England. As a historical pastiche, this book is a selectively representative portrait of the fourteenth- and fifteenth-century milieu and seeks to illuminate the religious world of late medieval England.

In this world, suffering is transformed from being a sign of powerless victimization to becoming the central signifier of the presence of a loving and merciful God who acts on behalf of humans. The suffering of Christ is not simply a historical event, completed at some point in the past. Rather, in the medieval world, the Crucifixion is ongoing as it is reenacted in the Mass, in liturgical drama, and in the minds and bodies of people who meditate on it. Viewers and readers learn to respond to the Passion of Christ as a present event. They are encouraged to cultivate a relationship of personal connection with the suffering Christ, so that the motivation for the sinner's reformation is friendship and alliance with the Crucified One and not just fear of damnation. A perception of humanity's deep need for mercy and a fascination with the visage of divine mercy pervade late medieval English spiritual life. The Passion of Jesus points to the re-creation of the universe as God's space, in which the merciful action of Jesus Christ provokes viewers of his life and death to imitate his mercy through their own inter-actions with their neighbors. In addition to fostering social uniformity in a world dominated by the church, the suffering Jesus image also empowered believers to undertake the radical, controversial, and dramatic action of calling people to recognize their own need for mercy and spiritual transformation.

All of this is not to suggest, of course, that the Christian society of late medi-eval England was a completely cohesive world of spiritually aware and engaged religious practitioners. Tens of thousands of petty larcenies and assaults were committed in England each year; robbery, fraud, forgery, and violent bloodshed abounded.[24] We have only to recall Margery Kempe's rebuke of the archbishop of York for his wickedness[25] and Chaucer's tales of carpenters and prelates ir-reverently swearing by Christ's wounds, his heart, his blood, his arms, and his feet to recognize how broken was the world in which these texts were embed-ded. This literature and art emerged in a world that its authors and creators deemed to be in desperate need of transformation. In this book, I explore how this image of the Passion of Jesus functioned to preach change and consolation to a sinful and suffering world.

The Dynamics of Divine Appeal

The Suffering Jesus in the Literature of Spiritual Guidance

Sermons and Spiritual Guidance Literature

The Suffering Jesus and the Offer of Divine Mercy

In a sermon, the preacher and ecclesiastical reformer John Mirk tells the story of a good man and an evil liar who are friends. The good man does what he can to persuade his wayward friend to confess and seek forgiveness for his heinous ways, but the friend refuses, always putting off confronting his sin until another day. "I'll do it when I'm near death," he says, and goes on with his life. Eventually, the evil man falls ill; his friend redoubles his efforts to persuade him to confess. Still he refuses, saying, "I've lived in sin for so long that I won't be forgiven." The good friend assembles priests and friars in a vain attempt to win confession from his friend but to no avail. One night about midnight, while sleeping in the sick man's room where a light burns through the night, the friend sees Jesus Christ with his bloody wounds standing in front of the sick man's bed. The wounded Christ addresses the ailing sinner: "My son, why won't you confess and receive my mercy; I'm always ready to give mercy to anyone who asks for it meekly." The sick man answers, "I'm not worthy to receive mercy, so you won't give me mercy." "Ask for it meekly, and you'll receive it," Jesus insists. But still the sinner refuses. Then Jesus reaches into his side wound, pulls out his hand, now covered with dripping blood, and holds it over the unrepentant sinner: "You child of the Devil, this will be a sign between you and me on Judgment Day: I would have given you mercy, but you wouldn't take it." And he casts the blood into the dying man's face. Crying out, "I am damned," the sinner dies. The friend, petrified, lies trembling in his bed in terror for a long time. Finally he gets up and lights a candle at the lamp. He peers down at his companion and finds him dead, the red blood staining his face.[1]

Most late medieval English devotional texts presume a common theological schema. The fundamental tenet is that the fall of Adam and Eve fractured the relationship between God and humankind. In the order of justice, humanity deserved condemnation for its affront to the Divine. Nevertheless, God sought to overcome the rift by responding with mercy while reckoning with the claims of justice. Medieval sermons and devotional literature frequently recount with dramatic flair this struggle to reconcile righteousness, truth, and mercy.[2] In one sermon, the preacher narrates the response of Righteousness, Truth, and Mercy, who are God's three counselors, to Adam's appeal for divine mercy. Although Adam is "will by-louyd" by God, Righteousness rebukes him, warning him not to hope for Righteousness's grace: "For þou shalte haue as þou haste wrought."[3] Truth echoes this castigation, saying Adam's guilt is so great that there can be no reconciliation.[4] Finally, Adam's last hope, Mercy, succumbs to his appeal: "I will not, man, þat þou die; / But with my bodye I will þe bie,"[5] thus accepting the harsh judgments of Truth and Righteousness and responding to humanity's pleas for help. Again and again, the same Anselmian insight is generated on the basis of medieval narratives. Instead of abandoning human persons to the consequences of their misdeeds, God intercedes through the work of Christ and establishes a new order of mercy while satisfying the demands of justice.

The suffering Christ embodies the offer of mercy to humanity by a loving God who willingly permits and endures pain on behalf of humans. The First Person of the Trinity loved Jesus Christ: "Þe Fader of Heuen hade but one sonne þat he loued passyng alle þyng,"[6] yet to "buy" humanity from the devil's domain, God sent Christ into the world and wrote a charter of freedom for people "wyth his owne hert-blod."[7] In spite of the claims of historians like Jean Delumeau, the God depicted here is not a fear-provoking tyrant but rather the loving source of all grace and mercy: "For he loued þe world so wele þat he ȝaf þerfore his owen geten sone, þe which vochidsafe for to dye for hem þat were enmyes to hym and mysdoers."[8] Through the life and death of Jesus Christ, the loving God reconciles justice, mercy, and truth by exercising compassion and forgiveness toward all persons.

Yet the late medieval English public theology of sermons, art, and drama was not overly concerned with exploring the justice of God as such; rather, the authors and artists considered here are characterized by their focus on how mercy is *experienced* in the lives of believers. In the pre-Fall situation, "Adam and Eve" had only to lose the assurance of salvation that had already been given to them. In the post-Fall world, the work of Christ brings about a situation in which the offer of salvation is once again extended to now sinful humanity. However, the prelapsarian situation has been altered in a fundamental way. In postlapsarian history, salvation is no longer an accomplished fact which can only be lost; it is rather an offer which must be accepted. In general, humans must avail themselves of divine mercy: in the suffering Jesus Christ, God extends an offer of mercy, and, as the above tale so graphically illustrates, humans must *respond* to the Divine offer or suffer the consequences of their refusal.

In the story, the liar not only persevered in his evil actions but also spurned Jesus Christ's personal offer of forgiveness. In the post-Fall world in which Jesus Christ offers mercy and a person must ask for it and accept it, the scandal of those like this sick man is not that they sin, because sin can always be rectified. Rather, the scandal is that they disdain the wounded Christ's offer of mercy. Mired in their sin, they refuse to ask for mercy, which is plentiful but still must be sought. Refusal to seek forgiveness becomes despair and is a manifestation of pride; so Christ reminds the sick person that those who set aside their pride and ask meekly are granted forgiveness. In the medieval worldview, with its blurring of the boundaries between the living and the dead, this literature is quick to remind people that the offer of mercy will not always be there. The last of the ubiquitous fourteen articles of faith (a fundamental feature of English medieval spiritual life) reminds its reciters that at the end of time Christ will come to judge the living and the dead.[9] The portrait of a God who is merciful now but will not be merciful at the Day of Judgment is a cornerstone in late medieval English spirituality:

> And ilkman answer of his owen dedis
> And be dampned or saued whethir-sum he deserves,
> For als his right wisenesse is now menged with mercy . . .
> So sal it han be withouten merci.[10]

Now, mercy is boundless. Indeed, if Judas had asked forgiveness for his betrayal of Jesus, even he would have received mercy.[11] One homilist's conclusion is that by praying Adam "vanne mercye out of heven,"[12] and this becomes a model all believers can use to pray for mercy. Fundamental to this literature is the claim that humans must *accept* the offer of mercy. The *offer* of mercy is ubiquitous, but mercy is granted only when it is sought and accepted through the decision of the disciple. By and large, the message of late medieval English homiletic literature is not that grace comes unexpectedly when people are least expecting it but rather that the offer of salvation and forgiveness is always extended, so people must respond to that offer and accept what can be rightfully theirs.

The Appeal of the Suffering Jesus

In the late medieval context in which the believer's response to the offer of mercy is crucial for salvation, much of the confessional, sermonic, and devotional literature is written to *provoke* the appropriate response. The bleeding and wounded Christ of sermons and devotional literature is the embodiment of divine mercy and love for humankind. Depictions of the suffering Savior seek to stir humans to respond with love to the Divine's love for them by portraying sorrow as the appropriate response to humanity's affront to the Divine, by awakening compassion in the face of Christ's suffering, and by urging merciful action toward other Christians in imitation of Christ.

John Mirk explains that images are important in churches (in opposition to the Lollards' claims that images promote idolatry) because looking at the wall paintings and the crucifixes above chancels and altars reminds congregants of Jesus' Passion. Mirk suggests that there are thousands of people who could not imagine (and consequently not respond to) what happened to Jesus on the cross unless they see it in images and paintings.[13] Artistic and verbal depictions of the suffering Jesus are much more than simple reminders of a historical event; in sparking believers' imaginations, this material seeks consistently to intensify the personal relationship between Christ and humans by stimulating believers' affection and compassion for Jesus' suffering. Christ's wounds bear witness to divine love, and, in the voice of the preacher, the suffering Christ appeals directly to humans to accept God's love. What God wants in return is love: "Sonne, ȝyf me þi hert, and þat is ynoȝe for me."[14] This theme echoes throughout medieval English sermons and devotional texts. God's expression of love for humanity seeks a corresponding love for God. The cross is not solely a symbol of Satan's defeat, but, even more, it is a poignant plea for people to respond to a divine offer of love and mercy:

> Loo, I am lyfte up on hyȝe up on the cros for the, synfull creature, that thu scholde here my voyce, turn to me a ȝene, and I wyll ȝiffe the remission and mercy. loo, myne armys ben sprede a brode for to clyppe the and to take the to grace, and myne hedde I bow doune for to gyfe the a kisse of luffe. And my syde is openyd for to schewe how kynde I have ben to the, and how lovyng, and myne hertt is clyfte a two for the love of the, my hondys and my feete bledythe for to schewe what I suffyrde for the. And ȝit thu turneste a wey, and wil not come to me at my callyng. ȝit turne to me, and I wil gyfe the joy and reste perpetually.[15]

Sermons like this often portray Christ recalling the sufferings he endured for the love of humankind and asking for a response of love. One sermon explains that the fourth and final time Jesus wept was on the cross because some sinful people were yet unmoved in spite of his suffering on their behalf.[16] At times, Jesus contrasts the pain he endures with the revelry of vain Christians, comparing the crown of thorns on his head to the garland of flowers on theirs, his bloody and wounded hands to theirs draped in white gloves. Christ is grieved by Christians' spurning his love for them.[17] The sermons consistently portray this central theme in a myriad of ways: "Be ȝe not vnkynd to your God, þat þus suffryd for you."[18]

In a sermon that echoes the common late medieval English encouragement of people to seek mercy now, the preacher explains the state that the cultivation of the seeking of mercy is meant to evoke: "Now God ȝeue us grace to vse kyendnes aȝeyne and loue hyme þat so many signes of loue haþ shewed to vs all, oure Lorde Ihesu Criste."[19] A response is called for whereby the believer replies with kindness and love to the love proferred by the Divine.

An assumption that it is specifically the *wounded* Jesus who makes this transformative impact on viewers pervades the literature. Homiletic and devotional literature seeks to impel people to respond to God's offer of mercy by concretizing and personalizing the figure of the wounded Christ. As indicated by the opening story in this chapter, the physicality of Jesus Christ is central in evoking this response. In medieval tales, the shocking appearance of blood flowing from Christ's wounds makes tangible the doctrinal claim that the Divine became human, reinforcing the presence of the Divine in human form and manifesting Divine love for humanity. The intensified physicality of medieval sermonody, with all of its blood and pulsing flesh, makes literal or somatizes the spiritual truth at the heart of medieval spirituality: the medieval God is not abstract and distant but is radically immanent in the suffering Savior whose wounds are an invitation to compassionate response and engaged relationship.

This carnal, fleshy understanding of Jesus becomes the very source of the manifestation of divine presence. Homilists narrate stories in which doubters have their faith revived through an intensified enfleshment of the presence of Jesus Christ—in the literalizing of the eucharistic presence of Jesus Christ.[20] Relating a story purportedly from the time of St. Gregory, Mirk narrates the account of a woman named Lasma who baked the bread used in the Eucharist. When the pope offered her the host, saying, "Take here Godis body," she smiled. Noticing this, Gregory withdrew his hand, placed the host on the altar, and inquired of Lasma why she had smiled. She replied that she had smiled when Gregory called "Godis body" the very bread that she had made with her own hands. Seeing her unbelief, Pope Gregory asked people to pray for a miracle; when he turned back to the altar, he found the host turned into raw, pulpy, bleeding flesh. Upon witnessing the bloody presence of Christ, the woman believed.[21] A similar story which Mirk says he read in the narrative of Ode, Bishop of Canterbury, tells of two clerks who did not believe in transubstantiation in attendance at mass with a bishop who was aware of their unbelief. When the bishop broke the host, he noticed blood dripping from it into the chalice. He motioned to the doubters to come and see. Aghast at seeing the bishop's bloody fingers and the blood running from the host into the chalice, they recognized that this was "Godis body, and his blod þat dropet þer into þe chalis." As they prayed that God would not exact vengeance for their doubting, the sacrament turned back into bread.[22]

These folk tales and others like them are shocking manifestations of the meaning of transubstantiation: the bread and wine literally "become" the body of God. It is small wonder that in the face of Lollard dissent on the nature of the Eucharist, religious leaders like Mirk would emphasize the literal presence of Jesus Christ in the eucharistic bread and wine. Yet while these stories are a part of the genre of miracle tales that somatize the medieval doctrine of the Eucharist, they also number among the more broadly construed myriad of stories that intensify the physicality of Christ as a way of manifesting divine presence. This physicality is demonstrated most graphically through verbal and pictoral representations of Jesus' bleeding flesh and is directed toward evoking a response of deepened faith on the part of observers.

A series of stories which evoke transformation through the radical physicalization of the reality of the God-human, in particular through the highlighting of the blood of Christ, occur in Mirk's *Festial* narrations of events surrounding the purported conversion of Jews. The virulent anti-Semitism of the *Festial* pervades these stories, in which Jews are characterized as hating Christ with such passion that they even seek to reenact the Crucifixion of Jesus through the inflicting of wounds upon images of Christ.[23] In one etiological narrative about the origin of the relic of Christ's blood at the Abbey of Hailes, a Christian leaves a crucifix "whech þat Nychodemus made in worschip and yn mynd of Crist" in a house where a Jew comes to live. Jewish neighbors come to visit the new resident, and in looking around the house, one of them comes upon the crucifix and accuses the other of being a Christian who worships the cross. The resident denies the charges but cannot convince the neighbor, who stirs up the Jewish neighbors against him. Furious, they beat him, then turn on the cross, saying that just as their fathers killed Christ, they will now inflict the same injuries upon the image. They blindfold the image, beat it, whip it with scourges, crown it with thorns, then nail it again to the cross. To their stunned amazement, when they thrust a spear into its heart, blood and water flow from the wound and run down the side of the crucifix image. Horrified at what they have done, they decide to collect a pitcher full of the blood to take to the temple to see whether the blood will cure people, and, if it does, they will be baptized. The cure works, and they proceed to the city, where the bishop who baptizes them puts the blood into vials of crystal, amber, and glass and sends it around to different churches.[24]

This story appears in a series of sermons in Mirk's *Festial* in which he tries to persuade his audience to be respectful of the cross by portraying its miraculous powers. It fits into a pattern of stories in which images of Christ come to life and exhibit the characteristics of living flesh. In another story in the section on the exultation of the cross, Mirk cites from the *Golden Legend* the story of a Jew who enters a church and, overcome with the envy he has of Christ, slits the throat of an image of the crucified Jesus. Blood spurts from the wound, bespattering his clothes. He hides the crucifix and tries to hide what happened, but he eventually tells it all to a Christian, is baptized and becomes a holy man.[25]

As this discussion of the bleeding image stories makes clear, late medieval homilies and guidance literature continually personalize the circumstances of the human as sinner, trying to construct a world in which the reader or listener is brought to a new understanding of her or his relationship to God and neighbor by encountering the living flesh of the wounded Jesus. The reality of the sin-based alienation of the person from God and from those around her or him is made tangible in the details of the encounter.

The nature of sin as a personal affront against Christ is graphically portrayed in the exemplum of a justice and his followers who permitted, and even encouraged, taking oaths by God's Passion, as well as his arms, sides, and bloody wounds. One day, a woman appeared carrying in her lap a child "blody and all tomarturd."[26] She asked the justice, "Of what are they worthy who have done this to my child?" When the justice replied, "They are worthy of death," the woman responded, "You and your men with your horrible oaths have dismembered my son Jesus Christ." She accused him of teaching all the land to swear such oaths and warned him, "You shall have your own judgment." At this point, in view of all the people, the earth opened and the magistrate fell down into hell.[27] The people were aghast and began to change their ways. Mirk concludes by urging his listeners, "syrs and dames," to abandon their oaths and to do reverence to Christ's Passion and wounds.

This story makes palpable the impact of human offenses against the Divine (and also Mary in this case) by rendering the effect of the offenses physically visible and concrete. In the above example, the words of sinners are literally *written* onto the body of Christ as bloody wounds, just as the blood flung from Jesus' wound onto the sinner in this chapter's opening story marks the sinner's own implication in the wounding of Jesus, as well as his refusal to seek mercy.[28] The meaning of the stories is straightforward: Jesus' body bears the scars of humans' many transgressions. Jesus' body is a *text of flesh*, as it were, upon which is written in blood every sin committed by humanity. These narratives confront readers and listeners with a visual rendering of the effects of their actions and constitute a reminder that the medieval God, in and through Christ, is profoundly impacted by the acts of humans. The dramatic confrontation of persons with the consequences of their actions visibly displayed on the body of the suffering Jesus shocks them into an acknowledgment of their alienation from the Divine. As in the previously related tales of the fate of the unrepentant ill sinner and of the justice who initiated the swearing of oaths, the stories often trade on fear of the consequences of inflicting hurt on the Divine. In the latter story, the people who adopt and persist in swearing and, by extension, the hearers of the sermons in which the exemplum is narrated are spared the descent into hell. However, the expectation is that they will be horrified at what they hear and see, respectively, and will be motivated to reform their lives—their speech in particular—while they have the chance, so that they do not become perpetrators of evil who deserve the same end as the unfortunate magistrate.[29] But often, as we shall see, the personal connection between the suffering Savior who loves humanity and the thoughtless or careless sinner who has only to see how her or his action impacts the Divine provides the impetus to stir up a compassionate response and a personal desire to reform. In most cases, as in this chapter's first story, the medieval sacrament of confession is offered as the initial, formal step in the process of reformation.

Confession and the Individual

The call to confession generally accompanies the homiletic challenge to recognize that humanity's sins impact the Divine, on the one hand, and to acknowledge the divine offer of mercy, on the other. After confronting the physicality of Christ in Eucharist and symbol, medieval sermonic materials consistently encourage the practice of confession as the basis of the transformative process for people who respond to the appeal of the suffering Christ. The focus on contrition and confession had a long and varied history in the medieval tradition, with papal involvement dating particularly from the *Omnis utriusque sexus* pronouncement of the Fourth Lateran Council of 1215, which required all persons to attend confession at least once a year.[30] Confession functioned in many cases as a catechetical as well as a penitential event, and repentance and the call to penance were among the most popular sermon topics of the day.[31] Numerous manuals were written to guide priests in leading people through confession. The importance of compulsory confession also led to heated disputes between the mendicants and secular priests over the question of who had responsibility for the care of souls and the right to hear confessions. The central place of confession in medieval culture is also reflected in the fact that many of the fourteenth century's leading religious figures struggled with what they called "scruples," that is, the ever-present danger of a failure to balance the acute and excruciatingly precise awareness of sin with an equally acute awareness of forgiveness.[32] Spiritual guides repeatedly warn of the temptation to pride in those who place unequal weight on their own sinfulness without balancing it with an equally acute awareness of divine forgiveness. Contrition and confession were frequently accompanied by visible displays of emotion. Peter of Luxembourg sometimes wept so profusely at confession that "he would leave a puddle where he knelt, as if someone had poured water in front of him."[33] Like Margery Kempe, who is considered in the second part of this chapter, Bridget of Sweden and Dorothy of Montau both sobbed and grieved loudly at their sinfulness in the face of God's mercy.[34]

Although the use of indulgences and excessive legalistic cataloguing of sins sometimes led to abuses, the most theologically aware literature, such as Mirk's *Instruction for Parish Priests* and Robert of Brynnying's *Handlyng Synne*—as well as the highly regarded spiritual leaders of the time such as Julian of Norwich, Bridget of Sweden, and Dorothy of Montau—did not advocate penance for its own sake; rather, penance and the contrition associated with it initiate the process by which believers participate in the work of Christ and are restored to a right relationship with the Divine. Sermons and devotional texts agree further that forgiveness is available only in this life. In this world, God has mercy on anyone who seeks forgiveness and repents for her or his sins, but in the next, as we have seen, there will be no mercy:[35] "Here he [God] is mercyfull, and þere he is a iuge; here he is esy, and þer he is dispitous and cruell."[36] But the motivation for confession differs according to whether the sermons emphasize divine justice or divine mercy. Although in sermons of divine justice the order of justice is not contravened because confession satisfies the God of justice, these sermons consistently focus on the dire consequences of the guilty who do not partake of mercy. The "fire and brimstone" sermons of medieval English Christianity portray the terrifying visage of divine justice weighing souls on the scale of good and evil. Those found wanting are released into the horrors of hell:

> "Go, ȝe curselyngs, to evere-lasting fier, whiche is maad redy to the devil and to his aungels!" And sodeinly thei shuln be cast doun into helle with the devil and his aungelis, and the ȝates of helle shul be schut for evermore that thei go nevere out. And ther thei shul [be] bulyd in fyr and brymstone withouten ende. Venemous wormes and naddris shul gnawe alle here membris withouten seessyng, and the worm of conscience, that is grutching in her consience, shal gnawe the soule. . . . Wepe ȝe nowe, and ȝelle! . . . Now ȝe shul have everlasting bittirnesse; ȝour pley is tornyd in to moorning, ȝoor lauȝing is turned in to sorwe, and ȝour wepyng shal be withoute conforte and everlastyng. This fyr that turmentith ȝou shal never be quenchid, and thei that turmentyn ȝou shul never be wery, nether dye.[37]

Sermons of this type presume that awakening the listeners' fears to the pains of hell will motivate their reformation: change is preferable to risking the terrors of hell as the consequences for sin.[38]

While reformation of the sinner's life can protect her or him from grievous sins in the future, only confession can free believers from the sins of the past, so sermons like those of Richard Alkerton, cited in the excerpt above, urge people to seek divine forgiveness while they can. Gruesome tales within sermons of divine justice warn against unconfessed sin and, even worse, against the prospect of death without confessing. One narrative tells of an avaricious man who had gathered so much gold that he filled a chest which sat at the foot of his bed. Greedy for more, he set up a second chest which he intended to fill as well, until God, aware of the man's covetousness, sent a sickness upon him. His wife and children then begged him to confess his sins and bequeath his goods, but he paid no attention to them, and, in spite of the discomfort of his illness, he would not even move for fear that if he so much as turned his eyes away from the coffer someone might steal the gold. After he died, his family, curious about what was in the chest, opened it and found it full of gold. On top of the gold there lay a heart, "all fresh in blood. . . . Thereby they knew well that he was damned, for making his treasure his god."[39] In this and other tales like it, divine mercy is not absent, but the consequences of divine justice loom large; the narratives emphasize the fates of those who refuse to avail themselves of the divine offer of forgiveness.[40]

This triadic constellation of themes—the just and judging God, sinful humans, and the possibility of confession as a way to avoid the horrors of hell—appears throughout medieval sermons and in a wide variety of other literary and artistic genres, from devotional writings and lyrics to manuscript illuminations and church wall paintings.

In sermons and religious literature that emphasize divine mercy, the theme of divine retribution fades into the background. It is supplanted by a focus on divine mercy in which a persuasive God, present through the suffering Jesus, woos and entices humans to a willingness to transform their lives and renew their Christian commitments. Unlike the medieval preachers of sermons of divine justice who caution against the laxity that might result from presuming God's patience, this second view maintains that it is only through divine persuasion that individuals will change in any significant way. Focusing solely on the wrath of divine justice may evoke a reformation of human behavior, but it is more likely to be temporary and superficial than deep-seated and enduring. The pain of Christ's death testifies to the depth of Christ's love for humankind, so sermons are filled with graphic depictions of the agonies and sufferings of Christ's passion:

> Byholde, thanne, that goede lord chyveryng and quakyng, al his body naked and bounde to a pyler; aboute him stondyng the wycked men, withouten eny resoun, ful sore scourgyng that blessed body, withouten eny pite. See how they cesse nouȝt fram here angry strokes, tyl they se him stonde in his blode up to the anclees. Fro the top of the hed to the sole of his fote, hole skyn saved they non. His flesch they rase to the bone, and for werynesse of hemself they him leevyd al-most for dede. . . . A garland of thornes they thrast on his heved, tyl the blode ran doun his eyȝen, nose and mouth and eeren.[41]

As this graphic description illustrates, intensifying the physicality of Jesus Christ through magnifying Christ's wounded body plays a key role in spiritual transformation. The presence of the suffering God is personalized by focusing on Christ's torn and wounded flesh; this focus initiates the process by which the person identifies in a personal way with the suffering Christ. In some cases, as we have seen, the presence of the wounded Christ leads to conversion, while in other cases it leads to the strengthening of faith. Most frequently, reflection on the injured Savior causes people to reflect on their own part in "causing," so to speak, the suffering Jesus endures. Reflection on the believer's own implication in Christ's suffering leads to contrition, sorrow for having harmed Christ, and resolution to avoid further offenses against him. Through encountering the wounded Jesus, believers are led to confession.

Persons accept the offer of the mercy embodied in the Christ who suffers on humanity's behalf through confession, a response by which believers renew their commitment to love God. Unlike the "fire and brimstone" exempla in which the horrors that await unrepentant sinners loom large, many stories of the persuasive type—sermons of divine mercy—portray Jesus as personally wooing people to confession. One fourteenth-century sermon, for example, tells of a woman who had committed a mortal sin and, though she went to confession yearly, left this one sin unmentioned because she was so ashamed of it. Christ knew that she could be damned for the deed, so he appeared to her one night and asked whether she knew who he was. She replied, "Yes, I think you are the one who died on the cross for me and for all people." Christ responded: "Now, so that you may know that this is really so, put your hand into my side." "Oh no, Lord," she cried out, "I am not worthy to do that." "I bid you to do so," said Christ. She reached her hand into the bloody wound in Christ's side, and she thought she felt Christ's heart and lungs. As she touched his heart, Christ said to her: "Lo, daughter, you have felt and seen my heart. . . . Why are you ashamed to show me your heart when I have shown you my heart's blood that I shed for you?" When she awoke the next day, her hand was red; in spite of her scrubbing, nothing would wash away the blood. Then, remembering what Christ had said, she went with a sorrowful heart and a sad demeanor to confession, where she repented of her sin. As she wept in remorse, the tears fell onto her hand, cleansing the blood until her hand was "white as ever before."[42] The preacher interprets this tale as a sign that "Christ does not want any man or woman to be lost if they will ask mercy and confess their sins."[43]

The guide for priests, *Speculum Sacerdotale*, reminds its audience that since they do not know the hour of their death, they must repent while they yet have time: "Clense it [synne] with the teris of thy yȝen, and sorowe for the vertu þat þou vsid noȝt in alle that tyme."[44] The process of repentance is carefully chronicled in medieval guidance literature such as the *Speculum Sacerdotale* and the *Layfolk's Catechism*. Compunction of heart, confession of mouth, and satisfaction by deed are consistently presented as the necessary components of good confession: "Sorow of our hert that we have synned . . . open shrift of our mouth how we haf synned, And . . . rightwise amendes makying for that we haf synned."[45] Unless the sinner renounces all "purpose of sinning," then all the deeds of satisfaction are performed in vain.[46] Moreover, if believers do not make a satisfactory confession now, they shall be purged "in the moste spitous fire of purgatorie."[47]

Sorrow of heart, as indicative of the internal state of the believer, is crucial for an effective confession: "Compunccion of herte is nedeful to a synner, scilicet, that he wepe and sorowe for his trespass, and that he be in wille no more for to turne there-to a-yene."[48] In the lengthy discussion of confession in Mirk's *Instruction for Parish Priests,* the state of the believer in relationship to contrition functions as a crucial determinant of the type of penance the priest shall impose.[49] The priest is to discern the nature of the penitient's contrition. If the penitent is sorry for the sin, is contrite, weeps, and asks for mercy, then the priest is advised to "A-bregge hys penaunce þen by myche,"[50] for this is the kind of sinner God readily forgives. If, however, the contrition is light, "þow, moste hyt vaunce."[51] The state of the believer's contrition becomes the determinant of the judgment the priest passes: "After þe contricyone þe dome moste passe."[52] (And yet not all uncontrite believers have a heavy penance imposed. Mirk urges priests to take into account the differences among people, and he counsels that it is better to put a person into purgatory with a light penance than to put a person into hell with too heavy a penance.)[53] The "confiteor" to be said at the end of the confession is a plea for divine mercy: "In werke and worde, & sory þoȝt / Wyth euery lyme of my body, / Wyth sore herte I aske god mercy."[54] Mercy is abundant, but the message of sermonic literature is that, invited by Jesus, people must ask for it.

Images of the suffering Jesus play a fundamental role in evoking the appropriate sorrow of heart. The author of the *Speculum Sacerdotale* explains that venerating the signs and shape of the cross calls to mind Christ's sufferings for humanity.[55] The cross and the crucified Jesus are immediately acccessible to audiences and confront the believer with the imperative to respond. The *Speculum Sacerdotale* author urges his readers to look at the image of the crucified Christ, who still "cryeþ and seiþ to vs yche day":

> Lystne, man, lystne to me,
> Byholde what I thole for the.
> To the, man, well lowde I crye;
> for thy loue þou seest I dye.
> Byholde my body how I am swongyn;
> Se þe nayles how I am þrouȝ stongyn.
> My body withoute is betyn sore,
> My peynes with-in ben wel more.
> All this I haue tholyd for the,
> As þou schalt at Domysday se.[56]

Here the crucified Christ appeals to believers to respond to his suffering on their behalf.

Sin, in and of itself, is not the chief issue in medieval devotional texts. Repentance reconciles the sinner with the Divine so perfectly that it is not the case that sin is simply forgotten but rather that in repenting, the spiritual demeanor of the believer is enhanced. Mirk narrates a story of a bishop who could discern the spiritual state of those who presented themselves for the sacrament of the Eucharist. The spiritual demeanor of the church-goers was evident in their visage, some with faces as red as blood (indicating envious and wrathful temperaments), others with faces black as "pyche" (indicating lecherous and unrepentant spirits), others with faces white as snow (forgiven sinners whose weeping has washed their souls), others fair and ruddy (who live by their own labor and avoid mortal sin). Among the congregants, the bishop saw two "comyn" women with faces shining as bright as the sun. These two women had lived an evil life, but upon entering the church they repented, vowing never again to act amiss. In response to their penitence, the merciful God forgave their sins and washed their souls so clean that their shining appearances surpassed all others. This narrative conveys the attitude toward forgiveness prevalent in medieval guidance literature: forgiveness washes penitents clean of their transgressions, not only removing the imprint of sin but also restoring the whole person to a state even more shining and brilliant than they might have obtained had they avoided sin entirely—as in the case of the "fayre and ruddy" hard workers noted above. The seeking of forgiveness leaves no stigma; only the perseverance in sin is responsible for the alienation of humans from the Divine. The Divine rejoices in the transformation of sinners to a life of love of Christ.

A central message of medieval devotional texts is that it does not matter how sinful a person is; anyone who is sorry for her or his deeds is worthy of receiving mercy. All that is necessary for receiving mercy is that the believer ask for mercy "wyþe a meke hert."[57] In Mirk's homily on the feast of Ss. Peter and Paul, he invites congregants to reflect on the figure of the seated Christ, with Paul on one side and Peter on the other. Jesus Christ's wounds are "opyn and bledyng, schewing to ych man and woymon þat he suffyrd þylke wondys þat byn fyve wellys of mercy yn v partys of hys body for soch men and woymen as Petyr and Poule werne."[58] Initially, Peter and Paul were grievous sinners: the early Paul was a fierce opponent of Christianity; although Peter believed himself to be a perfect disciple of Christ, according to the Gospels he denied any knowledge of him after Jesus' arrest. Both repented and relinquished their evil ways. Paul's cruelty was replaced by mercy, his pride by humility. Mirk preaches that Peter's sorrow at having denied Christ so marked him that although he repented, he still wept whenever he heard anyone mention Jesus. Each night when he heard the cock crow, he would get up and go to his prayers and weep so bitterly that his tears burned his face. His weeping was so profuse and frequent that he always carried a cloth with him to wipe the tears away. Once forgiven, the one-time sinner, Peter, became so holy that when he was out traveling, if his shadow fell upon anyone as he walked along, that person would be instantaneously healed.[59] Paul's sword symbolizes the cutting away of chains of mortal sin with the sword of confession, and Peter's keys signal his willingness to open heaven to repentant sinners. Medieval sermonic literature asserts that once forgiveness is received in response to the contrite repentance of the sinner, the slate is wiped clean, with the exception that now the contrite believer, like the shining woman in the exemplar of the bishop who could discern his parishoners' spiritual demeanors, may be united even more intimately with the Divine One: "But for he [Peter] was contryte, and byttyrly wepte, þerfor God þat ys full of mercy, foraf hym his trespas, and made hym more chere þeraftyr þen he dude byfore."[60]

Jesus as an Advocate for Humans and the
Social Dimension of the Believer's Response

We have seen that Jesus Christ *appeals* to people to respond to the divine offer of mercy. As figured in devotional texts and sermons, the wounded Christ also *advocates* on behalf of humans to the Divine. In sermonizing on the Ascension, Mirk alludes to Bede in explaining why Christ arose with his wounds "redy and fresshe, all blody."[61] Christ bears the still-bleeding wounds as a means of appeal for mercy to the First Person of the Trinity on behalf of humanity. Following St. Bernard of Clairvaux, Mirk explains the nature of the advocates believers have in heaven: Mary shows her breast to her son, and Jesus Christ shows the Father his beaten sides and his bloody wounds. The wounds of Christ embody his appeal to the Father on behalf of humans. By showing his wounds to the First Person, Christ both testifies to his love and appeals to God for mercy and forgiveness toward humankind.

A person's success in obtaining divine mercy is frequently paired with a second theme: that is, just as certain individuals have received mercy, so they must have mercy on other Christians.[62] At the end of the world, Jesus Christ will display his bleeding wounds, along with the instruments which inflicted them (the cross, the nails, the spear), and people will be judged according to whether they responded to the wounds or whether they "dispised þe price of his precious bloode."[63] Response to the wounds is measured according to whether people saw Jesus Christ in their neighbors and carried out works of mercy or whether they ignored the pleas of those around them. "And þerfore, dere breþeren, lete vs biwarre þat we may be of þe nombre of hem, that we dele of oure goodus amonge the pore and þat we cloþe þe nakyd and fede þe hungrie and visit the seke."[64] The specific deeds measured are the seven works of mercy drawn from the Gospel of Saint Matthew carried out in relationship to people's neighbors: feeding the hungry, giving drink to the thirsty, clothing the naked, harboring the homeless, visiting the sick, helping those in prison, and burying the dead.[65] The English version of the *Layfolk's Catechism* adds seven spiritual works of mercy which were not in the Latin original. One of the sermons in MS Royal 18 B. xxiii also lists them; they include teaching people how to come to heaven, counseling people to keep God's law, gently reproving sinners, keeping people from working ill, comforting the sorrowful with Christ's Passion, forgiving wrongs done to oneself, and praying for one's friends and enemies.[66] The refrain throughout late medieval literature is that those who are merciful shall find mercy, "and man withouten merci of merci sal misse."[67] The mercy expressed by believers becomes tangible as it is lived out in relationship to the community. In discussing charity in the section on the seven virtues, the author of the *Layfolk's Catechism* explains that the believer cannot love God without also loving her or his neighbor.[68] Thus, the medieval system of mercy advocates social responsibility in which the love of God and love of neighbor are inextricably linked.

Action is critical to the cosmos constructed here: as you sow, so shall you reap. Mirk relates one narrative in which a father has a son who was to be his heir. Unfortunately, the heir ends up in an altercation with another knight who, in fury, slays the son. The father seeks vengeance and calls out his company of knights to pursue the murderer relentlessly until he has no rest and must flee for his life. Good Friday arrives, and as people flock to church to worship God and give thanks to Jesus Christ who died on the cross for all humanity, the pursued knight follows them into the church. The word gets out, and his enemy, with his followers, rush into the church, with swords drawn, to avenge the murder of the son. The killer sees what he has done and realizes that he has trespassed against the father of the man he killed (and also realizes that his own death may be near). He approaches the father and falls to the ground with his arms spread out in the shape of a cross: "For love of the one who on this day spread his arms out on the cross, and died for me and all humankind and forgave those who killed him, have mercy on me and forgive me for trespassing against you." The father realizes that it would be a horrible deed to commit murder in a church against one who has sought mercy for Christ's sake. He thinks long and hard and finally answers, "Now, for his sake, love that died on the cross for humankind, I forgive you," and he helps the man up, kisses him, and together they venerate the cross. The father-knight creeps to the cross and kisses its feet. Marvelously, the image loosens its arms and embraces and kisses him, saying in a voice heard throughout the church, "I forgive you as you have forgiven for me."[69] Here the figure of Christ functions to transform these two knights' actions in the world. The one confesses and seeks forgiveness; the other forgives and is restored to a right relationship with God. And both, in imitation of the love Christ demonstrated toward humankind, receive forgiveness and mercy, which becomes, literally, the granting of life in the one case and the assurance of eternal life in the other. Mercy is gained by seeking it in alliance with the one who suffered on behalf of all humanity and by granting it to others.

Believers can seek divine help not only for themselves, but also for other Christians. The power of the Mass to influence the state of those in purgatory is expressed in the exemplum of a priest who sings masses for the dead every day. After he is suspended from this activity, the dead who are buried in the churchyard near a bishop saying matins on a feast day cry out, lamenting that the priest who said masses on their behalf was taken from them. The dead warn the bishop that unless he reinstates the priest, he will die "in an euel deþ."[70] In another story, fishers of St. Theobold haul in ice rather than fish. The bishop has gout, so he welcomes the ice to soothe his pain until he hears a voice from within the ice saying: "I am a sowle . . . that is turmentyd here in this frost for my synnes." The tormented soul says that he will be released if the bishop will say thirty masses on thirty subsequent days.[71] The author of the *Speculum Sacerdotale* explains that offerings, prayers, and the almsdeeds free souls from the pains of purgatory:

> Ȝit there schuld none trowe so harde relesynge or lewsynge to be a-bowte many þousand soules in the day of here commemoracion when þat alle holy chirche and peple crieþ and prayeþ to God for hem with oblacions, prayingis, and doyngis of almes deedes.[72]

The *Speculum Sacerdotale* specifically lists prayers, sacrifice of the sacrament, fasting, and the giving of alms as a means of helping the contrite dead. The Passion of Jesus points to the re-creation of the universe as God's space in which the merciful action of Jesus Christ provokes viewers of his life and death to imitate this mercy through their own interactions with their neighbors.

Medieval sermons and devotional literature depict a God of love, mercy, and justice and portray confession as the means of reconciliation with the divine life. In focusing on divine justice, some materials emphasize the hopeless fate of those who refuse to respond to God's love, while others, highlighting divine mercy, focus on the nature of God's love for humanity as it is embodied in the Passion of Christ. In general, late medieval homilies and guidance literature construct a world in which the reader or listener is brought to a new understanding of her or his relationship to God and neighbor by encountering the living flesh of the wounded Jesus. Sermons and literature of divine mercy convey the rich theological heritage of medieval England in language and images that capture the spiritual imagination and move the human heart to love and acceptance of the offer of mercy of God-in-Christ. This sermon and spiritual guidance literature portrays a God of unending mercy who grieves at the agony of Jesus but endures it for the love of humankind. It also portrays a human and divine Christ who suffers in order to urge women and men to seek forgiveness and renew their love for the God who loves them. The theological and emotional power of the images of the suffering Jesus, weeping for sinners, scourged, mocked, bloody, wounded, and dying, lies in its witness to the depth of divine love and empathy for humanity. As one medieval preacher said: "God loved in order to be loved, and asked nothing except that we love in return."[73]

Imitation of Jesus Christ in the Lives of Individual Believers:
Julian of Norwich, Margery Kempe, and Spiritual Anguish

The Spirituality of Suffering

We have seen the prominence of the suffering Jesus in homiletic and devotional literature in the first section of this chapter. Now we look more closely at responses to the suffering Christ in the lives of individual believers. We consider, in particular, the place of personal suffering associated with the wounded Jesus in the process of spiritual transformation described by the late medieval English spiritual guides Margery Kempe and Julian of Norwich.

My reading of Margery Kempe and Julian of Norwich suggests that three distinct types of suffering emerge in the relationships of humans to God: suffering born of contrition, compassion, and longing. Suffering in each of these progressive stages contributes to a comprehensive perception of the God who is Love, and each stage correlates with a part of the process of coming to understand that the Christ who suffered is God.[74] For Margery Kempe, the constellation of suffering of contrition, compassion, and longing can be correlated further with her understanding of the social roles that describe her relationship to God. In one of her dalliances with God, God says to her: "þow art a very dowtyr to me & a modyr also, a syster, a wyfe and a spowse."[75] As a daughter, she experiences contrition; as a mother and sister, she experiences compassion; as a spouse, she experiences the suffering of longing to be with her Beloved.

I explore these manifestations of suffering to demonstrate the progression from one type of suffering to another in the changing relationship to the Divine. I will briefly explore each of the three types of pain and suggest the nature of the interrelationship among them in order to show how Christians' identification with the suffering Jesus functioned in the process of spiritual transformation to deepen believers' relationships to God and to the world.

To this end, I consider the work of the late fourteenth- and early fifteenth-century English anchoress Julian of Norwich and the work of the lay pilgrim and spiritual guide Margery Kempe. Julian (b. c. 1342), about whom very little is known, lived for at least some time as an anchoress, a solitary in a small cell adjoining a parish church in Norwich. She cultivated her own spiritual life through private devotions, participating in liturgical services visible through a window in her cell, and praying for humanity generally. Julian also offered spiritual advice to people, among them Margery Kempe, who journeyed to see her.[76] Her *Showings*, the book discussed here, grew out of an experience she had at age thirty of a series of sixteen revelations connected with the stages of Jesus' suffering on the cross—from the crowning of thorns and the discoloration of Jesus' face, to the scourging of his body and the shedding of his blood. She first recorded the revelations in a brief, descriptive text, and then, about 20 years later, she wrote down her subsequent reflections on the meaning of the revelations in order to guide other Christians in their spiritual pursuits.[77] Her literary style and the theological sophistication of her writing suggest that she had extensive knowledge of scripture and classic theological and spiritual texts—some scholars hypothesize that her education and access to texts were gained in a monastic setting prior to her taking up the anchoretic life. She is assumed to have died soon after 1416, the date of the last recorded bequest to her in a local will.

In contrast to Julian, who lived out the monastic commitment to stability in the anchoritic form popular in fourteenth-century England, Margery Kempe's lifestyle reflects another growing trend in late medieval spirituality: the emergence of itinerant religious leaders from among laypeople with no ties to religious orders. Kempe—a laywoman, wife, and mother of fourteen children—narrates the lively drama of her encounter with the God of Love who guided her growth from a brewer of ale and unrepentant sinner to a pilgrim and preacher of repentance, compassion, and longing for God. Although we know nothing about her mother, Kempe (b. 1373) came from a respected family in Lynn in Norfolk. Her father, John Brunham, held a variety of public offices, including those of mayor and justice of the peace. At the age of twenty, she married John Kempe, also of Lynn, and records that after the birth of a child, she suffered a great physical and emotional illness, made worse by the fact that she had not confessed all of her sins. With Christ's intercession, she recovered from the affliction. She increasingly devoted her life to God and eventually (after the birth of fourteen children) convinced her husband to take a vow of chastity with her. In her lively book, she narrates the journey of her spiritual growth and describes the adventures and adversities of her pilgrimages throughout England, as well as Jerusalem, Rome, Norway, Venice, and Germany, among other places. Her loud crying, her devotional weeping, and her frank narrative method of teaching gained her many loyal friends but also many enemies (her traveling companions stole her sheets on one occasion and set off from a foreign town without her on another). She was accused of heresy numerous times, but she successfully defended her orthodoxy, and her *Book* suggests that the charges were never substantiated. Unlike Julian of Norwich, Margery Kempe could not read, but, as was common in the fourteenth century, she had developed a capacity for memorization. She had priests read to her regularly and enthusiastically attended sermons of local and renowned visiting preachers. It is therefore not surprising that her *Book* exhibits a remarkable familiarity with scripture and church tradition.[78] She apparently began dictating her *Book* to the first of her two scribes in the early 1430s and finished it sometime before her death in about 1438.

These two spiritual virtuosi are united by a theological focus on the suffering of Jesus Christ common to many Christians in the late fourteenth and early fifteenth centuries. I consider the significance of their identification with the "suffering Jesus," and I explore how experiences of Christ's Passion, whether through sorrow or physical duress, play such an important role in their spiritual life.[79]

The writings of both Margery Kempe and Julian of Norwich depict a Christian life-journey directed toward an experiential love and knowledge of God. For both authors, the imagery, metaphors, and stories used to describe God are united in the central theological affirmation that God is Love. Kempe and Julian are typical of many late medieval spiritual guides in that they lead their readers toward a deepening relationship of love and knowledge with the God of Love. They do not seek momentary ecstatic experiences of God, nor do they write disinterested ontotheological analyses of the divine life; rather, they envision a holistic lifelong path on which a growing relationship with the Divine is coupled with a deepening love of self and neighbor.

Suffering functions within this larger context as a part of the process by which a person learns to perceive God as Love. The experience of pain functions as a way to God, as a means to religious understanding. My claim is that underlying the manifestations of spiritual and physical duress in the works of medieval authors is a recognition that the believer's Jesus-identified emotional and physical suffering is not an end in itself. This tradition consistently critiques situations in which pursuit of pain is viewed as an autonomous goal; rather, an experiential understanding of the suffering of the earthly Jesus is always directed toward—and complemented by—an understanding of the divinity of Christ. This eventual recognition of Christ as the God-human who re-presents the God of Love to humanity enables the physical identification with Jesus' Passion to be a fundamental part of the believer's spiritual journey to God, even though this identification is never an end in itself.

For both Julian of Norwich and Margery Kempe, Jesus Christ is the most important guide in the growth of the God-human relationship. Sin ruptured humans' ability to perceive the loving God and alienated people from their proper spiritual goal. Julian emphasizes, though, that even when people do not experience the nearness of the Divine, God remains with them always. In the Incarnation, God presents the greatest possible sign of love to the world. In his Passion and death, Christ overcomes the devil, the sign of evil's power over humans, cleanses sin by the shedding of his blood, and frees people to experience the loving God once again. Thus, Christ's Passion is the critical restorative act in the God-human relationship. As a human, Jesus is accessible, someone with whom individuals can identify; as divine, Christ presents God to humanity. Exclusive focus on either the humanity or divinity of Jesus Christ misses the integrated relationship of the loving God to humankind. Julian and Margery are different from ethical mystics like their contemporary Walter Hilton (d. 1396), but like the flamboyant Richard Rolle, they center their spirituality not so much on the general life and service of Christ in the world but more specifically on the suffering of Jesus in his Passion and death on the cross.

Julian of Norwich's 1373 collection of sixteen revelations and her subsequent theological reflections on them record the successive stages of Jesus' suffering and death on the cross—including the crowning of thorns, the discoloration of Jesus' face, the scourging of his body, and the shedding of his blood. Significantly, each stage in this suffering reveals something of the nature of God and God's relationship to humans. Julian's process of reflection begins with consideration of what Christ suffered and for whom he suffered, which leads to reflection on why Christ suffered and, most important, causes the believer, in Julian's words, to "know that he is god that sufferyd."[80] The images of Jesus' agony and death which appeared to Julian and which she records in the *Showings* graphically portray the pains he endured. Meditation on the details of the suffering heightens awareness of what Christ endured for humanity and, along with this, prompts the observer to reflect on why Christ chose to undergo such pain. The answer emerges that Jesus suffered out of "love" for humanity. Thus, the believer reflects on the nature of the love that undergirded the events of Christ's death and is led to recognize, in the magnitude of the love, Christ's divinity. Recognition of the love which motivated Christ's work reveals Jesus Christ's divinity; once believers perceive this motivating love, they are reminded that at Christ's Resurrection, suffering was transformed to joy and bliss. In the world to come, humans will be heirs to the joy effected through Christ's suffering.

Three Types of Suffering

It should be noted at the outset that just as Augustine's *Confessions* records his spiritual autobiography and does not dwell on his day-to-day activities or family relationships (except insofar as they contribute to his spirituality), Julian of Norwich and Margery Kempe always treat suffering within the parameters of their relationship to God.[81] They do not linger over cataloguing the varieties of suffering that plague humans because they are not interested in the pain that often accompanies discipleship for its own sake. The type of physical suffering that may come readily to mind is very different from the type of suffering these women considered significant. In fact, Margery Kempe tells of being struck by a falling beam in a church not because of the physical suffering but because, miraculously, she did not suffer physically.[82] The suffering that most concerns these women is the physical and emotional (including mental and affective) anguish that emerges in their relationship to God. And it is their identification with Jesus' suffering that produced these women's exhortations advocating compassion for the suffering of the world around them.

CONTRITION   Initial reflection on humanity's relationship to the Divine reveals only the vast gulf of human sinfulness that separates people from God. Confrontation with this sinfulness exposes believers to their weaknesses; but meditation on sinfulness alone can lead to despair, the greatest of all medieval sins, unless contrition opens believers' eyes to the merciful God who forgets sin from the time that humans repent.[83] When the disciple clearly sees the futility of sole reliance upon the self, she or he can recognize that God is the foundation of all being and can seek the help offered by the God who reminds humans when they are going astray yet mercifully protects them in spite of it (667). Repentance in the face of a merciful God initiates the healing of the breach between God and humankind. The healing process is painful and beset not only with the sorrow and shame of having offended the Divine but also with further suffering which may occur as the contrite person willingly accepts penance in the form of physical illness, sorrows, or the world's contempt—all of which are part of the cleansing process. While acknowledging its importance in initially drawing attention away from the world and toward God, Julian does not dwell long on the matter of contrition but advises her readers against unreasonable depression or despair. She suggests that the reader meditate instead on the manifestation of the merciful God and proceed from being made clean by contrition to being made "ready" by compassion to come to God (451–52).

Margery, writing within a generation of Julian's *Showings,* and representative of the common tendency to highlight contrition in late fourteenth- and early fifteenth-century spirituality, deals at length with this early stage. While at times Kempe, louder and more demonstrative than Julian in her contrition, struggled painfully with "scruples" (a spiritual problem which does not seem to have afflicted Julian of Norwich) and is constantly reassured by God that her sins are forgiven, both she and Julian of Norwich affirm the critical place of contrition and its associated suffering in the God-human relationship. For Kempe, suffering functions both as a signal and as a response to the presence of sin. She associates her experience of intense suffering with the presence of unrepented sin within her.[84] Like Julian, she also depicts the suffering of contrition as remorse brought about by the repentant recognition of her sinfulness. Margery describes the early stages of her conversion as a time when she struggled with temptations, falling back into greed as she pursued careers as a brewer of ale and manager of a grain mill. But as the years passed, she more successfully centered her life around God: "And þis creatur had contrycion & gret compunccyon wyth plentyouws teers and many boystows sobbyngss for hir synnes & for hir unkyndnesse a-geyns hir Maker" (13). Throughout her spiritual autobiography, Margery Kempe describes weeping for her sins and suffering great anguish over having offended the loving God.

She associates her suffering of contrition with her growth in her relationship as a daughter of God: "Whan þow stodyst to plese me, þan art þu a very dowtyr" (31). Kempe maintains that at the initial stage of reformation, the most efficacious remedy for the distortions of the human's sinful relationship to God is symbolized by the obedience of a child to a parent.

For both Julian of Norwich and Margery Kempe, contrition signals the re-orientation of the human toward God. At this first stage, suffering arises from the awareness of the sinner's "unkindness" toward Jesus, whereas repentance reveals the God of mercy. Suffering emerges in the environment of contrition as a person experiences the disjunction between glimpses of what the healed relationship with God could be like and the present perception of sin hindering that relationship.

COMPASSION   Once a person has established God as a priority, the next stage of preparing for life with God can begin. Through compassion and its related suffering, the believer experiences the depth of her or his love for Christ, Christ's unity with humanity, something of what it means to say that Christ is divine, and a sense of Christ-identified unity with other humans.

Julian advises her readers not simply to recall the suffering of Jesus, but to remember actively what Jesus suffered:

> Crist shewde a parte of hys passyon nere his dyeng. I saw the swete face as it were drye and blodeles with pale dyeng and deede pale, langhuryng and than turned more deede in to blew, and after in browne blew, as the flessch turned more depe dede . . . the swet body was so dyscolouryd, so drye . . . so dedly and so pytyous as he had bene sennyght deed, contynually dyeng. (357–59)

She "remembers" Jesus' Passion as if she were there, identifying her love of Christ with that of Mary, Mother of Jesus; the disciples; and all "tru lovers" of Jesus (366). In imaginatively reenacting the Passion of Christ, the believer suffers with Christ just as the contemporary friends of Jesus had (692).

As indicated in the discussion of sermons in the first section of this chapter, the practice of active remembering characterizes medieval spirituality. The purpose of this recollection was to arouse the meditator's affections, to bring the message of Scripture into the present.[85] Julian relives Christ's Crucifixion so that her body reinscribes the pain of Christ's physical suffering: "I felte no peyne, but for Cristes paynes. . . . For me thought my paynes passyd ony bodely deth" (364). She experiences the pain of physical identification with the suffering Christ and the agony of watching a loved one suffer: "Here felt I stedfastly that I louyd Crist so much aboue my selfe that ther was no peyne that myght be sufferyd lyke to that sorow that I had to see hym in payne" (365). The intensity of her pain in watching Jesus suffer reveals to her the depth of her love for him.

As well as revealing the believer's love for Christ, suffering enables the believer to participate in the unity Christ's suffering created between him and the whole cosmos, because when Christ was in pain, not only did humans suffer, but "þe fyrmamente and erth, feylyd for sorow in ther kynd in the tyme of Cristes dyeng" (367). As Christ suffered for humans, thus linking himself with humanity, so individuals ally themselves with the benefits of that suffering by suffering with Christ. The pain is salvific: "But of alle peyne þat leed to saluacion, thys is the most, to se the louer to suffer" (365). The more believers identify with Christ's pain, the greater will be their reward in heaven.

For Julian, the most important point to grasp about Christ's Passion is that the "one who suffered is God," a perception conveyed by the nature and intensity of this suffering. Christ suffered in response to the physical agony inflicted on him as he redeemed the sins of humanity. The perception of the immensity of Christ's suffering to deliver humankind from sin that undergirds Julian's reflections on the Crucifixion is apparent in a fifteenth-century devotion in which Christ speaks to an unrepentant sinner, a devotion Julian herself could well have written:

> I foormede þee and sette þe in paradys. þou dispisedist mi comaundementis and /
> / deseruedist dampnacioun of deeþ. I hauynge merci on þee took fleisch. þat is bicam
> human. See þe woundis þat i took for þe. See þe hoolis of nailis bi þe whiche i was
> piȝt on þe cros. . . . I receyuede buffetis and spetyngis forto ȝelde to þee þe swetnesse
> of paradys. . . . I suffride peyne for to ȝiue glorie to þee. I suffride deeþ. þat þou
> schuldist haue heritage of liif. I lai hid in þe sepulcre. þat þou schuldist regne in
> heuene. What schulde i do gretter þingis þan þese. Where is þe fruyt of mi woundis
> so greet. Where is þe fruyt of mi wrongis so greete. Where is þe priis of mi blood.
> þat i ȝoure soulis. Where is ȝoure seruice þat / / ȝe han doon to me for þe priis of
> mi blood. I hadde ȝou aboue mi glorie. Aperinge man whanne i was god.[86]

As consideration of homiletic and devotional literature in the first section of the chapter indicates, Jesus Christ suffered because of human sin and in response to the physical agony inflicted on him as he redeemed the sins of humanity, and he expects believers to respond to that suffering. Christ suffered also, and no less significantly for Julian, in compassion for human sorrow and anguish at his suffering: "Every mannes sorow, desolacion and angwysshe he sawe and sorowd, for kyndnes and loue. For in as mech as our lady sorowde for his paynes, as mech sufferde he sorow for her sorowse" (376). Jesus' suffering in community with believers as they suffer in witnessing Jesus' pain manifests God's compassion for humanity. The God revealed in the Passion of Jesus is a God of mercy but also a God of compassion, reminding believers that they never suffer alone (411). Meditation on the nature of the love expressed in Jesus' suffering leads Julian to recognize that "though the swete manhode of Crist myght suffer but oonse, the goodnes of hym may nevyr seese of profer" (385). Christ's willingness to suffer reveals that Christ is endless love.[87]

Meditation on the compassion of Jesus, and the experience of compassion for Jesus, leads the believer to live in the world with compassion. For Julian, compassion toward, or suffering with, others manifests the presence of "Christ in us" (410).[88] Although this theme of communal love is present in Julian, she does not dwell on the painful nature of this compassionate identification with neighbors to the extent that, as we shall see in chapter 4, Margery Kempe does.

Margery Kempe's suffering of compassion also functions to deepen her understanding of Jesus by leading her to reflect on his motivation in suffering for people; eventually, this results in a recognition of Christ's love for humanity and in a perception of Christ's divinity, as well as his humanity. Kempe presents her growth in understanding of Jesus' humanity as a precursor to her eventual understanding of the Godhead: "Aftyrwardys whan . . . sche [Margery] . . . [had] suffyrd mech despite & repref for hir wepyng & hir criying, owr Lord . . . drow hir affeccyon in-to hys Godhed, & þat was mor feruent in lofe & desyr & mor sotyl in vndirstondyng þan was þe Manhod" (209). After perceiving the Godhead, Kempe was often filled with demonstrative sorrow over Jesus' life and death. She notes that the violence of her weeping was mitigated: "It was mor sotyl & mor softe" (209), she writes.

For Julian, but even more dramatically for Margery Kempe, compassion extends beyond compassion for Christ's suffering to compassion for the sin and pain of other Christians (Julian of Norwich, 408). This is paralleled by Christ's compassion for the suffering witness of those who love him. Kempe's emotional and physical suffering of identification with Mary, of compassion for Jesus' suffering, and of suffering with and for other sinners in her world functioned dramatically in a public way to re-present Christ's work to the world. As Christ had appeared different from those around him and had been ridiculed by many of his contemporaries, so Kempe herself becomes a "fool" for Christ.[89] This sense that suffering on behalf of Jesus and in identification with Jesus strengthens the believer's bond with him pervaded late medieval spirituality and is evident, for example, in the following fifteenth-century medieval poetic rendering of the beatitudes:

> Blessed be men þat mornen for synne
> þei shul be comforted her soule wiþ ynne . . .
> Blessed be men þat suffren for ryȝte
> þe rewme of heuene to hem ys dyȝte
> Blessed soþely schal ye be
> Whan men schul pursewe you for me.[90]

Christ informs her that God will take the "gift" of tears away if Margery no longer wants to suffer. Kempe refuses to relinquish the gift which not only brings her pain but also the "merriment" of doing Christ's work in the world. God explains to her why she suffers so visibly by saying that her anguish should remind people of Christ's suffering and of Mary's sorrows; Kempe's *Book* affirms, as do Julian's revelations, that the service of sorrowing is a way to salvation.[91] As the discussion in chapter 4 will indicate in more detail, Kempe's public commitment to bringing other people to God extends to weeping for the souls in purgatory, for those in mischief, for those in poverty and diseased, and for Jews, Muslims, and heretics. In this suffering of compassion, Margery experiences her relationship to Christ as that of caring sister and loving mother: "Whan þu wepyst & mornyst for my peyn & for my Passyon, þan art þow a very modyr to haue compassyon of hyr chyld; whan þow wepyst for oþer mennys synnes and for aduersytes, þan art þow a very syster" (31).

In the stage of suffering borne of compassion, the experience of pain reveals the believer's love of Christ, fosters unity with Christ and the world, and begins to draw the believer beyond the physical Jesus who suffered on the cross to an understanding of the immensity of the love that motivated Christ in the world to suffer on humanity's behalf.

LONGING   Contrary to what the emphasis on pain here might suggest, Julian's and Margery Kempe's appropriations of Christ do not stop at Christ's death on the cross:

> And I lokyd after the departyng with alle my myghtes, and wende to haue seen the body alle deed; butt I saw him nott so. And right in the same tyme that me thought by semyng that the lyfe myght no lenger last . . . sodenly I beholdyng in the same crosse he channgyd in blessydfulle chere. (Julian of Norwich, 379)

Yet perception of the risen and joyful Christ also gives rise to a further and final form of suffering.

Christ suffers for humanity from compassion, but he also suffers from thirst; Julian, like Richard Rolle before her, interprets this as spiritual thirst, a longing to gather all people into him, "to oure endlesse blysse" (418).[92] Believers are drawn to God by responding to Christ's longing for them by longing to be with God. The longing for the joy made possible by Jesus' suffering creates its own pain of desire which can be satisfied only after this life: "I had grete longyng and desyer of goddys gyfte to be delyuerde of this worlde and of this lyfe. . . . yf there had no payne ben in this lyfe but the absens of oure lorde, me thought some tyme þat it was more than I myght bere, and this made me to morne and besely to longe" (619–620). Julian knows the painful longing will remain until she sees God clearly in God's appearance of joy, yet God encourages her to endure, reminding her that eventually she will be filled with joy and bliss (662).

Margery Kempe's description of longing to be with God parallels Julian's. At this stage, Kempe relates to God as Spouse, which grows out of her experiences of both the humanity and divinity of Christ. She desires to be with God, even going so far as to say that she longs to leave this world. God reminds her, though, of her social commitment and responsibility to testify to the goodness and work of God in the world. But God also reminds her that her sorrow will be transformed into joy. The intimacy of this stage of the relationship is noted when God says to Margery: "And, whan thow sorwyst for þow art so long fro þe blysse of Heuyn, þan art þu a very spowse & a wyfe, for it longyth to þe wyfe to be wyth hir husbond & no very joy to han tyl sche come to hys presens" (31).

The pain here is pain of separation from the risen Christ who longs to gather all people "to our endless joy," an event which can never be fully experienced in this world, a longing which cannot be fully satisfied until the world to come.

❦

In conclusion, then, this discussion of Julian of Norwich and Margery Kempe suggests that experiences of emotional and physical suffering can lead to and be a part of deepening love of God and neighbor. And yet pain is not pursued for its own sake but rather emerges as a part of a spiritual process of renewal. The revelation and deepening perception of the God of Love that emerge out of suffering are critical for their religious transformation. Kempe and Julian suffer first in the face of their own sin and distance from God. They move from this to experience the suffering of Mary and particularly to experience the suffering of Jesus. The process of cultivating compassion for Jesus' work awakens them to Christ's love for humanity—but the process does not stop there. As they experience the suffering of Jesus, they come to recognize Jesus Christ's love for humanity; this leads both, but Margery Kempe especially, to testify publicly to that love in the world. Through a transformation of suffering, Julian of Norwich and Margery Kempe move beyond the historical Jesus to speak of the God of Love, who is merciful and compassionate and who longs for humanity and with whom humanity longs to be united.

The sermons and spiritual literature discussed in this chapter testify to the immense power of the central image of the suffering Jesus in medieval Christian culture. The presence of the bloody, tormented Savior awakens viewers and readers to their complicity in his wounding; his suffering and anguish engender contrition and compassion in them and open their eyes to recognize who it is who suffers and why. In the wounded Jesus, readers and viewers are offered divine mercy, and they are urged to respond to the offer by confessing their sins and imitating the divine mercy and love manifest in the torn and wounded flesh of Jesus Christ.

TWO

The Aesthetics
of Suffering

Figuring the Crucified Jesus in Manuscripts
and Wall Paintings

This chapter sets before us the visual world of medieval reflection on the figure of the suffering Jesus. I consider images of the suffering Jesus in two media: medieval church wall paintings and manuscript illuminations, particularly illuminations from Psalters and Books of Hours. My analysis of representative settings in which artistic depictions of the suffering Jesus appear demonstrates that for medieval Christians, the portrayal of the suffering Jesus made tangible and palpable the mercy of God. The suffering Jesus was the primary expression of the deep and abiding love of the medieval God for the world, a love so great that it foreordained the death of God's son. This worldview is, I think, alien to many of us in the late twentieth century who consider the association of love and suffering to be deeply problematic at best. Be this as it may, I seek in this chapter to reconstruct the medieval context for understanding the transformative power of religious suffering and to offer a glimpse of how a different culture and time might have understood and appropriated the central christological symbol of Jesus' Passion and death.

I consider portrayals of the Passion of Jesus in a variety of artistic forms to demonstrate the sophistication of medieval piety which, far from dwelling on the humanity of Jesus in an "excessively" sentimental way, perceived Jesus' suffering and the deeply emotional and empathetic experiencing of that suffering to be at the heart of the meaning of human life. Further, the medieval doctrine that Jesus Christ is one "person" who has both a human nature and a divine nature was crucial to medieval religiosity. As I will suggest, the narrative of Jesus Christ's life, death, and Resurrection—with the Crucifixion at the center—was perceived as the source of humanity's, and indeed of all creation's, healing, nourishment, and reconciliation with the Divine. I articulate how in the context of medieval piety, literary and artistic sources functioned together so that the process of re-calling Jesus' death and its cause reoriented viewers' lives and demanded that they respond to the cry of love expressed in the Crucifixion.

The placement of the portrayals of the suffering Jesus in Psalters and Books of Hours provides the visual key to the medieval understanding of the Hebrew Scriptures and of the New Testament. Further, in Books of Hours depictions of the suffering Jesus function to reconfigure *time* so that the cycle of day and night becomes a re-creation of salvation history centered on the sacrifical, healing, and nourishing work of Jesus Christ. The depictions of Jesus' life, death, and Resur-rection that cover the walls of even the most modest of medieval English churches locate worshipers in the center of the narrative of Divine love for humanity. The spatial and temporal transformation effected by the suffering Jesus opens medi-eval believers to the possibility of a renewed relationship with God and people. In this chapter, I seek to convey the religious depth and theological sophistica-tion of religious iconography and of the lived responses to this iconography.[1]

Psalters, Missals, and Books of Hours

The Passion Narrative as Hermeneutical Key to the Reading of Scripture

In their recent work, James Marrow and Jeffrey Hamburger have explored the medieval interconnectedness between the Hebrew Scriptures (the Old Testament) and the New Testament.[2] The New Testament and, in particular, the figure of the suffering Jesus provided the hermeneutical key to the medieval reading of both testaments. The use of images was one of the most powerful forms in which this key was transmitted to readers of medieval manuscripts. Medieval Psalters (collections of Psalms), contained no written introductions to remind readers to keep the New Testament in mind when reading and praying. Readers were never-theless guided to do so—visually, not verbally. The consistent use of artistic depictions of New Testament events to illustrate Hebrew Scripture visually in-structed medieval readers to understand that the Hebrew Bible has New Testa-ment themes embedded in it. This method of orientation is often immediately apparent in one of the most significant decorative features of medieval Psalters: the illumination which centers around the first letter of the first word of the Psalter, the B of the opening Psalm 1: "Beatus vir qui non abiit in consilio impiorum" ("Blessed is the man who has not walked in the counsel of the un-godly").[3] The Jesse Tree (cf. Isaiah 11:1)—the genealogical record of Jesus' lineage from Jesse through David, Solomon, and Mary, mother of Jesus, and leading, finally, to Jesus himself—was one of the most common features of this page.[4] The visual presentation of the Jesse Tree set the context for the inaugural reading of the entire Psalter; this artistic opening to the Bible conveyed, with visual immediacy, that the Hebrew Scriptures (the Old Testament in the medieval mind) were in reality the story of the lineage of Jesus Christ. All of the events of the Old Testament had meaning insofar as they pointed to the figure of Christ, whom they prefigured and whose life, death, and Resurrection they foretold.

The thirteen-line historiated initial "B" of the Beatus of Psalm 1 in the Vaux Psalter (fig. 2.1) establishes a theological template for the interpretation of the Psalms that follow.[5] Though the tree which emerges from the back of the sleeping Jesse includes figures such as David (with his lyre) and Solomon, the central trunk of the tree depicts in three quatrefoils the following: the crucified Jesus Christ flanked by the mourning Mary and the beloved disciple, John, pointing to the cross; Mary with a scepter and the child Jesus with the world in his palm; and, at the top, Christ enthroned. The crucified Jesus appears at the beginning of the Psalter to establish the christological subtext to the readings that follow. The eleven-line historiated initial of the Jesse Tree on the Beatus page of the Gorleston Psalter demonstrates a similar point.[6] Here, again, the focal image in the Jesse Tree is the crucified Jesus, hands outstretched and curved, head slumped to the left, bleeding profusely as Mary points to his wounds.[7] Thus, readers begin the Psalter with the image of the suffering Jesus graphically set before them, and they are encouraged to overread the text accordingly.

The depictions of Jesus' life and death in the Beatus page are echoed in many of the historiated initials of other commonly illuminated Psalms. In the St. Omer Psalter, Psalm 110 begins with the standard "Dixit Dominus Domino meo" ("The Lord said unto my Lord"). Here the historiated initial "D" of "Dominus" depicts the Last Judgment in which Christ, with prominent wounds in his side, hands, and feet, sits in judgment as the dead below emerge from their graves (fig. 2.2).[8] The border medallions from bottom left to top right depict the Passion, Death, Resurrection, Ascension, and Pentecost. This christological typology figures the "Lord" understood by the New Testament–guided readers of the Old Testament as the suffering and resurrected Jesus Christ who comes to judge the living and the dead. In the Ormsby Psalter, the historiated initial of Psalm 38 ("Dixi custodiam vias meas ne peccem in lingua mea"; "I said, I will take heed to my ways: that I sin not with my tongue") depicts Christ before Pilate, again indicative of medieval attentiveness to the New Testament backdrop for understanding the Psalms.[9] The point here is to see that for medieval Christians the suffering Jesus was ubiquitous, made present as much by visual images as by written texts. Artistic as well as literary sources testify to the Christ-saturated character of the Hebrew Scriptures, as well as of the New Testament.

Suffering and Liturgical Time

Manuscript illuminations position the figure of the suffering Jesus as the hermeneutical key to the Hebrew Scriptures. Further, the suffering Jesus orients ecclesial time. This is especially clear in Books of Hours, collections of prayers for laypeople organized according to the Divine Office that included matins, lauds, prime, terce, sext, none, vespers, and compline. These books generally consisted of the following parts: a calendar, four gospel lessons, Hours of the Virgin, Hours of the Cross, Hours of the Holy Spirit, the "Obsecro te" and "O intemerata" (two prayers to the Virgin Mary), the penitential psalms, the litany of the saints, the Office of the Dead, and suffrages (prayers to saints).[10] Series of illuminations in Books of Hours, especially in the Hours of the Virgin and the Hours of the Cross, frequently correlated the successive stages of Jesus' suffering with the eight liturgical hours which oriented the days of many religious and laity in fourteenth- and fifteenth-century England. This linking of Jesus' suffering with temporality charges all life with sacred purpose. Through recalling the suffering of Jesus at each of the liturgical hours, time was consecrated as God's time, and medieval worshipers were reminded of the ongoing significance of Jesus' presence in the world. The *Mirror of St. Edmund* divides meditation on God into seven hours modeled on the liturgical hours "þat non houre þe passe þat þou ne haue þin herte ocupyed."[11]

The liturgical hours are often demarcated in Books of Hours with depictions from the infancy narrative of Jesus or the life of Mary, beginning with the Annunciation to Mary at matins.[12] In fourteenth- and fifteenth-century English Books of Hours, it is also common to find scenes from the Passion cycle used to mark the movement through the day. In general, these images marked the transition from one hour to the next following a consistent pattern: the Agony in the Garden or the Betrayal of Judas initiated matins, and the Betrayal or Christ before Pilate initiated lauds. This was followed by Christ before Pilate or the Flagellation at prime, the Flagellation or Christ Carrying the Cross at terce, Christ carrying the Cross or the Crucifixion at sext, the Crucifixion or the Deposition at none, the Deposition or the Entombment at vespers, and the Entombment or the Resurrection at compline.[13] At times, as I will point out, scenes from both the infancy and Passion cycles are mixed, although, as in this case, the cumulative effect of the scenes is often to emphasize the suffering in Jesus' life.

In the early fourteenth-century Cambridge University Library MS Dd. 8.2 Hours of the Virgin, the liturgical hours sequence is punctuated by nine-line historiated initial scenes from the life and Passion of Jesus.[14] Although the Annunciation (and not the Agony in the Garden) is depicted at the beginning of matins, viewers are reminded of the suffering to come by the depiction in the bas-de-page of a hunter shooting an arrow toward a rabbit. The arrow passes through the red tendrils decorating the "D" of Dominus, portending the red blood which will appear when the arrow hits the rabbit, and evoking the suffering of Jesus to which the Annunciation points.[15] The infancy narrative continues at lauds, which is preceded by a five-line initial depicting the Nativity. Then, in traditional fashion, prime depicts Christ before Pilate, terce the Flagellation, sext Christ Bearing the Cross, none the Crucifixion, vespers the Deposition, and compline the Entombment.[16] Through these visual portrayals presented in conjunction with the psalms and prayers in the text, the hours and days of commonplace existence are invested with religious meaning and purpose. Temporality itself is made sacred and transformed into a continuous reminder of the suffering of Jesus in the world.

In a monastic setting, the recitation of the eight hours would generally have been spread out over seven different times of the day, beginning with matins and lauds at daybreak, prime at 6:00 A.M., terce at 9:00 A.M., sext at noon, none at 3:00 P.M. vespers at sunset, and compline in the evening.[17] Roger Wieck and Virginia Reinburg suggest that most laypeople did not follow this rigorous schedule; it is more likely that Books of Hours were used in the morning, often upon first awakening, and also for private prayer during mass.[18] The structure of the *Horae* and the manner in which they were composed to mark the passing of time, and even to transform the meaning of the passing of time, while not necessarily strictly observed by laypeople, were built into the structure of Books of Hours so that those who regularly read *Horae* could observe the patterns for making time sacred.

Through the continual call to recollection which such manuscript illuminations evoked, readers were inculcated in the knowledge that their prayers and meditations were not simply remembrances of past events, but, even more, they were reflections on the ongoing presence of the suffering Jesus in the world. The hours of each day were a reminder that all time has meaning insofar as it participates in the salvation history made possible by the wounded Savior. It is in this sacred time that the believer lives out a relationship to the Divine and responds to the suffering Jesus in the world.

Polysemy of the Crucifixion

The christological body becomes the site where the believer experiences the transformation of time into the meeting place of the Divine and the human. This intersection challenges the believer to respond to the divine offer of mercy present therein. But what happens at this bodily center? What does the viewer see? The meanings ascribed to the Crucifixion in the Middle Ages are endless. I illustrate here three primary valences to give some sense of the richness of medieval reflection on the suffering Jesus and to illustrate that images of Jesus, in their theological and emotional richness, are intended to generate love in the viewer, a love which responds to Christ's act of love wherein the devotee is encouraged to practice loving God and neighbor. In what follows, I comment on the themes of sacrifice, nourishing, and healing. First, however, I begin with a brief reflection on

Jesus' identity in response to the medieval question, Who is the one who suffers? Here, I note briefly medieval art's attention to both the humanity and the divinity of Christ.

HUMANITY AND DIVINITY   Although upon initial reflection, late medieval illuminations might seem to focus particularly and even exclusively on the humanity of Jesus, in general medieval images of the suffering Jesus attended to both his humanity and his divinity. This presentation of divinity and humanity was achieved in a variety of ways, including the juxtaposition of images of suffering with images of victory, the manner of depicting the Trinity, and, as I will suggest in later sections of this chapter, the details included in the images of suffering.

In many Books of Hours, the pictorial narration juxtaposes scenes from Jesus' life with scenes from Jesus' Passion in such a way as to convey not only the humanity of Jesus but also the kingly and divine reality of his being. This recognition of Jesus Christ as human and divine is depicted in some contexts through the use of two-tiered miniatures which juxtapose scenes from Christ's Passion with scenes from earlier events in Christ's life.[19] The visual impact of the pairing of scenes of suffering with scenes which remind viewers of the divinity of Jesus creates a rich christological context in which viewers perceive the unity of Jesus as human and divine. Medieval viewers understood the suffering Jesus as the blessed one, God on earth. Frequently, this juxtaposition results from the technique of "mixed Hours," that is, a particular form of Books of Hours in which the various Hours of the Virgin, the Cross, and the Holy Spirit are interspersed rather than organized in complete cycles after one another. In "mixed" Hours of the Virgin and the Cross, for example, the Matins of the Hours of the Cross are placed immediately following the Matins and Lauds of the Hours of the Virgin. The Prime of the Cross follows the Prime of the Virgin, and this cross-fertilization proceeds all the way through the compline.[20] Often, the opening illuminations to the two Hours are placed together so that, for example, the opening depiction for the Terce of the Virgin and the Terce of the Cross are placed together at the beginning of the Terce of the Virgin.

The British Library MS Add. 16968, a Book of Hours and Psalter, contains an intermingled Hours of the Virgin and Short Office of the Cross (two of the major formats for prayer often found in Books of Hours).[21] This blending of two distinctive subgenres creates an ongoing juxtaposition of illuminations and text which reminds the reader of Christ's humanity and royalty. A depiction of Christ before Pilate, which initiates the Prime of the Cross, is paired with a depiction of the Annunciation to the Shepherds, which illustrates the Terce of the Virgin.[22] The appearance of Christ before Pilate, then, is understood in the context of the divine favor and presence manifested in the birth of Christ. The juxtaposition of Christ Carrying the Cross (Terce of the Cross) and the Adoration of the Magi (Sext of the Virgin) (fig. 2.3) makes clear that the divine and kingly

Jesus visited by the Magi is also the blood and flesh human being who suffers—even though his divinity may initially be obscured for those who perceive only the suffering person.[23] At the Sext of the Office of the Cross and None of the Hours of the Virgin, the Crucifixion is conjoined with the Massacre of the Innocents to recall the fear that the royal Jesus' birth instilled in King Herod and to signal the innocence of the crucified enfleshed Jesus (fig. 2.4).[24] Medieval viewers perceived the Passion of Christ within the history of divine presence on earth. Visual images of the God-human depicted who it was who suffered and displayed the innocent nature of his suffering.

Pairings of the "Standing Virgin and Child" on one page with the Crucifixion on the next identify the one who suffers as the miraculously conceived Son of God. The Hours of Alice de Reydon and the Peterborough Psalter open with a series of full-page miniatures, including a Virgin with Child miniature facing a Crucifixion.[25] In the Alice de Reydon Crucifixion, Jesus' head falls onto his right shoulder against the green cross, a symbol of the Tree of Life (fig. 2.5).[26] Blood drips down his arm to his elbow and then drips off his body, and blood spurts out of a wound in Jesus' chest beneath his right nipple and flows down his side to just above his waist. While Jesus' eyes are closed, blood from his feet flows down the cross to the ground. The scene bespeaks pain and death, the suffering of the dying Jesus. Mary holds the palms of her hands open and up as if gesturing, and she looks up at Jesus. John's right hand is raised, paralleling Mary's, as he holds a green book in his left hand.[27] The book symbolizes life and is a reminder that Jesus Christ is the Logos, the Word of God. The placement of the Crucifixion page adjacent to the Virgin and Child page transforms the viewers' perceptions of the Crucifixion by emphasizing the nature of the one who suffers: he who was miraculously born of Mary (fig. 2.6).[28] A regal Virgin with a green crown and a golden halo holds the child Jesus with her left arm. He touches her, a sign of the human nature that he shares with her and a gesture that symbolizes their physical connectedness. In her right hand, Mary holds a small green tree with white fruits, a reminder of the lineage leading up to the birth of Jesus. She bears the Tree of Life so that, viewed together, these two pages provide a visually succinct crystallization of the double nature of Jesus Christ.

This evocation of divine presence in the body is also echoed in one of the more common Psalter illuminations in the historiated initials of Psalm 109 ("Dixit Dominus Domino a meo"; "The Lord said unto my Lord") which depicts the Trinity. Images of the Trinity take a variety of forms, such as an image of the first and second persons seated side by side, with the Holy Spirit in the form of a dove between them (fig. 2.7).[29] The medieval association of divinity with the figure of the suffering Jesus is powerfully manifested in portrayals of the Trinity in which the Second Person of the Trinity is the crucified Jesus Christ (fig. 2.8).[30] Such depictions of the Trinity become even more common in Books of Hours as shown, for example, in the full-page illumination at the beginning of the Hours of the Trinity in the Grey-Fitzpayn Book of Hours.[31] Images of the Second Person of the Trinity—bloodied, wounded, and nailed to the cross—signal the medieval identification of the suffering Jesus with God. Further, the *trinitarian* framing of *Crucifixion* scenes tells viewers that the one who suffers is divine. For example, in the Abingdon Missal (fig. 2.9) Crucifixion, Mary and John lament the bleeding and tormented Jesus; the "truth" of what Mary and John perceived, namely that Jesus Christ is God, is conveyed to viewers by the inclusion of the other two persons of the Trinity in the scene—the Spirit is perched on the top of the cross and looks toward the Father above who holds out his hands in a double gesture of acceptance and offering.[32] In a variety of ways, then, through the pairing of infancy and suffering scenes and through depictions of the Trinity in which the Second Person is the wounded Savior, illuminated manuscripts testified to the theological cornerstone of medieval religiosity: the one who suffered was both God and human.

LITURGICAL SACRIFICE   As I suggested in the preceding chapter on sermons and devotional literature, one of the main effects of the suffering of Jesus in the medieval setting was to call Christians to participate in the sacramental system of reconciliation and its celebration of the intimate relationship between God and humans. Manuscript illuminations also direct viewers toward the sacraments, and particularly toward confession and the Eucharist; illuminations frequently testify visually to the meaning of the sacraments. For example, illuminations that appear at the central point of the medieval Mass, the Canon of the Mass, visually demonstrate that the Crucifixion of Jesus provided the key to understanding the significance of the sacrament of the Eucharist. In the Litlyngton Missal (fig. 2.10),[33] the Canon of the Mass is preceded by a full-page Crucifixion miniature that includes depictions of angels with chalices catching blood from Jesus' hands, feet, and chest—a clear reference to the doctrine of transubstantiation in which God's Son becomes present in the Eucharist. Occasionally, at the Canon of the Mass, as in the Pierpont Morgan Library M. 107 (fig. 2.11), illuminations depict the elevation of the host with the Crucifixion above it, making the christological and eucharistic connection between the suffering of Jesus and the meaning of the Mass even more explicit.[34]

The meaning of the Eucharist is often further emphasized through the pairing of the Crucifixion with what prefigures it in the Hebrew Scriptures: the Sacrifice of Isaac. In the Abingdon Missal, the Canon of the Mass immediately follows the Crucifixion page with a historiated initial depiction of the Sacrifice of Isaac in which the angel stays the sword of Abraham, and Isaac, hands folded, prays while a ram peeks out of the woods.[35] The juxtaposition of the Abraham-Isaac narrative with the Crucifixion renders transparent what is only implicit in the medieval drama we will consider in chapter 3. The contrastive pairing emphasizes the nature of Jesus' death: he died as a sacrifice on behalf of all humanity—

like a ram in the thicket awaiting slaughter. In this case, unlike the Abraham-Isaac drama, the Father looked at the sacrificial victim and did not stop the suffering inflicted upon the Son. This pairing appears also at the Canon of the Mass in the Litlyngton Missal, suggesting a common means of communicating to viewers the pain and poignancy of the sacrifice of Christ on behalf of others which is at the heart of the medieval liturgy.[36]

At times, as in Trinity College MS B.11.3, a historiated initial depicting the Abraham and Isaac story, unaccompanied by a Crucifixion, opens the Canon of the Mass.[37] In missals such as this one in which we also often see literal illuminations—where, for example, a historiated initial of a priest at the altar opens the Preface to the Mass and a historiated initial of the Resurrection marks Easter—we know that the figurative rendering of Abraham's near sacrifice of Isaac evoked the Passion narrative in the minds of medieval viewers.[38] The divine interruption in the Abraham cycle that protects Isaac in only this one case was a clear reminder of the absence of divine intervention to stop death in the other.

The connection we noted in chapter 1 between Jesus' body and his divine presence can be observed in artistic depictions of the Crucifixion, as, for example, in the case of the Psalter of Robert of Lisle, the Litlyngton Missal, and the Taymouth Hours—all of which locate the source of eucharistic wine in the liquid blood of Jesus' wounds. Most often, as is the case in these three manuscripts, the blood flows into chalices held by angels (fig. 2.9) or into a chalice held by Adam (fig. 2.12), seated at the foot of the cross; more rarely, it flows into a chalice held by Mary (fig. 2.13).[39] The Bodleian Library MS Laud Misc 165 shows water and blood flowing from Christ's chest, illustrating the source for the mixing of water and wine enacted in the medieval Mass during the eucharistic celebration.[40] These illuminations in Psalters and in missals at the Canon of the Mass demonstrate the centrality of the figure of the bleeding and suffering Jesus to liturgical practice.

In Crucifixion scenes, artists often rendered Christ's giving of self on behalf of others by depicting a pelican reviving its offspring. Medieval aviaries suggested that the pelican kills its own offspring in anger when the offspring attack it; "then, moved by compassion, he pierces his own body to his heart with his beak, and his offspring, sprinkled with his blood, come to life again."[41] Christ was like the pelican when, moved by compassion, he shed his own blood to bring "sinners back to the life of grace after they had spiritually died by offending God."[42] In the Psalter of Robert of Lisle (fig. 2.12) and in the Litlyngton Missal at the top of the Crucifixion illumination (fig. 2.10), a pelican in a nest pierces itself to revive the four young which rest below it with beaks raised.[43] The pelican signifies Christ's self-sacrifice on behalf of others. As the pelican revives its young with its own blood, so Jesus Christ revives the world with his life blood. The pelican symbol bears out the theopaschite maxim "Deus passus est" by graphically symbolizing God's self-wounding through placing the Son of God on the *via dolorosa*.

In its pictorial rendering of the creation story, the Holkham Bible picture book links Crucifixion scenes that include pelicans with the original tree of Eden and the promise of Christ from the beginning of time (fig. 2.14).[44] The Holkham artist, known for drawing lush bird life with extravagant attention to detail, illustrated the Garden of Eden with depictions of a number of trees. Each, with one exception, had a lone bird at the top. The exception, the central tree in the garden, depicts a nest in which a larger bird, a pelican, pecks itself so that red blood flows from it into two young birds' mouths. Lest the viewer miss the connection with Christ, the Creator points his forefingers upward to the trees as if to signal the true meaning of the Tree of Life, which would be realized only in the future but was implicit even at creation.

THE NOURISHING SAVIOR   The pelican's reviving of its young is often depicted as a feeding of the young—a symbol of the spectator's need to take Jesus into herself or himself just as the young birds take the blood of their parent into themselves to be revived and nourished. The eucharistic valences of the Crucifixion—the feeding of believers—are graphically displayed in manuscripts like the Gorleston Psalter (fig. 2.15), in which Mary Magdalene clings to the cross and raises her face to Jesus as blood streams from his feet, down the cross, and onto the rocks below.[45] She places herself in the path of the blood flow and appears to be drinking the life-giving plasma straight from Jesus' body. In the Taymouth Hours (fig. 2.13), Adam is shown with red lips, drinking the blood which falls on him from the cross above.[46] Deposition scenes also sometimes portray this drinking from the wounds of Jesus. In the Gough Psalter, Joseph of Arimethea drinks the blood pouring from the dead Christ's chest wound (fig. 2.16).[47] This appears again in the Trinity College MS 0.4.16, in which Joseph touches his lips to part of the wound while he holds Jesus (fig. 2.17),[48] and in British Library MS Add. 16968, in which the Deposition shows Mary close to the hand wound and Joseph close to the wound in Jesus' chest.[49] By drinking Jesus' blood, the penitent feeds on Jesus' body and is nurtured and transformed during the sacred meal.

Although we often discuss the wound in Jesus' side, iconographic evidence suggests that the wound was not in Jesus' side at all but in his chest or just below his breast, as shown in the Litlyngton Missal, Abingdon Missal, Psalter of Robert of Lisle, and the Gorleston Psalter. We see this iconographic detail again and again in artistic depictions of the Crucifixion in the fourteenth and fifteenth centuries. Mary is often depicted nursing the baby Jesus in infancy scenes, and there is a clear association between her feeding and the feeding Jesus who offers the "milk" of his blood through his suffering on behalf of humanity (fig. 2.18).[50] It is often suggested that depictions of the nursing Mary and the Crucifixion symbolize Mary's intercession on behalf of humankind; she reminds Christ that she nursed him and she pleads that, remembering this, he should be gracious to the world. Although this may be the case, depictions of the *Virgin Lactans* in the context of the Crucifixion are also reminders that just as Mary fed Jesus with milk, so now Jesus feeds the world with his blood-milk (fig. 2.19).[51] After all, in the Middle Ages milk was understood to be made from processed blood so that, in a sense, Jesus' followers were getting milk in its pure and original form.[52]

This theme is also conveyed in many depictions of the circumcision, one of the central "types" prefiguring the Crucifixion. It was understood as the first shedding of Jesus' blood on behalf of the world and a reminder of the sacrifice which lay ahead in the Crucifixion. Mary is frequently depicted nursing Jesus at the circumcision, as in Fitzwilliam Museum MS 259 and Trinity College MS B.10.15 (fig. 2.20).[53] Mary's nursing of Jesus as he first sheds blood prefigures the Crucifixion in which believers are fed with the blood of Jesus.

The feeding motif in situations in which Christ's blood seems to flow from his breast, and in contexts in which he is described as a mother nourishing a child, links the flesh of Jesus with the flesh of women, the flesh of mothers. At times, this connection is made explicit, but generally it is portrayed with the same am-biguity and anxiety about "flesh" we see reflected in Mary's identity as simulta-neously virgin and mother. In discussing the age at which "God suffered" ("Deus passus est"), the author of the *Fasciculus Morum* emphasizes his "tender age," say-ing that on account of this Christ suffered even more, because that which is ten-der suffers more than that which is not tender. Here, Jesus' suffering is under-stood to be especially severe because of its identity with the flesh of women: "And keep in mind that the flesh of [a hu]man is tenderer than that of a wild animal, and among [humans] the flesh of a woman is tenderer than that of a man, and among women, that of a virgin more so that than of a woman who has lost her virginity. But Christ's flesh was taken and formed out of the most pure blood of the Virgin and he himself lived in the most pure virginity until his death."[54]

These reflections on the traditionally female images used to describe the work and person of Jesus Christ exemplify the common use of cross-gendered sym-bolism to understand the figure of Christ and, in this particular case, to high-light the issues of feeding and nourishing so crucial to medieval understandings of the Eucharist and of the relationship between God and humanity.

THE BLEEDING HEALER   As I have suggested throughout this book, the bleeding flesh of the suffering Jesus also functions to convey *healing* in the medieval religious system. In many depictions of the Crucifixion, the blood of Christ has special medicinal properties. The presence of the figure of Longinus, for example, in the vast majority of late medieval English Crucifixion scenes demonstrates the miraculous powers of the suffering and dying Jesus Christ. According to the medieval story, a blind soldier, Longinus, thrust a spear into Christ's side at the time of the Crucifixion and was reputedly healed by the blood which fell upon him. The blood of Christ accomplishes the healing, as is evident in scene after scene which depicts blood on Longinus, often on his spear or on the finger which points toward his eye (fig. 2.17)[55] and sometimes on his spear, hands, and face (fig. 2.13).[56] This pictorial witness signifies on a literal level the healing of Longinus' physical blindness and on an allegorical level the healing of his spiritual blindness. The visual allegory reminds viewers that the healing powers of Christ are powerfully manifest in even the most grim scenes of the Crucifixion, which seem at first glance to acknowledge only his death. The story reminds observers of Jesus Christ's divinity.

Responding to the Wounds of Jesus

The Crucifixion portrays the heart of medieval Christian belief that Jesus Christ died on behalf of humans to bring spiritual healing and nourishment to them and to reconcile people to the Divine: "Christ comes to the earth . . . as a good physician to heal us, second he comes as a loving mother, to nourish us, and third he comes as a knight to save us."[57] But the meaning of medieval iconography of the suffering Jesus does not end here. Crucifixion scenes that emphasize the pain and suffering of Jesus and the need to partake of his wounds are exercises in the aesthetics of response: believers are made whole through imitating the devotion of the holy persons figured in these manuscripts. In the many depictions of the Crucifixion in which Mary points to Christ, sometimes she points even more specifically to Jesus' wounds; sometimes to the side wound, as she appears to do in the Bohun Hours;[58] and at other times, as in the Abingdon Missal, to the wounds in Jesus' feet (fig. 2.9).[59] Mary is a model of the power of the grief experienced by those who respond to Jesus' love and have to watch him suffer. As in Glasgow University Library Hunter 231 (fig. 2.21), the depth of her grief is sometimes portrayed through an illustration of Simeon's prophecy to Mary in Luke 34: "and a sword will pierce through your soul also."[60]

Much as the medieval sermons considered in chapter 1 cultivated compassion as the appropriate response to the suffering of Jesus, so guidebooks which led readers through meditation on the hours also sought to inspire compassion and pity in believers. The selective Middle English translation of the Bonaventurean *Meditations on the Life of Christ* counsels those meditating at prime to recall Jesus' torments and the crowning of thorns: "Be-holde hym nowe with compassione & tendirness of herte hou his heued was thurghe-prikked with sha[r]pe thornes." Readers are encouraged to respond at terce "with gret pete and compassione" to the pain and agony of the bearing of the cross.[61]

Last Judgment scenes which prominently feature the Christ in Judgment as the wounded Christ make this need to respond to Jesus' suffering abundantly clear. The saved are separated from the damned insofar as the saved responded to the suffering of Jesus; the damned are marked by their refusal to act with compassion toward those who bear the wounds of Christ. The Bohun Hours artist closely links the Last Judgment with the suffering of Jesus Christ, depicting the Christ in Judgment with wounds and flanked in panels on both sides by angels who carry the instruments of the Crucifixion, including the cross, the whip for flagellation, a lance, the gall sponge, and the crown of thorns. One angel blows a trumpet and, below, the dead awaken (fig. 2.22).[62] In British Library MS Royal 6.E.VI–6.VII (fig. 2.23) and in the St. Omer Psalter (fig. 2.2), the Christ in Judgment is depicted with wounds and flanked by angels who hold the symbols of the Passion.[63] In these portrayals, we learn visually what many sermons and dramas had conveyed verbally: the suffering of Jesus calls viewers to respond with compassion to the suffering they perceive in the Passion and Crucifixion. "But I fear that with many people it goes as it does with a deranged child: the more his loving mother worries about his illness, the more he laughs and roars without any feelings for his mother. In the same way, when Christ sheds his tears and is bled for the sake of sinners, the latter not merely forget his Passion like ungrateful people, but like deranged persons laugh at him and blaspheme. . . . We must not act thus, beloved, but instead have compassion for his suffering, together with all creation. For at his death the sun had compassion and withdrew its rays, the earth quaked, rocks were split, tombs opened up, and bodies of saints rose."[64] Medieval Christians learned to inhabit the "world" portrayed by the manuscript traditions of their religious communities. Becoming denizens of this world, they were called to remember actively the events of Jesus' death, to enter into these events, and to weep and mourn at Jesus' suffering along with and in imitation of Jesus' first-century followers and their compassion for others.

Wall Paintings

Church Art as Creating Christological Space

Now that we have considered manuscript illuminations, we might be tempted to restrict the implications of this material for understanding medieval culture to those wealthy enough to own or educated enough to read Psalters and Books of Hours. In the second section of this chapter, however, I consider the liturgical environment of the majority of medieval Christians in England and suggest that the meanings and images I have discussed in the case of manuscripts were often writ large upon the walls of the very churches in which believers worshiped. The architectural infrastructure of the church in late medieval England was enormous: for the two-and-one-half to three million people engaged in a variety of Christian practices in about 1500, there were nineteen cathedral churches, nine thousand parishes, six hundred and fifty abbeys, and two hundred mendicant houses or "establishments."[65]

Far from being drab stone caverns, as we sometimes imagine, medieval churches, including the smallest local churches, were frequently brightly colored decorative settings for communal worship. Church walls, especially above the arches on the side aisles, were richly covered with wall paintings, often displaying larger than life-size local or favorite saints such as St. Christopher, St. Margaret, and St. Katherine and depicting such scriptural narratives as the life of the Virgin and the infancy, Passion, death, and Resurrection of Jesus Christ. By the thirteenth century, rood screens generally separated the church nave from the chancel. Although a vast number of these screens were destroyed during the years of Cromwell, evidence indicates that the screens were often colorfully decorated with pictures of saints, local patrons, and scriptural figures.[66] These screens generally supported a great rood or carved wood cross with the crucified Christ, often accompanied by life-size wooden statues of the Virgin Mary and St. John (fig. 2.24). In even the smallest of churches a crucifix was generally placed over the high altar.[67] Many churches also had stained glass windows, decorative roof bosses (fig. 2.25), elaborate baptismal fonts, painted hangings, and painted statuary and pulpits.[68] In some more well-endowed churches, a retable or raised shelf sat atop the altar; it was a picture or a series of depictions which could be closed with shutters (fig. 2.26).[69] Church colors were bright and images were dramatic, so that, in fact, the dark, unpainted stone of contemporary church buildings gives a very misleading impression of the environment of medieval worship.

In what follows, I consider mural paintings, one of the dominant decorative features in late medieval English churches and a powerful medium through which believers were visually encouraged to respond to the figure of the suffering Christ. I consider church wall art as an aesthetic device for inculcating the meaning of the suffering Jesus in the community. Wall paintings functioned in a didactic way to teach and remind people of the familiar and central narratives of the Christian tradition. Further, while in the discussion of Books of Hours I suggested that images of the suffering Jesus often marked and oriented *ecclesial time*, now, in considering wall paintings, we see that the narrative of the suffering Jesus also oriented *ecclesial space*. The artistic rendering of the stories of central events of Christian identity in a sacred space located worshipers within the narrative space and time of the Christian symbol system. In their pictorial renderings of the drama at the foundation of Christian belief, these monumental narratives give structure to and shape sacred space and bring salvation history into the present by enjoining viewers to become participants in the events the paintings depict.

Surviving English mural paintings generally have a more simplified narrative structure with less attention to detail than their manuscript illumination counterparts. Yet both manuscript illuminations and mural paintings depict the main liturgical feasts of the church year and the story of the life, death, and Resurrection of Jesus Christ, which was at the theological center of the medieval Mass.[70] Great similarities emerge in the aesthetics of suffering which characterize these two media. In both cases, the figure of the suffering Jesus takes a central role, embodying a similar meaning and evoking the ongoing presence of Jesus Christ. Both forms seek to kindle a response of compassionate identification on the part

Figure 2.1. London, Lambeth Palace Library, MS 233 (Vaux Psalter), f. 15v. Historiated initial "B" of "Beatus" in Psalm 1 with the Jesse Tree and crucified Christ. Reprinted by permission of The Archbishop of Canterbury and the Trustees of the Lambeth Palace Library.

Figure 2.2. London, British Library, MS Yates Thompson 14 (St. Omer Psalter), f. 120. Historiated initial "D" of "Dominus" with the wounded Christ in the Last Judgment and with scenes of the Passion through the Ascension in medallions. Reprinted by permission of the British Library.

Figure 2.3. London, British Library, MS Add. 16968, f. 20. Christ Carrying the Cross paired with the Adoration of the Magi. Reprinted by permission of the British Library.

Figure 2.4. London, British Library, MS Add. 16968, f. 21. Massacre of the Innocents paired with the Crucifixion. Reprinted by permission of the British Library.

Figure 2.5. Cambridge, Cambridge University Library, MS Dd. 4.17 (Hours of Alice de Reydon), f. 12. Crucifixion. Reprinted by permission of the Syndics of Cambridge University Library.

Figure 2.6. Cambridge, Cambridge University Library, MS Dd. 4.17 (Hours of Alice de Reydon), f. 11v. Mary and Infant Jesus. Reprinted by permission of the Syndics of Cambridge University Library.

Figure 2.7. London, Westminster Abbey, MS 37 (Litlyngton Missal), f. 120. Trinity. Reprinted courtesy of the Dean and Chapter of Westminster.

Figure 2.8. Cambridge, Trinity College Library, MS B.10.15, f. 33v. Trinity. Reprinted by permission of the Master and Fellows of Trinity College Cambridge.

Figure 2.9. Oxford, Bodleian Library, MS Digby 227 (Abingdon Missal), f. 113v. Crucifixion with Trinity. Reprinted by permission of the Bodleian Library.

Figure 2.10. London, Westminster Abbey, MS 37 (Litlyngton Missal), f. 156v. Crucifixion. Reprinted courtesy of the Dean and Chapter of Westminster.

Figure 2.11. New York, Pierpont Morgan Library, M. 107, f. 142. Elevation of the Host. Reprinted by permission of the Pierpont Morgan Library.

Figure 2.12. London, British Library, MS Arundel 83 II (Psalter of Robert of Lisle), f. 132. Crucifixion. Reprinted by permission of the British Library.

Figure 2.13. London, British Library, MS Yates Thompson 13 (Taymouth Hours), f. 122v. Crucifixion. Reprinted by permission of the British Library.

Figure 2.14. London, British Library, MS Add. 47682 (Holkham Bible), f. 3v. Creation. Reprinted by permission of the British Library.

Figure 2.15. London, British Library, MS Add. 49622 (Gorleston Psalter), f. 7. Crucifixion. Reprinted by permission of the British Library.

Figure 2.16. Oxford, Bodleian Library, MS Gough liturg. 8 (Gough Psalter), f. 61v. Deposition. Reprinted by permission of the Bodleian Library.

Figure 2.17. Cambridge, Trinity College Library, MS O.4.16, f. 113v. Crucifixion and Healing of Longinus. Deposition. Reprinted by permission of the Master and Fellows of Trinity College Cambridge.

Figures 2.18 and 2.19. *Left:* Glasgow, Glasgow University Library, MS Hunter 231, p. 62. Virgin and Child. *Right:* Glasgow, Glasgow University Library, MS Hunter 231, p. 89. Virgin Lactans, Nolo me tangere, Crucifixion. Both reprinted courtesy of Glasgow University Library, Department of Special Collections.

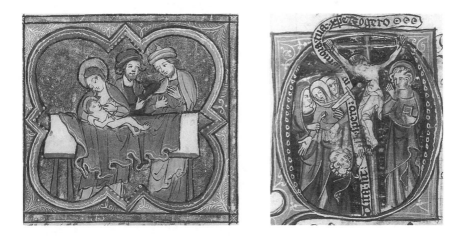

Figures 2.20 and 2.21. *Left:* Cambridge, Trinity College Library, B.10.15, f. 7v. Circumcision. Reprinted by permission of the Master and Fellows of Trinity College Cambridge. *Right:* Glasgow, Glasgow University Library, MS Hunter 231, p. 53. Crucifixion with Mary with Sword of Sorrow. Reprinted courtesy of Glasgow University Library, Department of Special Collections.

Figure 2.22. Oxford, Bodleian Library, MS Auct. D.4.4 (Bohun Hours), f. 169. Last Judgment. Reprinted by permission of the Bodleian Library.

Figure 2.23. London, British Library, MS Royal 6.E.VI–6.VII, f. 14. Christ in Judgment. Reprinted by permission of the British Library.

Figure 2.24. Eye, Suffolk. Restored rood screen. Reprinted by permission of the RCHME © Crown Copyright.

Figure 2.25. Norwich, Norwich Cathedral. Roof boss depicting Crucifixion. Reprinted by permission of the RCHME © Crown Copyright.

Figure 2.26. Norwich, Norwich Cathedral. Retable depicting the Passion through the Ascension. Reprinted by permission of the RCHME © Crown Copyright.

Figure 2.27. St. Mary-the-Virgin, Chalgrove. Exterior. Reprinted by permission of the RCHME © Crown Copyright.

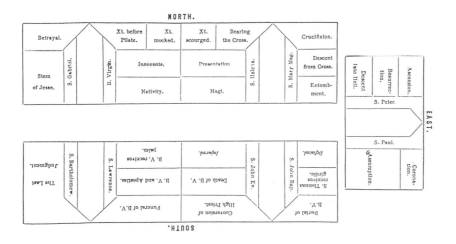

Figure 2.28. St. Mary-the-Virgin, Chalgrove. Diagram of wall painting arrangement. Diagram by R. W. Heath-Whyte, Brochure of St. Mary-the-Virgin, Chalgrove.

Figure 2.29. St. Mary-the-Virgin, Chalgrove. Resurrection.
Reprinted by permission of the RCHME © Crown Copyright.

Figure 2.30. St. Mary-the-Virgin, Chalgrove. Ascension. Reprinted by permission of the
RCHME © Crown Copyright.

Figure 2.31. St. Michael and All Angels, Great Tew. Crucifixion with Healing of Longinus. Photograph by author.

Figure 2.32. St. Michael and All Angels, Great Tew. Descent from the Cross. Photograph by author.

Figure 2.33. St. Pega's, Peakirk. Crucifixion with Healing of Longinus. Reprinted by permission of the RCHME © Crown Copyright.

Figure 2.34. St. Peter Ad Vincula, South Newtington. Passion and Crucifixion. Photograph by author.

Figure 2.35. St. Peter Ad Vincula, South Newtington. Virgin with Child. Reprinted courtesy of The Conway Library, Courtauld Institute of Art.

Figure 2.36. St. Albans, St. Albans Abbey. Crucifixion with Virgin and Child. Reprinted courtesy of The Conway Library, Courtauld Institute of Art.

Figure 2.37. St. Albans, St. Albans Abbey. Crucifixion with Virgin and Child. Reprinted courtesy of The Conway Library, Courtauld Institute of Art.

Figure 2.38. St. Albans, St. Albans Abbey. View of columns with wall paintings. Reprinted courtesy of The Conway Library, Courtauld Institute of Art, and Fred H. Crossley and Maurice H. Ridgway.

Figure 2.39. All Saints, Turvey. Crucifixion with Mary and John. Reprinted by permission of the RCHME © Crown Copyright.

of viewers. The creators of these images sought to produce a rhetorical aesthetic in which viewers would be stirred to respond cathartically with deep emotion, empathy, and sentiment—and through the process of responding, they would be healed, nourished, and reconciled with God and one another. The author of the *Fasciculus Morum* describes the process as one in which the Passion leads believers to perfect love.[71] The pictures rarely stood on their own: on the contrary, they were part of an ongoing dialectic between the images which visually awakened the imagination to reflect on the stories depicted, and thus shaped how believers heard the sermons and readings, and the sermons and readings which taught the viewers how to "see" and understand the paintings that surrounded them.[72] For example, while wall paintings in general have fewer sacramental directives than their manuscript illumination counterparts, the connection between the sacramental system and the narrative of the Passion of Christ was nevertheless closely maintained in a preaching environment in which viewers of the paintings were reminded how to interpret the narratives they saw depicted around them: "Notice that the shedding of [Christ's] blood is a very strong remedy because it leads the sinner to the sorrow of contrition, the shame of confession, and to the labor of satisfaction."[73] In conjuction with the sermons preached under their canopy, the pictures taught compassion by compelling observers to respond to the suffering of Jesus. Wall images set the table for the main themes in late medieval sermonody, even as the sermons explicated in more detail certain features of the Gospel accounts pictorially symbolized on the walls of the church.

As Marilyn Aronberg Lavin's recent study of patterns of Italian wall painting demonstrates, wall paintings were an integral part of the worship context, closely related to the architectural space which they adorned.[74] While we have no architectural analysis of English wall painting arrangements comparable to that of Lavin, scholars such as Charles E. Keyser, E. W. Tristram, and A. Caiger-Smith have extensively documented the content and placement of English wall paintings. Although I analyze only selected church sites, I am certain that the ongoing study of English mural painting will reveal that these works of art were not haphazardly put together, but rather that their arrangement suggests thoughtful attention to the narrative potential and liturgical orientation of church wall art, on the one hand, and to the architectural structure of the buildings in which they were placed, on the other hand. At St. Mary-the-Virgin, Chalgrove, for example, the pointed nave arcades and windows are echoed in the paintings which depict figures under pointed canopies; this technique of artistic repetition linked the paintings with their architectural setting.[75] Further, attending to the symbolic potential of architecture, the mural painter at Chalgrove followed a common practice of depicting the Annunciation "across an architectural opening"—the muralist portrayed the messenger Gabriel on one spacious and deep-cut window splay and Mary on the other, with the natural light through the window between signaling the divine presence at the annunciatory event.[76]

THE PANORAMA OF PAINTINGS AT ST. MARY-THE-VIRGIN, CHALGROVE   The church of St. Mary-the-Virgin in Chalgrove (fig. 2.27) houses an extensive mid-fourteenth-century narrative series chronicling salvation history. It focuses on the life, Passion, and Resurrection of Jesus Christ, as well as on the life, death, and coronation of the Virgin Mary. This extensive collection of paintings—with stories drawn from the New Testament and the Golden Legend and covering most of the wall space in the church—gives some sense of the magnificent theological and physical scale of the painting schemes that covered medieval churches. It suggests the variety of sources that inspired wall painting, and it illustrates the artisans' attention to space and to the physical construction of narrative time. Surrounded by the familiar stories of the central events of Christian identity, worshipers prayed and reflected in this space and became collective participants in the narrative world of the Christian symbol system.[77]

The three-tiered series (fig. 2.28) starts on the north wall at the entrance to the building so that congregants start "reading" the murals as soon as they enter the church.[78] The cycle begins with a Tree of Jesse covering the first and second tiers. The first tier includes King David, and the second the Virgin and Child. Within the splays of the window just east of the Tree of Jesse is an Annunciation (celebrated in the liturgical year on March 25) with, as indicated above, Gabriel on the west and the Virgin holding a book on the east. This is followed on the first tier of the wall to the east by a Nativity (celebrated on December 25) and then an Adoration of the Magi scene (celebrated on January 6). The liturgical associations of this scene are evident in the fact that the mural painting chronicles the events commemorated on January 6, the feast of the Epiphany, an important feast day in the church year. But even more specifically, the Magi's bearing of gifts to offer Jesus is traditionally associated with the bearing of gifts to the altar during the offertory of the Mass; the Magi's adoration of the infant Jesus thus corresponds to the congregation's adoration of the body of Jesus in the Eucharist.[79] The series continues on the second tier after the Tree of Jesse and the Annunciation window with the Massacre of the Innocents (commemorated on December 28), in which a soldier holds a child impaled on a spear as a woman struggles with another soldier to save her child. This is followed by the Presentation in the Temple (celebrated on February 2). The narrative then shifts to the Passion (commemorated beginning on March 25) as it continues on the third tier immediately above the Tree of Jesse with a scene of the Betrayal in which Judas kisses Jesus, and Peter cuts off Malchus's ear. The first mural east of the window depicts Christ before Pilate. The juxtaposition of Christ before Pilate with the Massacre of the Innocents immediately below reminds viewers that once again the Innocent One is subjected to the condemnation of the ruling political powers. The narrative continues with the Mocking of Christ, the Flagellation, and then, after the window break, the Carrying of the Cross and the Crucifixion (of which only traces remain).[80] After having read the narrative series upward and across, following the story line, the viewers' eyes symbolically move downward to the Descent from the Cross which is depicted immediately beneath the Crucifixion, with (as in many manuscript illuminations) Joseph of Arimethea lifting the body from the cross as Mary holds the dead Jesus' extended right arm and Nicodemus extracts the nail from Jesus' feet. Beneath this in the first tier is the Entombment, and, proceeding east, the window houses depictions of St. Helena and the Cross (feast day on May 3) and an unidentifiable female saint who points with her left hand to the Crucifixion scene to the east.[81]

The cycle then continues at the front of the church on the east wall. Here in the lowest tier we see the Harrowing of Hell in which Christ, with the bleeding wound in his side clearly visible, leads Adam and Eve, followed by other souls, from the mouth of hell.[82] Now, in contrast to the downward movement of the death scenes, the viewer symbolically looks upward to the Resurrection in the second tier (fig. 2.29) and, immediately above this, to the Ascension (celebrated between May 14 and 25) in the third tier (fig. 2.30).[83] The window splays on the east wall are decorated with a depiction of St. Peter holding the keys and St. Paul with his sword (feast days celebrated on June 29 and 30, respectively). The area south of the window depicts the Assumption (feast day celebrated on August 15) and, above this, the Coronation of the Virgin Mary; these two paintings complete the Death of the Virgin series which adorns the south wall. While the Resurrection and Ascension depictions complete the Christ cycle on the north wall, and the paintings of the Assumption and Coronation complete the cycle of paintings connected with the Life of the Virgin Mary on the south wall, these two sets on the east wall are artistically paired with one another because they both move upward, directing spectators' attention to the heavenly realm above.

Beginning again at the west end of the south wall, a Last Judgment in all three tiers parallels the Tree of Jesse (directly opposite on the north wall). This juxtaposition highlights the meaning of the Last Judgment as the outcome of the lineage of Jesse. Jesus Christ sits in judgment, displaying his wounds as the dead are depicted in the two tiers below rising from their tombs. Tristram identifies the figure kneeling beside Christ as the Virgin Mary praying in intercession on behalf of the souls below.[84] After window splays depicting St. Bartholomew (feast day on August 24) and St. Lawrence (feast day on August 10), the wall continues with a series of paintings commemorating the events surrounding the Virgin Mary's death, followed by window splays depicting John the Evangelist and John the Baptist (feast days probably celebrated on June 24).[85] This is followed on the east by the burial of the Virgin Mary and a scene of Thomas receiving the girdle which testified that Mary had been assumed bodily into heaven.

As even this cursory reading of the Chalgrove murals suggests, the scenes projected on church walls correspond to the feast days and liturgical celebrations that punctuate the church year.[86] The cycle of paintings around the church interior mirrors the progression of the liturgical year, so that the walls themselves chronicle the cyclical passage of time in which the past determines the present and the future. Sermons surrounding these festival days taught people how to "see" the paintings around them. For example, sermons at Epiphany regularly emphasized Christ's royalty. In proclaiming Christ the King's power, a preacher expounds Isaiah: "He is a vondirfull counselere, þe mighty God, and Prince of Peace."[87] Mirk explains the significance of the gifts from the three Magi: "Knowlechyng by þe gold þat he was kyng of all kynges, and by ensens þat he was veray God, and by myrre þat he was veray man, þat shuld be ded, and layde yin grauue wythout rotyng."[88]

As with the illumination series in many English Books of Hours considered at the beginning of this chapter, late medieval wall painting cycles focus on the events surrounding Jesus' birth, Passion, and death. As in the manuscript cycles, in the wall paintings the events of Jesus' birth and Passion are often paired with one another to reveal the double identity of the one who suffers. In this cycle at Chalgrove, for example, the Massacre of the Innocents is placed directly below the depiction of Christ before Pilate. This coupling reminds viewers of the innocence of the royal victim who suffers before Pilate.[89] When juxtaposed with events surrounding the Passion of Christ, in which the human suffering is most apparent, the events of Jesus' birth and particularly the Adoration of the Magi and the Presentation in the Temple, signal Christ's divinity as well as his humanity and function to set a context in which the identity of Jesus Christ as human and divine is evident to viewers at all times.[90] In these monumental narratives, history is portrayed as the ongoing commemoration of the heritage of Jesus Christ which seeks to shape the present and future even as it recollects the past.

Wall Paintings as Christological Narrative Cycles

In what follows, I describe the wall painting narratives in four churches located in various parts of southeast England to convey some sense of the common wall painting cycles found in even the most modest of medieval churches. I note also a number of examples of wall painting images of the suffering Jesus which parallel themes discussed in the first section of this chapter.

ST. MICHAEL AND ALL ANGELS, GREAT TEW   St. Michael and All Angels in Great Tew in Oxfordshire contains an even earlier (c. 1290) example of wall paintings than the St. Mary's, Chalgrove, cycle connected with the Christ narrative. Traces of paint throughout the church indicate that at one time the church housed an extensive collection of paintings, although the focus of the surviving three-tiered, twelve-panel cycle on the south wall is the Passion, death, and Resurrection of Jesus Christ. This cycle, which seems to proceed in either three or four tiers from west to east, includes the Betrayal of Christ on the top tier and continues on the second tier with the Crowning of Thorns, the meeting with Herod, a

Scourging, a Carrying of the Cross, the Crucifixion (fig. 2.31), Descent from the Cross (fig. 2.32), and Entombment. The third tier contains two or three panels which are difficult to decipher but which probably include a Descent into Hell and the Freeing of Souls, as well as a clear Resurrection and Noli Me Tangere. The movement of the narrative from the top tier to the bottom tier, as well as the left-to-right progression paralleling the reading of lines on a page, contrasts with the organization at Chalgrove and suggests the diversity of artistic structure Lavin observes in the Italian churches in her studies.

ST. PEGA'S, PEAKIRK   Near Peterborough and well north of Cambridge, at St. Pega's, Peakirk, is a small church dedicated to St. Pega who is commemorated in a stained glass window accompanied by the geese with whom she communicated. Traces of colors are not only on the walls in the surviving wall paintings but also on pillars, capitals, and arch mouldings—all of which convey some sense of the extent to which painted decoration covered the whole church.[91] Upon entering the south door, the most immediately visible painting is the huge St. Christopher (feast celebrated on July 25) painted in the spandrel between the first and second arches of the north arcade.[92] Over sixty St. Christopher paintings from the medieval period remain today, indicative of the popularity of this saint in the Middle Ages. Popular lore held that believers would be preserved from death on any day that they looked at St. Christopher, so many people have speculated about the placement of this figure within direct view of anyone entering into the church (giving the impression that perhaps some people concerned about their well-being might duck their heads into the church, catch a glimpse of St. Christopher, and leave!).

While there is evidence of thirteenth-century and even twelfth-century painting in this church, most of the images connected to the suffering Jesus are of fourteenth-century origin. A two-tiered Passion series begins to the east of St. Christopher and extends the length of the north wall of the nave. The series begins at the west end of the upper tier with a depiction of the Last Supper and continues eastward in five more panels. The first depicts the Washing of the Feet; the second shows a scene which is probably a Betrayal; the next two panels are nearly impossible to decipher; and the last panel may be a Mocking of Christ.[93] The narrative continues on the next lower tier, beginning again from the west and running east. The first panel may be a scourging scene, although it is difficult to decipher. The second is clearly Christ led to Calvary, followed by a Crucifixion in which the bearer of the vinegar and gall holds the sponge to Jesus' face as Longinus spears Jesus with his right hand and points to his eyes with his left (fig. 2.33). Next, in the Deposition, a figure who is impossible to identify but is usually Mary, Mother of Jesus, reaches out to hold the dead Jesus' arm while Joseph of Arimethea, his face pressed to Jesus' chest, lifts Christ down from the cross. This is followed in the next panel by an Entombment; on the next and bottom tier is the Resurrection, which includes the resurrected Christ, an angel kneeling at the tomb, and soldiers sleeping below. There are paintings and painting traces in the north aisle as well which include what Tristram identifies as a mid-fourteenth-century Tree of the Seven Deadly Sins and a similarly dated depiction of the Three Living and the Three Dead.[94] While there is evidence of painting on the east end of the south aisle, the subject of the painting is unclear.

ALL SAINTS, NORTH WALSHAM   We turn next to another narrative series in Crostwight at the Church of All Saints near North Walsham in Norfolk. Here, as at St. Pega's, Peakirk, there are a variety of subjects, including, on the north wall, a Tree of Deadly Sins and three amorous couples in the arms of a huge demon.[95] As at St. Pega's, a gigantic St. Christopher adorns the church wall, this time to the east of the doorway. Also on the north wall between two windows are three tiers of paintings including a Passion series which begins on the west end of the second tier with the Entry into Jerusalem, followed by a Last Supper and the Washing of the Feet, along with a depiction of the Agony in the Garden.[96] Starting again from the west end, the series continues on the third tier with a depiction of Christ before Pilate. The next panel is difficult to decipher, although given standard cycles it is probably a scourging scene. A Crowning of Thorns scene with half-size figures cuts into the boundaries between the second and third tiers. This is followed in the third tier by a Carrying of the Cross and a Crucifixion scene in which Longinus spears Christ, the bearer of the gall and vinegar holds the sponge to Jesus, Mary swoons, and Mary Magdalene is at "the foot of the cross."[97] An Entombment scene is partially visible at the edge of the window. The narrative probably continues in the lowest tier, although the only visible scene is the Ascension.

ST. PETER AD VINCULA, SOUTH NEWTINGTON   The final narrative series I mention here is the fifteenth-century Passion series on the north wall above the Norman arches of the nave in St. Peter Ad Vincula in South Newtington, near Deddington, north of Oxford. The wall paintings begin on the west end with a scene of Christ riding the donkey into Jerusalem, surrounded by spectators depicted on the wall above waving palm leaves. The next scene is a depiction of Christ praying in the Garden of Gesthsemane while the disciples sleep nearby. Following several scenes that can no longer be identified are a Flagellation scene with a crowned Christ covered with wounds, a scene of Christ Bearing the Cross, a Crucifixion in which the gall sponge is held to Jesus' mouth, another scene which is obscured, and a Resurrection with Christ grasping the vexillum in his left hand and holding his right hand upright as he steps out of the tomb while the soldiers sleep below (figs. 2.34). This is followed by a number of panels that cannot be identified. There are also three Trees of the Trinity with arms of the Passion, one on each side of and one between the Norman arches.[98]

The widespread whitewashing and destruction of wall paintings in the sixteenth century obscured many of the elaborate cycles which decorated medieval churches. Consideration of the above examples from a variety of local churches conveys some idea of the prevalence of mural paintings in general and, more specifically, points to the ubiquity of portrayals of the life, Passion, and Resurrection of Jesus Christ. The narrative images which traverse church walls create sacred space and reconstitute the world as the arena of divine presence. Just as the St. Christopher image functioned to preserve the well-being of those who brought themselves into its purview, those who gazed upon the sacred history of Jesus Christ's life, death, and Resurrection were invited to imagine themselves as among those whom Jesus came to heal, nourish, and lead to salvation. But in focusing on the Passion of Jesus, church murals become a violent tableau of agony and suffering. They constitute an affective theology that put less emphasis on the triumphant Christ of the church militant and more on the divine victim who willingly endured betrayal and execution out of compassion for humankind. Like the often-depicted blind Longinus who spears Jesus in the heart, every congregant in the church, through her or his daily transgressions, is a complicitor with Longinus in the Crucifixion of Jesus. Like Longinus, medieval believers suffered from spiritual blindness and needed the healing blood of Jesus to cleanse them of their sins.

SOUTH AND EAST ANGLIA MISCELLANY   As observed in the Chalgrove cycle, wall painting techniques often employ the method we noted in manuscript illuminations in which two or more scenes are paired so that each is seen in the light of the other and new meanings emerge from the juxtaposition. Annunciations and Crucifixions were commonly linked with one another, as when Annunciation scenes were depicted on splays of the east window in a church in visible connection with the Crucifixion scenes so often depicted in the carved or painted retable of the high altar.[99] St. Albans Cathedral houses a collection of five Crucifixion scenes painted on successive columns on the north side of the church (figs. 2.36, 2.37, 2.38).[100] These scenes evoke the Alice de Reydon Hours in that two of the paintings pair the Crucifixion with a depiction of Mary enthroned holding the infant Jesus. At Faversham in Kent, a Crucifixion is depicted on "an octagonal pillar in the eastern arcade"; an Adoration of the Magi is painted on the pillar immediately below it.[101] These images are clearly in view for people looking to the front of the church and have a visual effect similar to that of the Books of Hours pairings of the Bearing of the Cross with the Adoration of the Magi. The Adoration of the Magi scene, which celebrates the kingship of Christ and acknowledges his divinity, reminds viewers who it is who suffers in the Crucifixion, and as indicated above, the adoration of Jesus' body celebrated in the Magi image evokes the adoration of the body of Jesus Christ celebrated in the Eucharist.

We find some depictions of the Trinity on late medieval church walls, although this is unusual prior to the fourteenth century.[102] In Little Kimble (Buckinghamshire), a bearded figure holds a triptych above a St. Christopher image. The image on the left of the triptych is defaced, but the middle panel depicts the Virgin and Child, and the right panel portrays an image of the Trinity.[103] This juxtaposition of the Virgin and Child panel with the Trinity panel emphasizes the divinity of the Christ child held by Mary. At St. Andrew, Gorleston, Norfolk, the north chancel chapel contains a fourteenth-century "Easter Sepulchre" recess in which the First Person holds a cross with the Crucified Son; a dove, the Holy Spirit, also appears.[104] Nearby, on one side, is found a shield of the Trinity, and on the other side, a shield with the Emblems of the Passion.[105] One of the clearest remaining representations of the Trinity is at Canterbury Cathedral. The elaborate image provides a clue as to why we see so few depictions of the Trinity. The head of the First Person of the Trinity has been defaced; the depiction of the Second Person, Christ on the Cross, is also badly defaced; and the Spirit, in the form of a dove, is scarcely visible.[106] It is likely that iconoclasts of the sixteenth century and their successors perceived artistic displays of the Trinity as particularly offensive. Undoubtedly, Trinities were commonly destroyed and defaced; yet we find enough portrayals to indicate that in addition to sermons that identified the suffering Jesus Christ with God, pictorial renderings, such as depictions of the Trinity, also made this association clear.

Suffering Jesus images are also found in free-standing contexts, apart from narrative cycles. At the Church of All Saints, Turvey, near Bedfordshire, for example, a thirteenth-century Crucifixion with the grieving witnesses Mary and John decorates an alcove at the front of the east end of the south aisle (fig. 2.39). Jesus hangs on the cross, his body with the familiar and sharp "S" curve and blood flowing from the wound in his side. Mary grieves, her hands folded in front of her. John holds his right hand to his face in sorrow and holds a book in his left hand. This emotional painting bears witness to the agony of Christ on the cross and to the grief of those who recall his suffering. Viewers are stirred to remember actively the Crucifixion and the pain of the observers who watched their beloved Jesus Christ suffer.[107]

While the paintings we have considered decorate walls, extensive decorative schemas at certain times also covered ceilings and arcade columns. At the fourteenth-century Church of St. Mary-the-Virgin in Broughton (near Banbury in Oxfordshire), there is abundant evidence of a narrative series depicting the events surrounding the Death of the Virgin on the north wall, and one of the nave arcade columns holds a Crucifixion. The blood-red background to the Jesus figure conveys some sense of the original vividness of the church paintings and evokes the agony of the suffering Jesus.

It is notable that the panoply of christological images in South and East Anglia is widely present even in nondiachronic contexts. In addition to the monumental narrative histories chronicled on church walls, images of the suffering Jesus are also found on pillars, in ritual alcoves, and even in tombs. The presence of these often elaborate paintings on columns and walls in the worship space of congregants, as well as in ritual spaces like the Easter recess, suggest their connection to the liturgical practices of medieval congregations. Life-size images of the Crucifixion scene in alcoves, such as those at All Saints in Turvey, invite viewers into the transformative drama of the Passion. Spectators are summoned to imagine themselves present with the mourning witnesses at the scene of Jesus' death and to cultivate their apprenticeship to Jesus' mission. This process of being transported into the christological drama is aided by viewers' gazing on the distinctive permutation of images in church art. Crucifixion images are often juxtaposed with some of the central persons and events of the sacred history in liturgically and theologically evocative parallels. The eucharistic coupling of the Adoration of the Magi with the Crucifixion reminds spectators that the incarnate God worshiped by the Magi is the same Jesus whose crucified body is the center of the Eucharist. The pairing of the enthroned Mary with the Crucifixion tells spectators that the infant held by the regal Mary is the incarnate God, the same divine Savior who suffers in the Crucifixion. Along with the narrative depictions of Jesus in mural cycles, individual images and pairings of paintings shaped the devotional life of medieval church communities.

Responding to the Offer of Mercy

As did many thirteenth- to fifteenth-century churches, St. Peter Ad Vincula includes a Last Judgment painting (c. 1330–1340) above the chancel arch. Generally, Last Judgment scenes were painted in prominent places, most often, as in this case, in the space over the chancel arch where they symbolically manifested the connection between this world and the next. Significantly, although the chancel arch often housed the Last Judgment scene, in front of it or immediately below it stood the rood screen with its life-size depictions of the Crucifixion and of Mary and John: the Last Judgment, then, was read through the lens of the Crucifixion. Believers' responses to the Crucifixion determined their status at the Last Judgment. Although the painting at St. Peter Ad Vincula is in poor condition, it contains traces of Christ in Judgment, bodies rising from their graves, Michael weighing souls, and the torments of the damned. Seventy-eight examples of Last Judgment paintings, which became increasingly common in the fourteenth century, still exist.[108] They often included images of the Seven Deadly Sins and the Seven Corporal Works of Mercy. By the beginning of the thirteenth century, the Christ of Judgment, "often seeming to be endowed with familar human feelings," begins to be portrayed with the wounds of the Crucifixion, often prominently displayed.[109] As I suggested in chapter 1, the wounds of Christ are his means of appeal to believers. The author of the *Fasciculus Morum* compares Christ to a knight who goes to battle against the "enemy" of humankind.[110] As a knight who is so battle weary and wounded that "from the sole of his foot to the top of his head there is no soundness in him" (Isaiah) goes to his lady seeking refreshment, so Jesus comes to the believer:

> Yet nonetheless, as a most gracious and faithful knight he does not cease to knock and cry: "Behold my wounds," and so forth. "O, human soul, blush then, and . . . [open] the soul's affections for God and his favors, which are so firmly shut through sin, and do so with the keys of contrition, confession, love, and charity."[111]

The suffering Jesus calls on believers to respond to his bloody and tormented body. Depictions of the bleeding and crucified Jesus awaken viewers' compassion: those who turn away are condemned in the face of those wounds to which they did not respond. Last Judgment paintings functioned to jar Christians from their complacency and to goad them to respond with compassion to the suffering of Jesus.

Sometimes wall paintings made these points even more explicitly in the artistic rendering of Matthew 25:35–40, which names the works of mercy.[112] In the parish church of Arundel, the works of mercy are depicted in a wheel circling around an angel in the center. The angel, with "IHS" inscribed on its breast and surrounded by the works of mercy, represents what it means to have the love of Christ in one's heart.[113] In sermons about the works of mercy, medieval worshipers heard words similar to these of the author of the *Fasciculus Morum* in describing the meanings of charity toward the neighbor.

> Love and charity toward our neighbor consists in supporting him in the things he needs. . . . And if you ask what such charity is, I answer: now it is to bury the dead, now to feed and care for the sick, as the saintly Tobit did; now to give the poor shelter, as did Blessed Martha; now to clothe the naked, as did Blessed Martin; and other such works. These are called the deeds of mercy. . . . He who helps his needy neighbor, whether by giving or putting him at ease or forgiving him, surely in such a person is perfect charity, according to Blessed John in the Epistle quoted above: "God is love, and he who abides in love, abides in God, and God in him."[114]

Caiger-Smith describes a powerful fifteenth-century wall painting at Linkinhorne in Cornwall "where the figure of Christ rises up in the midst of the performers of these deeds, seeming to participate in both the suffering and the mercy depicted in the little scenes."[115] Jesus Christ is both present in the recipient of the good works as well as the model for the believer who carries out works of mercy; Christ is alternately the recipient of the love expressed and the source of that love. The religious message of these paintings, namely that believers link themselves to Jesus Christ through their works, is clearly communicated in a portrayal of the Last Judgment at Trotten in which Christ in Judgment rejects the wicked man on his left who is surrounded by sins such as gluttony and welcomes into heaven the good man on his right encircled by symbols of the works of mercy.[116]

This constellation of images provides the key to the taxonomy of salvation. In summary fashion, viewers perceive what distinguishes the saved from the damned. The emphasis in church communities worshiping under the shadow of the pictorial works of sin and mercy is on socially interactive public deeds of compassion. Pictures convey that what distinguishes the saved from the damned is the choice to sin, on the one hand, or the choice to carry out the works of mercy, on the other. The decorative schemes in church buildings provided the structure for supporting Christians in making choices to carry out deeds of mercy motivated by the love embodied by the suffering Christ.

Certainly, graphic depictions of the damned in the clutches of devils could have functioned to goad viewers to carry out works of mercy as an antidote to the deadly sins. This depiction of the consequences of not acting with mercy might seem to be part and parcel of the fire and brimstone sermons of judgment which I discussed in chapter 1. However, when the context of the paintings in narrative cycles such as those at Chalgrove, Great Tew, and Peakirk are considered, another perspective emerges. As depicted on church walls, the historical narrative of Jesus' life emphasizes that humans are the reason for which Jesus became human and endured the torments described in the mural cycles. Love, not fear, characterizes the world depicted on medieval church walls. In connection with this, the ubiquitous images of saints and what they endured on account of their love for Christ evoked not the terror of damnation but rather heroic ideals. These reminded viewers of the devotion of Jesus' followers, of the protection and assistance offered by these "friends of God," and perhaps also of the fact that not nearly so much was being asked of believers in the fourteenth and fifteenth century as had been asked of commonly depicted saints such as St. Katherine of Alexandria, St. Margaret of Antioch, and even St. Thomas of Canterbury in earlier times.[117]

Medieval Christians were awash in a cycle of narratives as they read their Psalters and Books of Hours, prayed, listened to sermons, and observed the paintings and iconography in their places of worship. Encircled by miniature and monumental scenes in words and paint of the central narratives of their faith, they were rendered participants in the tradition that began with the suffering Jesus and his followers; they were the next generation, the witnesses who carried out the work of Christ in the world. The dialectic between the paintings which created *sacred space* with their theologically and emotionally powerful images and the sermons and Books of Hours readings which charted the course of *liturgical time* awakened viewers' imaginative participation in the stories depicted and summoned them into the God-centered cosmos of medieval spirituality. The Word of the sermons and *Horae* gave voice to the images on church walls, and enlivened by the Word, the images urged believers to count themselves among the cloud of witnesses, the followers of Jesus, who carried on his work in the world. In the wall paintings and manuscript illuminations, medieval worshipers were reminded of what had gone before them, and they saw that the presence of Jesus was living and was continuing to shape the sacred space and time of the worshiping community. The illuminations and paintings were an integral part of the temporal and spatial world believers inhabited, inviting them to become participants in the universe projected therein and to risk identifying with the God-human Jesus Christ who had suffered on their behalf and who pleaded with them to respond to that love by loving others in return.

THREE

Dramas of Divine Compassion

The Figure of the Wounded Jesus and the Rhetoric of Appeal in the Mystery Plays

Medieval liturgical drama cycles were public spectacles. Often whole towns and cities participated in producing them, with different guilds and craftspeople taking responsibility for the staging of individual plays. At York, for example, the fishers and mariners produced the Noah play; the goldsmiths, the plays of the three Magi; the bakers, the Last Supper play; and the butchers were responsible for the death of Christ play.[1] Although written by the educated and undoubtedly by clerics in some cases, the plays were immensely popular with people in all strata of medieval society.[2] Along with their entertainment value, these plays were also a form of public education, much like medieval sermons, art, and poetry in their accessibility and widespread appeal.

Scholars such as Rosemary Woolf and Martin Stevens have challenged the common perception of late medieval spirituality as "decadent sentimentality" by illustrating the religious power and sophistication of medieval drama.[3] Yet despite the richness of their analyses, they do not go far enough in acknowledging the rhetoric of religious transformation that undergirds these plays. In what follows, I consider late fifteenth-century medieval religious drama and its implicit theology as portrayed in the York and the N-Town mystery cycles. In particular, I understand these cycle plays as *performances of persuasion* that appeal to the viewer's will.

First, the plays manifest a God of compassion who loves humanity. It is notably through an elaborate interweaving of descriptions of Jesus' suffering that this love is apparent. In the first section of this chapter, I highlight four of the central methods by which the plays focus attention on Jesus' suffering: prefiguring, prophecy, event, and recollection. The sheer magnitude of the manifestations of this suffering, always infused with a clear identification of who the sufferer is (God), creates a drama of extraordinary power and clearly defined theological purpose.

Second, the words and actions of the suffering Jesus Christ, literally and typologically portrayed in the plays, constitute a rhetoric of persuasion in which the audience is moved to *respond* to Christ's work of reconciling God's justice with God's mercy. In communicating how Jesus' physical suffering manifests divine love, the plays seek to evoke a compassionate response to Jesus' torment and torture. This response, often initiated by sorrow at the plight of the wounded Jesus, is channeled in the plays into the sacramental system of baptism, Eucharist, and, especially, confession. In this sense, the plays break down the wall between performance and audience by "cycling" viewers into the liturgical and sacramental rituals enjoined upon all regular members of medieval Christian society. Believers respond by sorrowfully repenting and reconciling their lives with God and are further motivated by the dramas to imitate Jesus Christ's living out the mercy of God through love of neighbor.

Testimony to the Immensity of Divine Love

Varieties of Testimony

In enacting the history of creation and salvation, the York and N-Town plays dramatize God's love for humankind. In these mystery cycles, as in much late medieval English spirituality generally, the figure of the suffering Jesus is the central symbol that conveys the depth of God's love for humanity. In Jesus' speech at the Mount of Olives, for example, his physical pain and anguish awaken viewers to the immensity of his love for them: "In peynys for [man] my body schal schake / And for love of man man xal dey . . . / My flesche qwakyth in ferful case . . . / It is not for me þis peyn I lede / But for man I swete bothe watyr and blode."[4]

This medieval focus on suffering is a dramatization of a central tenet of Christian faith: the Divine becomes physically present in the figure of Jesus Christ. "The story is itself the story of permission to witness the story of the sentient body of God being seen and touched by the sentient body of man."[5] In a thought-provoking analysis of *wounding* in the Hebrew Scriptures and the New Testament, a part of her insightful study of the human body and pain, Elaine Scarry maintains that in the Hebrew Scriptures the contrasting scenes of reproduction and wounding are often "signs" of Divine presence, whereas in the New Testament the healing of persons and the wounding of God emerge as central indicators of divine presence. Scarry emphasizes the radicality of the New Testament concept of the "wounded" Deity while acknowledging the crucial place of physicality in the relationship between God and humans in both testaments. In the Hebrew Scriptures, people are most immediately identified as "body" and the Divine as an absolutely unembodied "voice." Human bodies then become the location where divine presence manifests itself. So, for example, the stories of Sarah's and Rebekah's transformations from having no children to each being "with child" are narratives in which the fecundity of women's bodies manifests the presence of the Divine. God's presence is confirmed through the bodies of humans, and bodies become the site of divine presence.[6]

Furthermore, in the Hebrew Scriptures physical manifestations signal disbelief, as in "the stiffening of the neck, the turning of the shoulder, the closing of the ears, the hardening of the heart, the making of the face like stone."[7] As in the cases of reproduction above, now, in the face of disbelief, the presence of the Divine becomes manifest through the intensification of embodiedness. Just as scenes of birth and reproduction generally somatize divine presence, and thus confirm religious belief, in situations of disbelief the Deity asserts its presence and power through marking the bodies of disbelievers and through intensifying their bodily experience. "God's invisible presence is asserted, made visible, in the perceivable alterations He brings about in the human body . . . in a flood that drowns, in a plague that descends on a house, in the brimstone and fire falling down on a city, in the transformation of a woman into a pillar of salt, in the leprous sores and rows of boils that alter the surface of the skin, in an invasion of insects and reptiles into the homes of a population, in a massacre of babies."[8] Scarry's point is that wounded human bodies also manifest the presence of the Divine.[9] The scenes of wounding often happen in response to situations in which humans blur the distinction between body and voice, so in the making of the golden calf, for example, during which there is an attempt to give God a body, the Deity responds by commanding the sons of Levi to go throughout the camp "and slay every man his brother, and every man his companion, and every man his neighbor" (Exodus 32:27). God then sends a plague. These events, which follow the embodying of the Divine, result in intensifying people's physical experience, thus reinforcing the distinction between the unembodied Divine and the physicality of persons.[10]

Scarry argues that in the New Testament the manner of divine presence shifts, due not so much to events involving reproduction and wounding as to events involving healing, which are the primary signals of divine presence. In the Hebrew Scriptures, the transformation of the human body marks divine presence—for example, fertility which signals divine presence and confirms belief or the wounding of human bodies to reassert divine presence in the face of disbelief. In the New Testament, however, the wounding of Jesus becomes the foremost sign of the connection between the Divine and humanity. In contrast to the Hebrew Scriptures, in which the Source of the wounding is acknowledged and even becomes powerful through the act of wounding itself, in the case of the suffering of Jesus in the New Testament "the fact of bodily pain is not . . . memorialized as the projected facticity of another's power."[11] While Scarry's general distinction is thought-provoking, I believe she draws the contrast between the Hebrew Scriptures and the New Testament too sharply. As scholars such as Mark Wallace have explained, divine wounding as a means of asserting divine power continues also in the New Testament (as the stories of Ananias and Sapphira suggest [Acts 5: 1–11]);[12] and the presence of the Divine through reproduction (as in the stories of Mary and Elizabeth) continues as well. Also, the fact that the Hebrew Scriptures were not read as antithetical to the embodiment of the Divine and, even more positively, were understood to support this idea may be seen in the medieval reading of Hebrew Scripture stories as prefiguring New Testament stories about Jesus (so the Suffering Servant of Isaiah prefigures Jesus). Nevertheless, Scarry does aptly point to a tendency in the New Testament which medieval plays dramatize. In the figure of Jesus Christ, the New Testament creates a relationship among power, sentience, and pain in which the inflicting of pain does not indicate the possession of power, but rather "the greatness of human vulnerability . . . not the greatness of divine invulnerability. They are unrelated and therefore can occur together: God is both omnipotent and in pain."[13] In the New Testament, "human sentience is deeply legitimated by its having become God's sentience."[14] The Divine is present now in the wounded God who is an object that can be touched.[15]

Medieval mystery cycles seek to explore with vigor and power the meaning of this intersection between divinity and sentience and to develop the implications of this intersection for the relationship between believers and their God. References to the suffering of Jesus pervade the cycle plays and create the fabric that weaves the individual plays together. Prefigurings of the Passion link the Old Testament dramatizations of the Killing of Abel, the Sacrifice of Isaac, the New Testament Slaughter of the Innocents, and the Raising of Lazarus with the culminating events of the sacred history, the Passion and death of Jesus Christ. Prophetic foretelling, as in Joachim and Anna's words at Jesus' presentation at the temple and the preaching of John the Baptist, predicts the agonies that Jesus will endure on humanity's behalf. Detailed accounts of the buffeting and the Crucifixion as they happen reenact the pain and tortures of Christ before the viewers' eyes. (Indeed, two-thirds of the surviving York text focuses on the events of the Passion.)[16] Later recountings, as in the witness of the three Marys at the tomb and the testimony of the doubting Thomas, remind the audience of the ongoing meaning of the events. In these accounts, the pain and suffering of Christ is consistently presented as incontrovertible evidence that the God-Person acts on humanity's behalf. Moreover, both the cumulative assembly of christological events and the dialogue expressing these events manifest divine presence and persuade viewers of Christ's love for them.

PREFIGURING   The theme of sacrifice runs through the N-Town and York plays and reminds readers and viewers from the start of God's self-sacrifice in the Passion and death of Jesus Christ on behalf of humans. The early plays, based on Hebrew Scripture events, establish the tradition of sacrifice to God and move from Abel's pious sacrifice of the best of his goods to Abraham's painful near sacrifice of Isaac. Abel makes the connection between the best sheep in his flock, which he offers to the "god of gret mercy" (N 31/85), and the future sacrifice of Jesus Christ when he asks for God's grace "throwh þi gret mercy / which in lombys lyknes / þou xalt for mannys wyckydnes / Onys ben offeryd in peynfulnes / and deyn ful dolfoly" (N 31/74–79). Abel's offering prefigures the sacrifice of the Lamb of God on behalf of all people.

The contrast between Cain and Abel exemplifies the principle that runs throughout the plays, namely, that a sacrifice is acceptable to God only when it is included as part of an ongoing loving relationship to the Divine. Abel reiterates that he makes his offering with goodwill and professes his commitment to serve and worship God always (N 31/70; 32/119). Cain, on the other hand, jests that it makes no sense to promise the best to God and keep the worst for oneself because, after all, God does not even eat or drink. The innocent Abel, who promised the best sheep in his flock to God, is killed by the envious Cain: "What þou stynkyng losel and is it so / doth god þe lobe and hatyht me / þou xalt be ded I xal þe slo / þi lord þi god þou xalt nevyr se" (N 33/144–147). Viewers are reminded not only of Lucifer, who envied divine power, but also of the proud and vain Herod, who boasts that he is "þe comelyeste kynge clad in gleterynge golde" (N 152/9). When the three Magi seek his advice, hoping to be guided to the child, Herod boasts of his power, declaring that there shall be no king over him. After the massacre of the innocent male children, he reminds his followers and the audience that he is "kynge of myghtys most" (N 173/134–137). Just as the innocent Abel fell victim to the jealous Cain's wrath at God's preference for Abel's offering, so the innocent male children are murdered to preserve Herod's fragile hold on royal power. Viewers see prefigured here the innocent sufferer Jesus, who, like Abel and the innocent male babies, will be tormented and tortured by jealous enemies threatened by his power.

The prefigured dramatic portrayals of Jesus' physical and spiritual anguish manifest the love not only of Jesus Christ but also of the First Person of the Trinity. Here, as is the case so often in medieval drama, prefiguring takes its meaning from the typology so essential to it. Although the literal figure of the medieval God the Father appears rarely in the cycle plays, typological references to the First Person are numerous. In the Abraham and Isaac play, for example,

Abraham is the type of the First Person and Isaac of the Second.[17] The prefig-uring through typology is most obvious in the York cycle in which Isaac is not a boy but a man of "thyrty ʒere and more sumdele" (Y 93/82), which is to say Isaac is the same age as Jesus was at his crucifixion. The Abraham and Isaac plays evoke the pathos of the Abraham who loves Isaac and yet obediently yields to the command of God to offer as a sacrifice the one whom he loves most. Even before God asks for the sacrifice, Abraham affirms his love for Isaac by saying that no one could love a child more than he loves Isaac.[18] Though the York plays generally emphasize emotional expression less than the N-Town drama, in the York play Abraham's grief is poignantly displayed: "This is to me a perless pyne, / To se myn nawe dere childe þus boune. / Me had wele leuer my lyf to tyne, / Than see þis sight þus of my sone" (Y 96/239–242). The medieval audience, perceiving the tremendous relief of Abraham when the angel stays his hand from killing his beloved son, saw prefigured the situation in which the divine Son, beloved of the medieval God the Father, would be killed, and no angel would stop the hand of death.

Through the technique of prefiguration, these plays draw the Hebrew Scrip-tures into the New Testament arena in which the Divine itself becomes physi-cally present, and in which the wounding of the Divine becomes an expression of divine love for humans. As Erich Auerbach demonstrates, the mechanism of figuration assumes a "connection between two events or persons, the first of which signifies not only itself but also the second, while the second encompasses or fulfills the first."[19] We can see how this is the case in the prefiguration of Jesus in Isaac. Although the stories of the near sacrifice of Isaac and the Crucifixion of Jesus are separated in time, insofar as they are described as historical events, they are linked by their occurrence within the "stream of historical life."[20] The events point to one another, even as they also point beyond themselves to the future. New Testament events themselves "are not the ultimate fulfillment, but them-selves a promise of the end of time and the true kingdom of God. . . . All history . . . remains open and questionable, [and] points to something still concealed."[21] The Abraham-Isaac narrative prefigures the situation in which the First Person of the Trinity will suffer the pain and anguish of the Son on behalf of humanity. Yet even this is not complete. The outcome of what Jesus' coming means to believers will not be fully realized until the Last Judgment, a dramatized event of the future which, understood in light of the events which have preceded it, draws the plays' audiences into living in the present with an eye both to the past and to the future.

PROPHETIC FORETELLING   In the plays, the suffering and death of Jesus Christ do not come as an unexpected traumatic eruption of violence. From the beginning, through the technique of prefiguring, the plays prepare the readers and viewers for what is coming next, always pointing to the suffering and anguish of the innocent one who suffers on account of his love for God and humanity. Even more, Jesus' pain and anguish have been foretold explicitly in the prophecies of the Hebrew Scriptures, on occasions such as the purification of Mary, in the preaching of John the Baptist, and in the presentation of Jesus Christ himself as he enters Jerusalem.[22]

In the N-Town Prophets' play, Isaiah, Jeremiah, Solomon, Ezekiel, Daniel, and David, among others, prophesy elements of the Jesus narrative. Isaiah explains that Jesus will suffer death to save human lives (N 58/11); Daniel's words link the tree in the Garden of Eden with the cross on which Jesus will be crucified: "In fygure of þis I saw a tre / all þe fendys of hell xall been affrayd / whan maydenys ffrute þer on þei se" (N 59/60–62); and King Asa predicts that God will be born of a maiden "and vs to bryngyn to endles blys / Ruly on rode be rent and torn" (N 59/65–66). In both the N-Town and York cycles, after the angel appears to them, the shepherds recall the prophecies of Balaam that "out of jacob xuld shyne a skye / many ffolk he xulde bye / with his bryght blood / Be þat bryght blod þat he xulde blede / he xal us brynge fro þe develys drede" (N 147/38–42).[23] One of the shepherds greets Jesus by proclaiming, "Heyl god grettest I grete þe on grownde . . . þou wynnyst þis worlde with þi wyde wounde" (N 149/94–96). Upon seeing Jesus in the temple, Simeon and the prophetess, Anna, speak the words recorded in Scripture which tell the history of Jesus' work on behalf of humankind. As in the N-Town Adoration of the Magi play, this Purification play emphasizes the blood that Jesus will shed to "bye mankende" (N 164/68) and depicts the redemption that Jesus' suffering accomplishes on humanity's behalf as an expression of divine compassion to restore what was lost through the sin of Adam and Eve (N 165/82–95; Y 158/358–410).

The prophecy theme continues with Jesus' forerunner, John the Baptist, who greets him as the Lamb of God and recites the fate of the Lamb to those gathered at the River Jordan (N 189/46–52), proclaiming that Jesus will be beaten and will bleed for "mannys sake" (N 189/49). And in the York Entry into Jerusalem play, Jesus himself predicts the events to follow: "Man sone schall þer [Jersusalem] betrayed be / And gevyn into his enmys hende / With grete dispitte. / Ther spitting on hym þer schall þei spende / And smertly smyte" (Y 217/463–467). He endures this humiliation "For veray loue · man to revyfe" (N 241/301).

There are few secrets kept from the readers and audience in the plays. While the audience may enjoy the dramatic tension created when a figure like Herod at his expansive best settles down to a feast as Death (unbeknownst to him) arrives to carry him off, the knowing audience must brace itself for the death of Christ with the full knowledge that all the plays' dramatic lines lead to this final denouement. Not only does the audience anticipate the death which will come to Jesus, but also, as the plays progress, it is taught how to respond to the coming events. In particular, the audience is prepared to attend to the suffering which will overtake the Lamb of God and to know that the depth of Jesus' suffering reveals the depth of his love for humans. In this way, the self-understanding of the plays' observers is refigured through the ritual enactment of Jesus' life and death by the sacred performers.[24]

EVENT ENACTING   The plays prefigure and prophesy Jesus' suffering so that viewers and readers anticipate the events which unfold after Judas's betrayal on the night of the Last Supper. They know that Jesus will die. The dramatic tension mounts as Pilate hesitates to condemn Jesus and as his wife warns him not to kill Jesus, but the audience knows that the desires of Annas and Caiaphas will prevail and the innocent one will be persecuted. Jesus will keep the pledge he has made to humanity (N 181/101–104), and the plays plunge their audiences into the pain and anguish surrounding the sacrifice of the *Agnus Dei*. The N-Town stage directions indicate that as his captors lead Jesus from the Garden of Gethsemane, he should be jostled, pulled forward and backward, and yanked and tugged by captors who brandish weapons and wave lights. Mary Magdalene rushes to tell his mother what has happened, and the Magdalene's own sorrow so poignantly displayed at Lazarus's death is superseded as Mary, Mother of Jesus, takes into herself the full meaning of the events which will come to pass: "Þe swerd of sorwe hath so thyrlyd myn herte A-sondyr þei do rende" (N 268/1066–1068). After Caiaphas and Annas question and accuse Jesus, the stage directions indicate that his captors spit on Jesus and beat his head and body. When Jesus refuses to respond to Herod's demand that he perform a miracle, Herod lashes out at him in fury; "Þou knowyst I may deme All thyng / thyn lyf and deth · lyeth At my wylle" (N 285/415–416). He tells the captors to beat Jesus to make him speak. They scourge him until he is badly bloodied, but still he refuses to speak. Herod turns him over to Pilate, letting him determine "whether he wole hym [Jesus] dampne or sawe" (N 287/461). Pilate also tries to force Jesus to speak by reminding him that he has power over Jesus' life and death; he can condemn him to death on the cross or he can free him. Woolf suggests that Christ's silence here manifests his willingness to suffer, but, even more, it becomes "a sublime expression of his divinity, where elevated language could only fail, silence becomes a magnificent symbol of the inexpressible."[25]

In the N-Town play, which malevolently blames "the Jews" for Jesus' death, Pilate recommends that Jesus be released, but the "doctors," speaking on behalf of the people, decree that he shall be put to death. Pilate turns him over to his enemies to be stripped, bound to a pillar, scourged, beaten, and crucified.[26] His captors ridicule him, dress him in silk, crown him with thorns, thrust the heavy cross onto his back and neck, and then pull him forward with ropes. Sweat and blood blind him until Veronica wipes his face with a cloth. His captors strip him, lie him down on the cross, and pound the nails through his hands and feet, taunting him to free himself from the cross and mocking the state of his kingship. Jesus' suffering overwhelms Mary, and she mourns: "How mayst þou a-byde þis sorwe and þis woful þowth / A deth · deth · deth why wylt þou not me kylle" (N 299/776–777). Mary swoons, overcome with sorrow at Jesus' suffering, while Jesus cries out in pain to his "father in heaven," pleading to know why he has been forsaken and begging the Father to "lete deth my sorwe slake" (N 302/866). While John tries to comfort her, Mary can think only of Jesus' suffering (N 303/914–921).[27] In the York play, Christ speaks only twice after his captors begin the process of the Crucifixion.[28] First he speaks to the "Almyghty God," recalling that his "fadir free" bid him to act on behalf of humanity and petitioning that humankind might find favor with the Divine.[29] The second speech comes almost two hundred lines later as he hangs on the cross and calls out to all who are passing by to see his pain. He asks whether any other misfortune can equal his. He also seeks divine forgiveness for his persecutors.[30] In the N-Town play, as Christ's soul prepares to descend into hell, he reminds viewers that his body is dead, hanging on the cross, "rent and torn and all blody red" (N 305/983).

V. A. Kolve reminds us that it was undoubtedly difficult for medieval audiences to witness the dramatization of the torment and torture of Christ. He argues that the game imagery which runs throughout the scenes of the tormenting of Christ (interpreted by many scholars as a comic interlude intended to elicit the audience's laughter) functioned to make bearable an experience which otherwise might have been overwhelming for the audience. In ways similar to those Scarry describes in contemporary torture, Kolve describes how "game" language enables the torturers to distance themselves from the person tortured: "The craft of killing is revealed dramatically, step by step, and furnishes them with a subject of conversation, and a focus of interest; their deepest emotions relate to that, rather than to the other object of *our attention*, the grief and the shame of the dying."[31] Witnessing the torture of a person and being called to compassionate meditation on the spectacle had to be in some measure controlled "so that it could be understood as well as felt, so that feelings would not numb themselves through excess. . . . The action is deeply shocking. . . . The horror of the Passion is controlled by constantly breaking the flow of its action. . . . Christ dies in a chaos of noise, violence, jests, and laughter, in a series of spontaneous, improvised games."[32]

We have noted that the technique of prefiguring in these plays functions not only to link the past of the Hebrew Scriptures with the New Testament life of Christ but also to project viewers' minds toward the future time of judgment—the fulfillment of all that has gone before. The assignment of the plays (like the York and N-Town Crucifixion plays) which ritually reenact the torment of Jesus to certain performers based on symbolic affinities between the theme dramatized and the occupations of the performers links the plays about historical events with the present as well as the past. At York, for example, the pinners who dramatized the Crucifixion play did not enact a finished event of the past but, akin to the sermon exemplum of the justice discussed in chapter 1 whose oaths marked the body of Jesus, dramatized an ongoing event. The acts of persons over time wound the body of God. "Pinners, makers of pins, fishhooks, mousetraps, and other small metallic objects, put on the Crucifixion play. . . . The Pinners of York demonstrate their human culpability in the death of Christ, which, by extension, belongs to all persons. . . . York, the city, becomes a *theatrum mundi.*"[33] This allocation of plays "on the basis of the symbolic affinity between the occupation and the scriptural episode which the play represented" roots the plays in the world of their medieval audiences (which is to say that they did not create a new order *de novo*).[34] The Crucifixion of Jesus, therefore, lives on in the present as individuals and communities reenact the torment by assigning the dramatization to groups and individuals who have a symbolic connection with the events displayed therein.

LATER RECOUNTINGS   The nature and extent of Jesus' suffering are not forgotten after he dies but are recounted by the mourners immediately after his death, by his disciples, by Cleophas and Luke on the road to Emmaus, by the witnesses to the Resurrection, and by God at the Last Judgment. In the York Supper at Emmaus play, travelers recount the events of Jesus' suffering and death at length and in gory detail. The travelers mourning Jesus' death recount the torment he suffered; when Jesus appears and they do not recognize him, they tell the story of his sufferings again: "His bak and his body was bolned for betyng— / Itt was . . . a sorowfull sight" (Y 363/107–108). The N-Town play audience has always before it the visage of the suffering Jesus. After the Deposition, Joseph of Arimethea lays Jesus in Mary's lap, saying, "Here is þi son blody and bloo" (N 311/1141). Mary holds him, lamenting his death: "Þi blody face now I must kysse / þi face is pale with-owtyn chere" (N 311/1143–1144). After Christ's soul has released the souls from hell and rejoins the body, he again reminds viewers that he suffered on their behalf, and he recalls the suffering he endured. The three Marys go to Jesus' tomb, and they recount Jesus' suffering: the nails, the spear, the deep wounds. The angel tells them that Jesus has risen from the dead and lives "with woundys reed" (N 330/78). When the disciples tell Thomas that Jesus has risen from the dead, he refuses to believe them and recounts his witness to Jesus' death. Peter tries to persuade Thomas that only the power of the Godhead could have brought about this miraculous event. Thomas still refuses to believe and makes the tangible presence of the wounded Jesus Christ the only proof that the dead could have risen. As he details what he needs for proof, he recounts the suffering of Jesus (N 347/321–328). When the disciples try to persuade Thomas that Jesus had appeared to them, they recount the events of his visit and tell him of the physical presence of Jesus, the wet wounds, and the fact that he ate honey and fish with them.

When Jesus appears, he invites Thomas to behold the wounds which he suffered on behalf of all humankind and to feel his heart's blood (N 347/338–339), evidence of his faithful friendship: "So · ffeythffull a ffrend where mayst þou

fynde" (N 347/341). It is only when Thomas puts his hands into the still bleeding wounds that he believes. Thomas then recounts repeatedly that he has seen
proof that the one who died has arisen; he has washed his hand in Jesus' blood;
blood has run down his sleeve. The physical reality of the running wounds of
Jesus Christ persuades Thomas of the Resurrection. Thomas's gory recounting
of Jesus' agony serves to keep the reality of Jesus' physical and spiritual anguish
before viewers and readers, and the recounting of these wounds becomes a means
of persuading fifteenth-century audiences to become latter-day participant-
observers in the blood and Resurrection of Jesus Christ.[35]

In the York play, Mary Magdalene arrives at the tomb with the other Marys,
and they are told by an angel that Jesus has risen and that he is gone. Mary
Magdalene refuses to leave until she sees Jesus, and she tells her companions to
go on their way to preach; she will remain behind.[36] She recalls Jesus' suffering,
his feet and hands nailed to the tree, the wounds he endured: "Þe woundes he
suffered many one / Was for my misse" (Y 351/278–279). Jesus suffered because he loved her. As she walks along weeping, Jesus appears to her, asking whom
she seeks: "Mi lorde Jesu and God verray, / Þat suffered for synnes his sides
bleede" (Y 356/28–29). She still does not recognize him and says her sorrow will
abate only when "Goddis body founden myght be" (Y 357/45). As in the play of
the doubting Thomas, it is Jesus' wounds which convey his presence and his
solidarity with people: "Marie, of mournyng amende thy moode, / And beholde
my woundes wyde. / Þus for mannys synnes I schedde my bloode" (Y 357/
62–64). Then she recognizes Jesus and exclaims that his wounds are still wet.
He tells her: "Negh me noght, my loue, latte be / Marie my doughtir swete"
(Y 358/82–83). This is not a distant and condemning Jesus who made juridical
reparations for human transgression and now abandons humanity to its own
devices. This is "God verraye" whose love is "swetter þanne þe mede" (Y 358/
88). The intensified physicality of the wounded Jesus signals the divine presence: Jesus' body is essential for the salvation of humanity. The incarnation is at
the heart of medieval theology and religiosity; thus Mary addresses Jesus: "A,
blessid body þat bale wolde beete, / Dere haste þou bought mankynne. / Thy
woundes hath made þi body wete / Nayled þou was thurgh hande and feete, /
And all was for oure synne" (Y 358/110–115). Medieval theology is an exercise in
carnal salvation. God's love for humankind is inscribed in Jesus' broken body,
and each new audience that witnesses the recountings of Jesus' suffering is called
upon to exegete this text of flesh afresh and learn the meaning of the cross and
resurrection.

In an otherwise excellent study of medieval scenes of death in French Passion
plays, Edelgard DuBruck claims that the focus on the cross led to reflection on
"man's own sinful mortality and the decrepitude of the body. . . . Like Mathais
Grunwald's *Altarpiece*, the spectacle of the crucifixion teaches the onlookers to
despise the body . . . and to look forward to the hereafter."[37] DuBruck suggests

that as viewers looked at Jesus' worn and tattered flesh, perception of his suffering led people to reflect on their own mortality and to a hatred of human flesh. The study of medieval theater, however, would seem to indicate something quite different. Attention to Jesus' flesh testifies to the power of the human body: it was in and through corporal existence that the reconciliation between humans and the Divine was effected. Far from denigrating carnality, the cycle plays testify to the grandeur of humanity and to the majestic potential of the body to script the message of healing and forgiveness for all people. The prefiguring, prophesying, description, and recountings of events plunge the viewers and readers into the heart of the scriptural affirmation that the Divine became human. These dramatic modalities explore this affirmation, charting the intricacies of the meaning of the suffering Jesus for the medieval world. The audience is invited to reflect deeply on the spectacle of the Divine become human and is invited to "feel what is being presented in the playing area, for only when the Passion and Crucifixion are felt can the iconography of the tableau have its desired effect."[38]

Identity of Jesus Christ: Human and Divine

What is the desired effect of the theatrical tableau? The lavish attention to Jesus' suffering described here might suggest, as some scholars have argued, that the medieval focus on Jesus' suffering promoted devotion to the humanity of Jesus to the exclusion, or at least to the neglect, of his divinity. Such claims overlook a central tenet of medieval theater: a fundamental affirmation of Jesus Christ's humanity and divinity undergirds the plays.[39] The suffering of Jesus Christ derives its power and meaning from the fact that it is God who suffers. As Julian of Norwich explained, the most important thing to recognize in witnessing the Crucifixion is who it is who suffers, "for the hyest poynt that may be seen in his passion is to thynke and to know that he is god that sufferyd, seeyng after these other two poyntes whych be lower. The one is what he sufferyd; and that other for / whom that he suffered."[40]

The presentation of Jesus Christ as divine and human functions as a theological centerpiece in both the York and N-Town cycles, though the plays differ somewhat in their presentation of Jesus' identity. The York text refers to Christ most frequently as God's son, while the N-Town cycle often refers to Jesus Christ as "god and man." This contrast is apparent in the Raising of Lazarus play in which the York Lazarus testifies to Jesus Christ's power by saying, "Certayne singnes here may men see / How þat þou art Goddis sone verray" (Y 204/ 190–191), while the N-Town risen Lazarus hails Jesus by saying, "Ffor ȝe be god and man and lord of most myght" (N 224/427). Although both plays rely on prefiguring, prophesy, event enacting, and recollecting to convey the suffering of Jesus Christ, the N-Town cycle provides more details of the suffering through prefiguring and prophesying, and the York drama devotes much more time to

the Passion events and recollection of the suffering. The prefiguring and prophesying so integral to the N-Town-cycle structure contribute to the tone of the
plays, which chronicle the inexorable unfolding of events that lead to the reconciliation of humans with the Divine through the death and Resurrection of Jesus
Christ. While Jesus Christ's identity as God's son is also prefigured and prophesied in the York cycle, the identity of Jesus as divine emerges amid a plethora of
identities, unfolding with more drama in the York cycle than in the N-Town
cycle. The announcement of God's son is apparent early on in the Annunciation
play in the York cycle, for example, but the plays, while reiterating this, emphasize his life as a miracle worker and as a prophet until, in the Transfiguration
and the Raising of Lazarus plays, the divinity of Jesus is revealed to some of his
followers. The Passion plays are much more expansive and detailed in the York
cycle than in the N-Town cycle. The N-Town viewers have already had the
spectacle of the suffering and death prefigured and prophesied extensively in the
foregoing plays. They know just what to expect and why the events happen as
they do. In the York cycle, the full meaning of the work of Jesus Christ and the
motivation for his suffering is fully revealed only in the Passion plays in which
the lessons about this work's meaning are bluntly and poignantly conveyed to
the viewers.

Testimonies to the divinity of Jesus Christ based on the connection between
him and the other persons of the Trinity run throughout the York and N-Town
cycles. The N-Town cycle consistently presumes that even prior to the Incarnation, worship of the Divine was worship of the Trinity—"Father, Son, and Holy
Spirit" (N 66/90). Joachim and Anne, Mary's parents, who have been told of
their daughter's future by an angel, take her to the temple to dedicate her to "thre
personys and on god" (N 72/6). As Joseph searches for a place to rest with Mary,
he prays to find a place to stay, addressing the Divine as "trinité" (Y 125/1). When
Gabriel appears to Mary at the Annunciation, he tells her that she will bear "þe
sone of þe trynyte" (N 105/240) and that the child she bears "sall be God and
called God sonn" (Y 115/162). The shepherds greet the baby Jesus as the light of
the Trinity, saying, "Heyl god grettest I grete þe on grownde" (N 149/94).

The figure of Jesus Christ is portrayed in both cycles in a multifaceted way—
simultaneously as healer, comforter, teacher, miracle worker, and prophet, as well
as the one who ransoms humankind. In the play of Jesus in the Temple, one of
the doctors remarks, "I trow þis barne be sente / Full souerandly to salue oure
sare" (Y 177/135–136). Jesus' identity as healer is particularly apparent when upon
his entry into Jerusalem people begin to gossip about him: "He helys þe seke,
both ʒonge and olde, / And þe blynde giffis þam þer sight. / Both dome and
deffe, as hymselffe wolde, / He cures þame right" (Y 208–209/130–133). The
bystanders recite the litany of Jesus' miracles: the feeding of the five thousand,
the turning of water into wine, and the raising of Lazarus.[41] A blind person tries
to discern the source of all the excitement in the streets as Jesus enters Jerusalem,

and upon being told that a prophet has arrived, he calls out to Jesus to heal him. The apostle Philip attempts to silence the blind man so that he will not disturb the procession; still he shouts to Jesus to "haue mercy." Jesus heals him, saying, "þi faith shall þe saue" (Y 214/350). Then a lame person calls on Jesus for mercy and healing, proclaiming in his appeal that Jesus has healed the deaf and the dumb and restored the dead to life.[42]

In the N-Town play of the prophets, Isaiah predicts the Incarnation: "Flesch and blood to take god wyll be born" (N 58/14); King Asa says that God will be born of a maiden (N 59/64); and King Joras prophesies that after the Resurrection Jesus will return to heaven "both god and verry man ther endles to be" (N 60/82). Anne asks Mary if she is willing to live as a virgin and also as "goddys wyff." Mary protests that she is not worthy, and then, in one of the ironies that the medieval viewers and audience no doubt enjoyed, Mary replies that God should have a sweet mother, and she prays that she might live to see this woman (N 72/22–23)! Later, in a moment of humorous irony, she petitions God to allow her to see just once the woman who bears "goddys sone" so that she may serve her (N 79/221–222). After Gabriel appears to her, Mary describes the presence of Jesus within her when she says, "A now I ffele in my body be / parfyte god and parfyte man" (N 107/293–294). In the York cycle she says, "now will be borne of my body / Both God and man togedir in feere" (Y 126/52–53). She addresses Jesus by saying, "hayle God and man in erth to wonne" (Y 126/60), and she calls him "My God, my lorde, my sone so free" (Y 128/149). Elizabeth greets Mary as the "modyr of god" (N 117/52, 61; 120/113). In the Purification play, Simeon announces Jesus, "Ffor goddys son as I declare / Is born to bye mankende" (N 164/67–68).

In the N-Town play, after explaining the narrative of the Fall and the nature of the process by which all will be restored, Christ begins to reveal his own identity in the play of Christ and the Doctors: "I am of dobyl byrth and of dobyl lenage / Ffyrst be me fadyr I am with-out gynnynge / And lyke as he is hendeles in his hyʒ stage / So xal I neuyr mor haue endynge" (N 183/157–160). He has his body from his mother, "but myn hyʒ godhede þis is no lesse / all thynge in þis world for sothe dude I make" (N 183/167–168). John the Baptist preaches that "cryst þe sone of god is be-come oure fere" (N 192/133). The Transfiguration play is one of the key acknowledgments of who Christ is in the York play: Elijah and Moses testify that Jesus Christ is the Son of God. A shining cloud appears, and God the Father announces that Jesus is his son: "Where he is, þare am I" (Y 197/177).

Women are often the first to recognize Jesus' identity in these plays, as in the N-Town play of the Raising of Lazarus in which Martha addresses Jesus as the "sone of god in blys" (N 220/312). The unveiling of Jesus' identity reaches a crescendo as he tells the gathered friends of Lazarus to roll the stone away from the grave "þe glorye of þe godhede a-non ʒe xal se" (N 223/400). Lazarus arises, prefiguring the Resurrection of Christ and testifying to Jesus Christ's identity as divine and human. Peter and John echo his recognition of Jesus Christ as "very god and man" (N 224/436).

With the Entry into Jerusalem play, the York cycle begins to pick up pace as events proceed inexorably to the death of Jesus. When asked who Jesus is, Peter replies that he is the King of the Jews and "both God and man withouten blame" (Y 207/83). The angel who appears to the anguished Jesus, who is sweating water and blood in the Garden of Gethsemane, greets him by saying, "Heyl bothe god and man" (N 264/945).

In the Passion plays, the affirmation of Jesus' identity comes almost as frequently from the mouths of his detractors as from the mouths of his friends and followers. Often, as with Annas (N 235/130), the statement of Jesus Christ's identity is made as if to ridicule him or to accuse him of a false naming of himself as an explanation for why he is being tried.[43] Even Jesus' enemies must affirm who he is. Caiaphas charges Jesus to say that he is God's son, and Jesus affirms this: "Goddys sone I am I sey not nay to þe" (N 276/149). Pilate taunts him, calling him a king, the son of God and lord of Earth. In the York Conspiracy play, one of the doctors explains that Jesus offends the Jews when he teaches people to call him "Grete God son" (Y 221/52). Caiaphas complains that "he lykens hym to be lyke God, ay-lastand to lende" (Y 221/60–61). Sometimes affirmations of Jesus Christ's identity come from people who suddenly realize who he is. At the Crucifixion, Dysmas, the thief on Jesus' right, recognizes him as the son of God (N 299/799), and after the Crucifixion, the centurion exclaims, "I knowe he is both god and man / be þis wark þat here is done" (N 307/1045–1046).

In the late medieval England of the liturgical dramas considered here, reflection on the humanity of Jesus was inseparable from the affirmation of his divinity. It was precisely through responding with repentance and compassion to the humanity of Jesus that Christian believers recognized the Divine's love for them and were empowered to respond to that love. Acknowledgment of the humanity of the suffering Jesus Christ opened the way to recognizing his identity with God and initiated the process of compassionate identification with the one who sacrificed his life so that others might live. Just as Mary Magdalene sought "Goddis body" in the York cycle (Y 357/45), so the plays themselves stage the belief we saw preached in the sermons of chapter 1: it is in the encounter with the bleeding body of the suffering Jesus that viewers and readers meet the Divine.

Divine Compassion: Reconciliation of God's Justice with God's Mercy

The Parliament of Heaven play is one of the most significant in the N-Town cycle for determining the identity of Jesus Christ and for revealing the divine compassion which lies behind the Incarnation. Rosemary Woolf described the play (a discussion among God's four daughters—Truth, Justice, Mercy, and Peace—and the Trinity) as having as its "poetic theme the encounter between man's wretchedness and God's burning love."[44] In evoking the medieval debate between God's justice and God's mercy, the play sets the theological stage for the resolution which follows: Contemplation begs God to be merciful, evoking images of sobbing and sorrowful creatures, contrite and crying, begging for divine mercy. The Virtues make their appeal, reminding God of the prophets and patriarchs who have made supplication on behalf of humanity. God responds by saying that now is the time for reconciliation: prophets have begged and contrite creatures called out for transformation. God's daughter, Truth, replies, pointing to the incongruity and impossibility of a situation in which the God who had condemned Adam and Eve to death and to hell for sinning should now reconcile with them: "Twey contraryes mow not to-gedyr dwelle" (N 99/64). The woe that comes to one who has despised the Creator cannot be excessive, so Truth advocates letting humans suffer forever. Mercy intercedes, urging God to have compassion on people who grieve for their transgressions. All heaven and earth cry out for mercy, says Misericordia (N 100/78). Mercy appeals to God to free humankind from the clutches of the devil: "Þi love man no lengere lete hym kepe" (N 100/88). Justice speaks up, reminding Mercy that God loves righteousness. Humankind chose the devil as master and spurned the maker; those who sin against the eternal one shall have unceasing punishment: "xulde he be savyd · nay nay nay" (N 100/95). Mercy interjects again, reminding her vengeful sister, Righteousness, that the eternal God may rectify eternal sin: the mercy of God is inexhaustible (N 101/112). At last, Peace enters the discussion and sides with Mercy, though she recognizes the great reason with which Truth and Righteousness speak. And yet, Peace concludes, if humankind is condemned to hell, then there will always be division between God and humanity "And than myght not I pes dwelle" (N 101/120).

Jesus appears and reiterates the themes which had appeared in the previous debate. Adam's and Eve's deaths were necessary, otherwise Righteousness and Truth would have perished. If, however, Peace were exiled, then Mercy, too, would perish. So reconciliation must be made. Jesus goes on to say that the one who repairs the breach must be without iniquity so that hell may have no claim on him. The Trinity decides that the Second Person, Wisdom, must become incarnate to effect the transformation. Justice, Peace, Mercy, and Righteousness are reconciled, and as the Father's first speech in the play suggests, the "mercy-seeking" Trinity is reconciled with all created beings, and the four daughters are unified in a loving unity. This Anselmian portrayal is of a God seeking to balance justice, mercy, truth, and peace. The four must always coexist in unity for the Divine to live in harmony. The Divine portrayed here responds to the pleas for mercy and recognizes the pleas of contrite sinners for comfort (N 99/48–56). Thus even before the Incarnation happens, the audience has been reminded that the loving and merciful Deity will become incarnate to effect reparation of the breach between God and humanity.[45]

Models for Describing How Jesus Christ Effects Reconciliation

These plays demonstrate a medieval celebration of the Divine become human. The power of these dramas is in their intricate exploration of what the encounter with the suffering Jesus Christ can mean for the late medieval audience. But the heart of their imaginative eloquence does not lie in their unified systematic theological analysis of how Jesus accomplishes what he does. Rather, a medley of explanations of the nature of Christ's work runs throughout the plays—including ransoming humanity from the devil, outwitting Satan, sacrifice, and Anselmian satisfaction—and it is impossible to isolate one trajectory as singularly describing the theological process for securing human salvation.

The themes of outwitting the devil and conquering the power of evil comprise what Gustaf Aulén refers to as the "classic" idea of atonement.[46] The plays do not delineate the precise nature of the devil's rights over people, though the implication (at least in the York cycle) is that Satan gained control over humankind through the Fall. Nor do the plays describe precisely how Jesus Christ's life and death overcome Satan, though both the N-Town and York cycles do make ongoing references to tricking the devil, who is ever uncertain of the identity of Jesus until it is too late.

In connection with this model of human captivity to Satan, the plays often draw on "ransom" language and suggest that the ransom price, Jesus' life, has been paid, presumably to Satan. Jesus describes himself as ransom in the York play: "From heuen to erth whan I dyssende / Rawnsom to make I made promys" (Y 205/8–9). The implication is that Satan, who has gained rights over sinful humanity, finds it impossible to possess the ransom offered in exchange for humanity's freedom because death cannot hold Jesus Christ. It is this theory that is evoked when the plays speak of Christ's blood buying the safety of humanity. In the York Harrowing of Hell play, for example, Jesus explains his rights to the inhabitants of hell: "I haue þame getyn agayne / Thurgh bying with my bloode" (Y 333/11–12). The plays may reflect the early Christian view that "the devil exceeded his rights in his treatment of Christ, and therefore was deprived of his rights and lost his kingdom."[47] In shedding Christ's blood, Satan punished an innocent one, exceeding his proper domain and thus jeopardizing and finally losing his rights over humanity.

Connected with this economic rhetoric of ransom and purchase, one of the unfolding subplots of the N-Town and York cycles is the Deity's resolve to trick the devil, who is uncertain about Jesus' true identity (which remains camouflaged under the veil of his humanity). Jesus Christ's divinity is hidden, and Satan "as a fish swallows the bait on the fish-hook . . . swallows his prey, and is thereby taken captive by the godhead, hidden under human nature."[48] In the York drama, the Divine intent to beguile the devil explains Mary's marriage before the birth of Jesus: "So was the Godhede closed and cledde / In wede of weddyng whare they wente" (Y 111/28–29; 339/249–252). The devil has heard people talking about one who will come to restore humankind to bliss. Though he claims not to believe the story, he nevertheless wants to survey the situation. Having heard that Jesus has been fasting in the desert for forty days, Satan decides to test him in this weakened state. He plans to tempt Jesus with gluttony. "For so it schall be knowen and kidde / If Godhed be in hym hidde" (Y 187/48–49). After resisting gluttony, vainglory, and covetousness, Jesus sends Satan away to hell. The N-Town Temptation play centers on the evil figures of Belyull, Belsabub, and Satan, who have heard Jesus referred to as the Son of God but are uncertain of his identity. They decide to tempt him with gluttony, vainglory, and avarice, the three sins which so easily lead people astray. When Jesus resists Satan's temptation and sends him away, Satan leaves in frustration: "What þat he is I kan not se / Whethyr god or man what þat he be / I kan not tell in no degre" (N 199/ 192–194). When at last Christ descends to hell and announces that he is God's Son, Satan is stunned and expresses wonder that one so exalted should have lived so simply. Jesus replies: "Þat was for hartely loue I hadde / Vnto mannis soule, it for to saue / And for to make þe mased and madde" (Y 339/245–246). The plays, and especially the York plays, at times, then, portray the image of Jesus Christ directly involved in transactions with Satan in order to overthrow Satan's hold on humankind.[49]

As is apparent in the Abraham-Isaac story which prefigures the Jesus narratives, and as I will suggest again in a later section on the Eucharist, Jesus Christ is also presented frequently as a sacrifice in these plays, another scriptural and early patristic christological device.[50] As the N-Town Parliament of Heaven play discussed above suggests, the plays also reflect the Latin doctrine of the Atonement that deemphasizes Satan and places the burden of reconciliation on the relationship between the Deity and humans. Humans must "make an offering or payment to satisfy God's justice."[51] Here the theme of juridical sacrifice sometimes emerges, and though the plays are unclear about the exact nature of the sacrifice in question, they may have been working with a model like that of Gregory the Great, who had argued that "human guilt necessitated a sacrifice; but no animal sacrifice could possibly be sufficient; a man must be offered for men. . . . The sacrifice must be undefiled. . . . The conclusion is that, in order that the sacrifice may be reasonable, a man must be offered, and that, in order that it may avail to cleanse men from sin, a sinless man must be offered."[52] The N-Town Parliament of Heaven play, though, reflects an Anselmian view of atonement in which the Divine tries to find a way whereby, in keeping with divine justice and mercy, satisfaction for humanity's dishonor to God can be made. Only a human ought to make satisfaction because it is the sin of humanity which is the source

of the dishonor; only God can make the satisfaction because the offense is infi-
nite and beyond the power of humanity to repair (since humans cannot give God
anything beyond the honor which is already due to God). Jesus Christ, then, the
God-human, makes satisfaction on behalf of humanity by dying innocently
and by attributing his merit to satisfy humanity's dishonor to God.[53] As Anselm
and the N-Town play construct this understanding of the Atonement, the motivation for the reconciliation comes from a loving and compassionate Deity.

The medieval cycle plays encapsulate a variety of views of the atoning work
of Christ. The brilliance of the plays is not so much in resolving the doctrinal
question of the nature of the Atonement as it is in exploring what all of these
theories presumed: that the Divine Logos became human and transformed the
lives of believers who responded to the reconciliation which the Deity made
possible.

The pathos of the First Person, as evident in the Abraham and Isaac play and
in the Parliament of Heaven play, and the willingness of the Second Person of
the Trinity to endure anguish and agony testify to the immensity of divine love
for humankind. But the dramatic enactment of that compassion goes beyond a
demonstration of God's love. The medieval cycle plays reflect the Abelardian
insight that Christ's redemptive work in living, suffering, and dying seeks to elicit
a *response* of love on the part of humans.[54] The flooding of viewers' senses with
extravagant depictions of pain and anguish in foreshadowing, prophecy, event,
and recollection comprises an urgent appeal to the audience to respond in discipleship to Jesus Christ's expression of love.

Response to the Immensity of Divine Love

The Appeal of the Suffering Savior

Awareness of Jesus' anguish and torment calls attention to the work of the Savior in reconciling humanity with the Divine. This leads to my second point in
this chapter: the plays urge believers to *respond* with compassionate love to the
Savior who suffered on their behalf. In keeping with common theological teaching, the cycle dramas portray the Fall as leaving humankind subject to the wrath
and judgment of the Divine. The life, death, and Resurrection of Jesus Christ
introduce the mercy of a loving God and reconcile and make possible the ongoing reunion of God and humanity through the sacraments. Late medieval liturgical dramas consistently promote the medieval sacramental system, particularly
the sacraments of baptism, confession, and Eucharist, for effecting reconciliation between God and the faithful.

As is evident in the Parliament of Heaven play, the N-Town cycle characterizes the Divine motivation for merciful response to humankind as springing in
part from people's pleas for mercy. This message—that human beings are advo-

cates for their own fate—runs throughout the cycle. The Creator loved the created world even though it spurned the Maker through the "abominable presumption" of trying to seize all that God had made. Mercy and Peace reflect divine love for humans and pave the way toward the reconciliation that the Trinity and the work of Jesus Christ make possible. With the depth of God's love for humankind manifest yet again—this time through Jesus Christ even more dramatically and obviously than through the creation—people are once more confronted with the choice of whether to respond to or to despise the offer of love. Just as the N-Town play describes God's response to human and angelic appeals and just as Mercy responds to the cries of "all hefne and erthe" for mercy after the Fall, humans, by being contrite and seeking mercy, must avail themselves of the peace offered them after Jesus Christ makes the reconciliation possible.

In the York Crucifixion play, Jesus' reasons for suffering become immediately apparent in his address to the First Person of the Trinity as the soldiers prepare the cross for the Crucifixion. Jesus announces that he suffers to save humanity from sin: "Here to dede I obblisshe me, / Fro þat synne for to saue mankynde . . . / And fro þe fende þame fende, / So þat þer saules be saffe / In welthe withouten ende" (Y 316–317/53–54; 57–59). As I have indicated, the York Crucifixion play excruciatingly details the Crucifixion process in which Jesus is tied and nailed to the cross and then the cross is hoisted to an upright position. When the cross is raised, Jesus addresses the audience from his lofty pulpit and urges passersby to reflect on his suffering: "Byholdes myn heede, myn handis, and my feete, / And fully feele nowe, or ʒe fyne, / Yf any mournyng may be meete, / Or myscheue mesured unto myne" (Y 321/255–258). In the Death of Christ play, Jesus speaks from the cross again to remind his viewers that he suffers on their behalf. How could he show more kindness? He urges his audience to "mende thy moode," to respond to the suffering they witness:

> Þou man þat of mys here has mente,
> To me tente enteerly þou take.
> On roode am I ragged and rente,
> Þou synfull sawle, for thy sake;
> For thy misse amendis wille I make.
> My bakke for to bende here I bide,
> Þis teene for thi trespase I take.
> Who couthe þe more kyndynes haue kydde than I?
> Þus for thy goode
> I schedde my bloode.
> Manne, mende thy moode,
> For full bittir þi blisse mon I by. (Y 326/118–130)

He repeatedly reminds onlookers that he suffers for their benefit and urges them to learn the spiritual meaning of his suffering.

With bittirfull bale haue I bought,
Þus, man, all þi misse for te mende.
On me for to looke lette þou noȝt,
Howe baynly my body I bende.
No wighte in þis worlde wolde haue wende
What sorowe I suffre for thy sake.
Manne, kaste þe thy kyndynesse be kende,
Trewe tente unto me þat þou take,
And treste. (Y 327/182–191)

He asks specifically that those perceiving his anguish respond to it: "Manne on molde, be meke to me, / And haue thy maker in þi mynde, / And thynke howe I haue tholid for þe / With pereles paynes for to be pyned" (Y 333/1–4).

Mary, the Mother of Jesus Christ, provides a model for sorrow as a response to Christ's Passion: "Alas Alas I leve to longe / to se my swete sone with peynes stronge / As a theff on cros doth honge / And nevyr ȝet dede he synne / Alas my dere chyld to deth is dressyd / now is my care wel more in-cressyd / A myn herte with peyn is pressyd / Ffor sorwe myn hert doth twynne" (N 303/899–906). In the York cycle, when Mary laments the death of Jesus, he tells her not to weep; he is doing the work of the Father. Yet she still mourns, asking how she could do anything else: "Allas, þat þou likes noght to lende, / Howe schulde I but wepe for thy woo?" (Y 326/148–149). Jesus tells her that John should be her son, but this is no consolation for her, and she weeps still more, crying that she would rather be dead than witness the pain of her son: "Allas sone, sorowe and siȝte, / Þat me were closed in clay. / A swerde of sorowe me smyte, / To dede I were done þis day" (Y 327/157–160). John tries to comfort her by saying that he is her son and by wishing her peace. Mary is amazed that anyone would even try to mitigate her misery in the face of her son's gruesome and painful death. "My steuen for to stede or to steere, / Howe schulde I, such sorowe to see, / My sone þat is dereworthy and dere / Thus doulfull a dede for to dye?" (Y 327/ 167–172). Readers and viewers remember the grief of Mary and Martha at Lazarus's death, which prefigures Jesus' death. Mary lamented that her brother "þat I loued most" (Y 203/151) is gone. Her mind and her strength fail her, and she and Martha ask why death does not take them. Mary's response to Jesus' death models the deep grief that wells up in those who witness the sufferings of Jesus. It is not only because she is his mother that she grieves; the play argues that the scene itself should evoke pain and sorrow. Mary urges the audience to respond to the Crucifixion by saying that even if he had not been her son she would have lamented "to se my ffrende with many a ffo / all to rent from top to too / his flesch with-owtyn hyde" (N 303/920–922). The lamentations expressed by Mary and the followers of Jesus "reinforced the pathos, the aspect of the suffering endured during Christ's agony. They voiced, in fact, the audience's compassion."[55]

John Elliott argues that medieval actors were much more dramatically sophisticated than historians of drama have generally acknowledged. They crafted skillful performances to stir viewers' emotions and evoke in them the desired responses. "The fourteenth-century *Treatise Against Miracle-Playing*, though antitheatrical in purpose, acknowledges that 'ofte sythis by siche myraclis pleying men and wymmen, seynge the passioun of Crist and of hise seyntis, ben mouyd to compassion and deuocion, wepynge bitere teris.'"[56] Love led Jesus to bleed and agonize on humanity's behalf, and, like the Jesus of the homiletic literature considered in chapter 1, the Jesus of medieval drama implores his audience to experience the divine love manifest in the torn and tortured flesh of the wounded Savior.

Sacraments

The plays suggest that during his life and ministry Christ instituted the sacramental system. They feature baptism, Eucharist, and, especially, confession as the means by which, after Jesus Christ's Ascension, his followers could still avail themselves of the mercy that he offered them.[57] As depicted in the plays, Jesus' suffering and death bridged the uncrossable chasm between life and death and made possible the ongoing divine assistance available in the sacraments. The angel in the N-Town Shepherd's play links the presence of the sacraments and the healing they proffer with Jesus' suffering: "Sacramentys þer xul be vij / Wonnyn þurowe þat childys wounde" (N 146/5–6).[58]

The suffering Christ, who reunites the justice of God that had demanded the condemnation of sinful humanity with the mercy of God that sought reconciliation, urges people to participate in the sacrament of confession. I differ from scholars such as Jean Delumeau who associate the medieval insistence on confession with a prevailing social conception of a wrathful and judgmental God.[59] I suggest that emphases that at first appear to be incongruent—the fear- and guilt-provoking God of justice, on the one hand, and the merciful and compassionate God of love, on the other—are inseparably related to one another in medieval religious life and, even more important, are linked in a critical way in the figure of the suffering Savior. Jesus Christ calls the observers of his sufferings to repent. Confession becomes the means by which, in keeping with the demands of a God of justice, believers can avail themselves of the merciful love of God which the Crucifixion expressed.[60] In the two medieval dramas considered here, as in hundreds of late medieval English narratives, lyrics, and sermons, the call to repent comes not from a threatening God but from a loving Christ who suffered on humanity's behalf.

Jesus suffers because of people's sins: "He suffereth death for our trespasses." This suffering on humans' behalf binds Jesus to believers; he says to the doubting Thomas: "Be-holde wele thomas my woundys so wyde, / which I haue sufferyd ffor All mankynde / Put þin hool hand in to my ryght syde / And in myn hert blood þin hand þat þou wynde / So ffeythfull a ffrend were mayst þou fynde" (N 347/337–341). The emphasis on the physical suffering of Jesus throughout late medieval drama manifests the medieval belief that the shedding of the Savior's blood was a pledge, a visible symbol of his ties to humanity. Thomas foresees his own forgiveness by linking himself with the shedding of Jesus' blood: "In his dere herte blood myn hand wasch I haue / Where þat þe spere poynt was peynfully pyght" (N 348/363–364). Longinus (whom we considered in chapter 2), the soldier who pierced the side of Jesus and whose blindness (both physical and spiritual) was miraculously cured when the blood dripped into his eyes, represents another response to Jesus' suffering and death. He recounts the agony of Jesus' torture and shedding of blood and teaches the audience to seek mercy: "Mercy, my treasoure, / Mercy, my sauioure, / Þy mercy be markid in me" (Y 330/310–312). Jesus' torment, endured on behalf of humankind, makes possible the pleas for mercy which emerge in the context of the Crucifixion. The centurion, marveling at the darkness which enshrouds the earth at Jesus' death, sees it as a "trewe token I trowe þat it is / Þat mercy is mente unto man" (Y 330/315–316).

The call to respond to Jesus Christ's suffering by seeking forgiveness appears throughout the N-Town and York cycles. In the Woman Taken in Adultery play, one of the central repentance plays in the N-Town cycle, Jesus says, "Man, I cam down all ffor þi loue / Loue me ageyn I aske no more / . . . haske þou mercy and þou xalt haue" (N 201/19–20, 24). The plays direct believers to respond to Jesus' anguish by asking for forgiveness and mercy and by loving Jesus Christ. The response of seeking forgiveness appears in the Abraham and Isaac play in which Isaac's last request before his near sacrifice is a prayer for forgiveness and mercy; this not only prefigures Jesus' request for the forgiveness of his killers but also provides a model for all humanity of the proper response to God.

The York and N-Town plays echo similar themes of confession and repentance, although at times they differ regarding what plays and characters express these themes. In the York scene in which the tax collector, Zacchaeus, repents and promises to return what he has taken, Jesus' reply articulates the power of confession: "Thy clere confessioun schall þe clense, / Þou may be sure of lastand lyffe" (Y 217/453–454). A similar emphasis on sorrowful contrition appears in the N-Town play of the Woman Taken in Adultery. The woman begs her accusers to have mercy on her, but they refuse. Then she asks mercy from Jesus Christ, saying that she repents of her sins and asking him to take compassion on her sorrow (N 209/269). This play can be seen as a continuation of the problem debated in the Parliament of Heaven play—that is, in confronting Christ with a woman caught in adultery, Jesus' enemies are trying to trap him in a situation in which justice and mercy cannot be reconciled so that he will be forced to acknowledge the contradiction. Jesus casts their own accusations back at them by reinterpreting the situation such that they cannot justly stone the woman. He forgives her and explains (as did the sermons discussed in chapter 1) that when a person is contrite, God does not keep "olde wreth in mynde" but loves them better "very contryte whan he them fynde" (N 209/290, 293).

There is a strong sense in these plays that people participate in determining their own destiny. God loves those who repent and express compassion for the suffering Jesus: "Mi God, youre God, and ilk mannes frende / That till his techyng will consente, / Till synneres þat no synne þame schende, / Þat mys amendis and will repente" (Y 377/157–160). "Christ's law is not cruel—characterized by love, grace, mercy, and forgiveness which flow to men through the sacraments."[61]

The Eucharist is constructed in medieval drama as a sign of God's ongoing love and nourishment of humanity, a visual symbol that manifests the meaning of Jesus' suffering for others and encapsulates what the Passion accomplishes for humanity. The portrayal of the Eucharist begins in the Old Testament plays in which God is depicted as food and nourishment for humankind. In the Moses play, for example, Moses urges the audience not to wallow in wordly goods but rather to focus their love on God "which bodyly ffood / doth ʒeve all day and gostly helth" (N 54/80–81). Before Jesus' birth, Joseph asks Mary at one point in their travels what she wants for sustenance. She replies that she does not want any food: "All-myghty god my fode xal be" (N 139/109).

As we might expect, the Last Supper functions as the central event during which the meaning of the Eucharist fully emerges. In the N-Town Last Supper play, Jesus calls the bread "god and man" (N 256/732), thereby establishing that the Eucharist is the body of God which has the capacity to nourish and trans-form humans. The play "transmute[s] the abstract dogma that maintained Christ's Real Presence in the Eucharist into images through which the identity of flesh and Host is vividly perceived."[62] Jesus engages in an elaborate interpretation of the original Paschal meal, giving a spiritual interpretation of the Hebrews' last meal as the Pharaoh's captives and identifying himself literally with the lamb. Just as under the old law the lamb was eaten and the Pharaoh destroyed, now in the new Christian era the lamb is eaten to destroy spiritual enemies. In his speeches in the N-Town play (the York text is missing here), Jesus forges connections with the sacrifices of the Hebrew Scriptures and identifies himself as the new Paschal Lamb, "a sacryfyce most of price" (N 255/693). The stories of old are now the examples of virtuous living; for example, the staff the Israelites once carried now becomes the "example" they teach to others. In interpreting the meaning of the Hebrews' Paschal feast, Jesus teaches that the bread is to be eaten in love, with bitter contrition, and that the lamb is to be eaten both head and feet:

> This immaculat lombe þat I xal ʒou ʒeve
> Is not only þe godhed A-lone
> But bothe god and man þus must ʒe beleve
> þus þe hed with þe feet ʒe xal receyve ech-on. (N 256/730–733)

Jesus repeatedly affirms that he is present in the Eucharist "Hol god and man" (N 259/826); through the power of the Father and Christ's blessing, bread is "mad my body" (N 255/701). Jesus feeds his disciples with his blood which he sheds for love on account of their sins: "This is my body fflesch and blode / þat for þe xal dey up-on þe rode" (N 257/770–771). As the Eucharist, a sign of divine love, makes Christ present, those who will be saved must believe that what appears as bread is actually Jesus Christ's flesh and blood.

The disciple Peter provides a model for how the new Paschal Lamb is to be received:

Ffor with more delycyous mete lord þou may us not fede
þan with þin owyn precyous body
Wherfore what I haue trespacyd in word thought or dede
With byttyr contrycion · lord I haske þe mercy. (N 257/766–769)

Peter asks forgiveness before receiving the Eucharist, indicating the crucial place of confession in proper preparation for the Eucharist in the medieval sacramental system. In contrast, the unrepentant Judas typifies the believer who receives the Eucharist in sin. Jesus says he will not deny the Eucharist to Judas, but tells Judas that since he presumes to receive Jesus' body, he shall receive it to his own damnation.[63]

When the soul of Christ descends into hell, the audience is again reminded that Jesus died for humanity; believers eat his body and drink his blood for strength and assistance (N 305/985–986). When Jesus rises from the dead, he explains that he suffered death because he loved humans and made his body into bread to feed the human soul (N 320/1426–1427). Later, when Christ meets Luke and Cleophas on the road to Emmaus, Cleophas reveals the true nature of Christ in the world when he says that to speak of Christ is food to him. Jesus' suffering and death frees people from their bondage to the devil; Christ nurtures and sustains his sheep and protects them from the evil one. The scene of the Last Supper evokes the depth of love which motivates Jesus to act as he does: "With my flesch and blood I haue ʒow fed / Ffor mannys love I may do no mo / Þan for love of man to be ded" (N 259/814–816).[64] The eucharistic references in medieval liturgical drama are not simply records of past events; they are an invitation to contemporary viewers to partake of the sacrament dramatized there: "We find, not merely dogma brought to the stage, but instead what must have been for its audience a fervent invitation to behold the body of Christ's sacrament and sacrifice and to see there the ever-present means of redemption."[65]

Love of Neighbor and the Cosmos on Stage

Although the plays portray the sacraments as necessary for the reconciliation of humans with the Divine and for the ongoing spiritual nourishment of believers, the sacraments were generally not sufficient for a renewed relationship with God, and particularly not for one which would lead to eternal life. (The story of Dysmas, the thief on Jesus' right, suggested that in some cases repentance at death would be sufficient.) In general, though, in addition to promoting the sacraments, the plays offer descriptive interpretations of biblical history that serve to prescribe relationships with other people as a crucial dimension of the life of Christian believers. Believers were called by the plays to enact their own belief, guided by the Ten Commandments, particularly the first two, which were thematically critical to the plays. Furthermore, they urged viewers to imitate the example of Jesus Christ as portrayed in the cycle plays. The combination of guidance by the love of God and neighbor and mimetic attention to Jesus was so central to religious life, as we shall see, that it became the means of distinguishing the damned from the saved. Attention to the manner of Jesus' living (as portrayed in the cycles) points to the significance of biblical historicity for medieval drama. As we have seen, Jesus Christ's identity as human and divine is fundamental to the meaning of the plays; at the same time, a deep familiarity with the pains and possibilities of the human condition courses through them. Mimetic attachment to Jesus Christ guided viewers deeper into their own humanity and potential for salvation. Jesus Christ's life, death, and Resurrection taught believers that the way to eternal life was through love of God, self, and neighbor. In other words, the message of the divine and human Savior for believers was not to measure themselves against a divine exemplar but rather to cultivate ever more deeply their own humanity, as well as that of their neighbors.[66]

The dramas urge the faithful to go beyond repenting for their sins and insults to the Divine—to make the merciful work of the Savior who was bound to them by his suffering a model for their own compassionate activity within the world. In the N-Town Last Judgment play, for example, the saved depict the suffering of Jesus as the merciful expression of God's love which made their bliss possible: "[We] wurchepp oure lorde þat mercyfful is / For thorwe his woundys þat be so wyde / he hath brought us to his blys" (N 375/58–60). The damned souls cry out for mercy, and God responds by asking them why they seek mercy: "to whom haue ȝe don Any mercyful dede?" (N 375/73). Christ invites the saved into heaven, recalling how they fed him when he was hungry, comforted him when he was sick, harbored him when he was homeless, clothed him when he was naked, and visited him when he was in prison. The saved ask when they perceived Jesus thus, and he replies that when they helped any who had need, they helped him. At the Last Judgment, those who did not carry out the corporal works of mercy and who were slaves to vices provoke the judgment of God, while those who cared for the poor, the sick, the imprisoned, and the hungry are invited into heaven.[67]

In both the York and N-Town plays, the drama of the Woman Taken in Adultery exemplifies Jesus' call to all people to repent, not only to seek forgiveness for themselves but also to forgive those who offend them. The woman seeks mercy from her accusers, but until Jesus reminds them of their own sins, they are unwilling to be merciful to her. He tells them to be merciful to one another because whoever is not merciful will not receive mercy. As in the homilies and art considered in previous chapters, social relations are also portrayed here as the source for distinguishing the damned from the saved. The York cycle play of the Woman Taken in Adultery highlights not the woman herself (a critical leaf is missing at the place where this might be found) but the response of the accusers to the woman, an example of the importance of social interactions in distinguishing the saved from the damned: "He þat will noȝt forgiffe his foo / And vse mekenesse with herte and hende, / The kyngdom may he noght come too" (Y 201/91–93). Jesus does not focus here on believers in a relationship only with the Divine. That relationship to the Divine undergirds but also depends on the believer's relationship with the world. One response to the magnanimity of mercy expressed in the Passion of Christ is compassion expressed in merciful action toward one's neighbors in the world. Zacchaeus, called down from the tree he climbed to catch a glimpse of the prophet, forsakes his sins and promises to give half of his goods to the poor. His renouncing of his sin and his reaching out to make recompense to the poor whom he "beguiled" renews his relationship with the Divine (Y 217/ 447–453). He provides a model of the life to which Jesus calls the witnesses of his life, death, and Resurrection.

The figure of Jesus as exemplar which runs throughout the York cycle is crucial here: "The example of Christ's life redefines the goodness acceptable to God, and as a result we have in the plays of the Final Judgment little reference to the written law, or even to man's obedience, but instead a more searching examination of the individual soul in terms of the seven deeds of corporal mercy. The saved are those who fed the hungry, gave drink to the thirsty . . . those, in short, whose lives followed Christ's example of perfect charity."[68] Often, Last Judgment plays are remembered for the fear they may evoke in the hearts of their viewers, and, certainly, the York and N-Town plays meant to strike fear into the hearts of unrepentant sinners. But this does not undercut or minimize the privileged place of divine love that I have pointed to throughout this chapter. We misunderstand the medieval context if we posit a "fear school," on the one hand, and a "love school," on the other. Rather, as reflected in the plays here, much medieval religiosity "tended both to accept fear as a good beginning to sorrow, and to want love as a proper culmination."[69]

Mary Magdalene represents the response Jesus seeks from those who love him. The response is not fear or dutiful but begrudging obedience. Instead, joy is the response to Jesus' love: "Alle for joie me likes to synge, / Myne herte is gladder þanne þe glee, / And all for joie of thy risyng / That suffered dede vpponne a tree" (Y 359/134–137). Kolve is right to point to the celebratory nature of the mystery cycles: "The corpus Christi cycles celebrated the salvation of [all]—the action of redemption achieved by Christ and available to all."[70]

I have focused here on the appeal of the suffering Jesus to the readers and viewers of the plays. While I will not develop this point here, I want to point briefly to
the cycles' important role in enacting social unity in the very manner of their performance, which necessitated the cooperation of a significant portion of the Christian
society within English cities and towns. Participation in these ritual performances,
whether as actors or spectators, functioned as a unifying event. Through their presentation of salvation history, which made demands on the late medieval Christian
community, the plays configured a world for their observers. The plays taught the
meaning of that world and models for living in that world and by calling their
audiences to respond to their claims, they attempted to make real the world they
dramatized. Robert Potter defines ritual as "a public observance of accepted truth;
more specifically, a collective activity in which past action is imitated and repeated
for a present purpose. . . . By rehearsing in an articulated and formal sequence the
correct attitudes, ritual causes the truth to 'come true.'"[71] The plays were an effort
to enact episodes and events for viewers, while at the same time inviting viewers to
inhabit the world they portrayed. The dramas taught the "grammar" of the language and the activities necessary for living in that world.[72] Viewers were invited
to participate in the temporal, spatial, and spiritual cosmos enacted on the stage.
Insofar as people already did this to some degree, their experiences were mirrored
in the dramatic activities portrayed, and they were reaffirmed and renewed in their
belief system. Because some people did not already participate, the plays functioned
as an invitation to enter the world made present there. Social values, such as the
sacraments and love of neighbor, were promoted by the plays, which were not only
didactic and catechetical events but also attempts to standardize religious practices
and to achieve uniformity of belief.

In conclusion, then, the N-Town and York cycles create the world of salvation
history in which God's love for humankind is the *axis mundi*. The pain and torment of Jesus Christ, enacted throughout the cycle plays, make present for the
audience God's expansive compassion in seeking reconciliation with humanity.
In foreshadowing, prophesying, enacting, and recounting the suffering of Jesus,
the plays appeal to the viewers to respond to the depth, grandeur, and pathos of
the Savior's suffering on their behalf by cultivating sorrowful contrition and
availing themselves of mercy. The members of the audience learn to imitate the
Purveyor of Mercy by renewing their lives through love of and merciful action
toward their neighbors. Mercy (now reconciled with justice) is abundant but must
be sought in this earthly life, as the figure of God concludes in the York Judgment play: "Thei þat wolde synne and sessid noght, / Of sorowes sere now schall
þei syng, / And þei þat mendid þame whils þei moght / Shall belde and bide in
my blissing" (Y 415/377–380).

FOUR

Body, Power, and Mimesis

Holy Women as Purveyors of Divine Presence

Previous chapters have considered portrayals of the suffering Jesus in public forums including sermons, Books of Hours, church wall paintings, and liturgical drama. In this chapter, I explore the frequent association between suffering and spiritual authority in writings by and about women in texts available in England during the thirteenth through fifteenth centuries. In the first section, I address the extravagant suffering of hagiographical narratives by considering two examples popular in Middle English literature: the lives of the fourth-century martyrs Margaret of Antioch and Katherine of Alexandria. In these narratives, Christ-identified suffering is associated with these women's public functions as conduits of divine power and as intercessors seeking divine mercy on behalf of humanity. In the second section, I consider the *vita* of the thirteenth-century Elizabeth of Spalbeek which, besides providing an example of medieval narratives in fourteenth- and fifteenth-century vernacular translation, demonstrates how devotion to the liturgical hours commemorating Jesus' Passion (also mentioned in chapter 2) can be integral to the spiritual lives of holy persons who are intimates of the Divine. Although we can move only with great caution from reflecting on particular saints' lives to making general claims about women's religious experience in late medieval culture, I suggest in this chapter that in the genre of hagiography, the female body is a theological trope for figuring Christ to the world. In keeping with the observations of the previous two sections, in the chapter's third section I examine the writings of the fifteenth-century laywoman, Margery Kempe, to demonstrate the significance of women's public suffering in identification with the suffering Jesus. I suggest that it is in and through her body that Kempe manifests the ongoing presence of the Divine by publicly calling others to spiritual growth and interceding with God on their behalf.

In each of the following examples, the personal suffering of the believer is directly linked to the figure of the suffering Jesus, but in none of this material is suffering pursued for its own sake. Behind the saintly identification with Jesus is the affirmation found throughout late medieval literature and art that the suffering of Christ is the unparalleled manifestation of divine love and that to suffer with Christ is to become a parable of divine compassion to a broken world. At the heart of the medieval spiritual milieu lies the claim that Jesus' suffering benefited all humanity: humans are saved by the suffering Christ endured with love. Although religious texts consistently affirm that Jesus could have saved humankind without suffering, they also maintain, using the knight/lady imagery common in medieval romance literature, that Jesus "let his shield be pierced, his side opened up, to show her [the church/soul] his heart, to show her how deeply he loved her, and to attract her heart."[1] Suffering to demonstrate love of another is portrayed as a powerful and persuasive means of expressing compassion and concern for the welfare of the other. For some people, and for many women, the personal experience of christological suffering was crucial to appropriating the work of Jesus Christ. Through the disciple's own suffering, she or he could hope to experience something of what it meant for Jesus Christ to suffer as he did; imitating Christ's manner of being in the world served to unite the believer with Jesus and his work. As Jesus' suffering initiated salvation, so the Christian's own Jesus-identified suffering could mimetically participate in Jesus' salvific work, not only on an individual level but also on the cosmic scale at which Jesus Christ functioned. In identifying with the wounded Jesus, the believer could participate in attaining not only her or his own salvation but also the salvation of others. In evoking a response of compassionate love on the part of the believer, Jesus' suffering proffered the possibility of reconciliation in the God-human relationship, and, as the examples which follow indicate, women's suffering functions in a variety of ways to further that reconciliation.

Women's Bodies as Inscriptions of Divine Love:
Margaret of Antioch and Katherine of Alexandria

We have only to recall the painful cry of the Hebrew Psalmist lamenting abandonment by the Divine and ceaseless persecution by enemies to remember that religious texts plunge us into the heart of both the anguish and the joy of human existence. To medieval theologians, a person is "the world in little," and to an even more magnificent degree, medieval saints are microcosms of the macrocosmic relationship of the Divine to creation. Saints express in and through their bodies—

with extravagance and grandiosity—the struggles and joys of persons in the world. Hagiographers do not create literal records of historical occurrences, but rather through sensual, physical, and visual images, they seek to edify readers by constructing a universe charged with God's presence. In many female and male saints' lives, Christ becomes visible to the world through imprinting his suffering onto the holy person's body. The possibilities of human interaction with the Divine One are inscribed on saints' bodies; their bodies function as "texts" to be read by a world in need of spiritual transformation.[2] Saints' bodies carry a double valence: through them saints not only experience ecstatic intimacy with God but also become bearers of the sin of the world and embodiments of the alienation of the human from the Divine. In their imitation of Jesus Christ, saints are healers who carry on Jesus Christ's work in the world—they enter into the realities of suffering and joy to heal the breach between God and humankind.[3]

The prominence of suffering in the saints' lives that were repeatedly translated and retold throughout the Middle Ages testifies to the immense power of the central image of the suffering Christ in medieval Christian culture. Some sense of the tenacity and awesome character of this symbol can be conveyed by considering the reciprocity between the Divine and humankind that is apparent in the narratives of both Margaret of Antioch and Katherine of Alexandria.[4] The power of Christ's love for these holy women and of their love for him is demonstrated in the theatrical testimonies of holy women who bear witness to their commitment to Jesus by suffering torture and death. These saints' willingness to die in defense of their commitment to Christ attests to the strength of their love. Furthermore, both narratives testify to the magnificence of Christ and to the power associated with the holy person's love of Jesus by recounting fantastical events like Margaret's emergence unharmed from scalding water and Katherine's defeat of a torturous wheel. The extravagance of these dramas summons the audience to taste the love of Christ—the love that motivates and empowers the heroic saints to undergo the trials recorded in the stories. Like the medieval dramas, sermons, and art we have previously considered, these narratives also summon the audience to place their hope and love in the one who suffered on their behalf. The narratives seek to persuade not so much by depicting the suffering of Jesus himself but by figuring the suffering of the saintly hero as virtuoso of mimetic identification with the Christ who bled and died on humanity's behalf.

The divine summons is not unilateral. By being branded with the suffering of Jesus on their own bodies, the holy figures summon the world on behalf of Jesus. But the saints' work is bidirectional: in an equally important way, the saints' endurance becomes an appeal to the Divine on behalf of Christian believers. For example, Margaret and Katherine each pray that God should hear the petitions of anyone who is mindful of their passion (Katherine, 542/290; Margaret, 301/275).[5] These literary texts suggest that the saints' intercessory powers derive from their willingness to suffer on Jesus' behalf and in imitation of him. The very suffering that is the basis of divine appeal to humans is also the basis for the saints' status as intercessors. The saints' suffering in mimesis of Christ's suffering provides access to Christ's Passion and all that it accomplished on humanity's behalf. Holy persons' endurance of physical—sometimes mortal—trauma wins them status as advocates on behalf of humanity and transforms them into patrons whose petitions the Divine One readily grants.[6] Thus, the texts constitute both a summons *by* Christ *to* people and an appeal *to* Christ *by* the saintly heroes. Crucial to both parts of the dialectic is the vision of suffering that provides the model for the holy person who seeks to change the world. It is also the basis for the saint's appeal on behalf of humankind.

As we have seen, medieval culture was a sensual and visual culture in which verbal and pictorial images often functioned to shape and express religious ideas. Literature and art consistently manifested the central medieval insight that "God is love" by way of a visual medium which centered on the wounded Jesus. In the early thirteenth-century text, "On the Custody of the Soul" (a homiletic English version of a Latin dialogue on the right ordering of the human), a messenger, Love of Life, comes from heaven to cheer God's four daughters—Prudence, Justice, Temperance, and Fortitude—who are pondering the difficulties of spiritual life. Love of Life describes *seeing* a vision (through a mirror) of the Trinity in which Jesus was seated in majesty, "And yet I *saw* plainly the places of his wounds, and how he *shows* them to his Father to reveal how he loved us" (emphasis added).[7] We have seen how Jesus Christ's love for humanity is described vividly in texts like Julian of Norwich's *Showings* and depicted in altarpieces and other works of art. In this chapter, I consider four narratives in which holy women embody the crucified Jesus; these women are purveyors of divine power who manifest the love of the one who suffered on humanity's behalf.

Margaret of Antioch and the Cosmic Struggle with Evil

The lives of martyrs were among the most popular of late medieval narratives about female followers of Christ. We know, for example, that over two hundred late medieval English churches were dedicated to the fourth-century martyr, Margaret of Antioch, and depictions of her were among the most popular wall paintings in these churches.[8] We must approach saints' lives with a hermeneutics of suspicion, however, cognizant that they are not literal representations of historical persons but patriarchal portraitures in which the events portrayed consistently promote ecclesiastically hierarchical practices. In other words, we cannot assume that these narratives provide direct access to how early Christian and medieval women understood themselves as purveyors of divine power. The texts do, however, convey some sense of what was presented to medieval believers through the perpetuation of tradition, and, as I will suggest in the third section of this chapter, we find some of these dynamics of power associated with the suffering Christ reappearing in the literary constructions of historical women (such as Margery Kempe) in the late Middle Ages.

The suffering Jesus is critical to the meanings conveyed in these martyr stories. Reflection on texts like the Life of St. Margaret reveals the narrative function of the female body as a literary figure for mediating Christ to the world. The saintly woman renders Christ visible through mimetic suffering; her endurance of torture evokes the suffering of Jesus, and the evils of the world and the glory of the suffering Jesus are inscribed onto her body for all to see and be edified by. Through her identification with Jesus, she comes to participate in the divine power Jesus possesses so that through this participation the holy woman becomes a purveyor of divine power herself, a representative of God *to* people. But she also becomes a representative *of* people, an advocate who, through her feats of bodily endurance, has earned special favor in the divine eyes and so is granted the privilege of being listened to by the Deity.

Martyrs' narratives are chapters in the ongoing saga of the work of Jesus Christ in the world; they are dramatic renderings of acts and scenes within the cosmic struggle of good against evil. Stock narrative patterns and literary devices often convey the drama of the story to the reading and listening audience. Among the generic narrative patterns common in hagiographical literature are the following: good confronts evil in the form of a holy person persecuted by a pagan emperor or imperial official; the heroic representative of good endures a series of trials, the very endurance of which reveals the immense power of good; the representative of good sometimes converts the evil opponent but generally dies as the innocent victim of intransigent evil without achieving the conversion; and after death, the saintly intercessor continues to aid those who invoke her or his name. Although death is the last word from the perspective of the evil system that battles against the saint, the narratives convey to the audience how short-lived and false the victory of evil over good really is. The stories tell how even death cannot conquer good—in fact, death only hastens the reunion between God and the beloved holy person. There are many permutations to this general hagiographic formula (which is itself only one of a number of patterns), but with this barest of outlines instantiated in the two examples to follow, we can discern the central place of mimetic association with the suffering Jesus in the literary construction of saintly heroes. Saints are theological tropes of the Divine, advocates for believers with God, and conduits of sacred power to believers.

In the narrative *vita* of Margaret of Antioch, Margaret is constructed from the beginning as being familiar with the stories of martyrs such as Stephen and Lawrence who endured pain and death (292/9–12); "He[o] ne wilnede noȝt so muche · as to be[o] hore yuere" (292/12).[9] Even before she encounters the evil Olibrius, Diocletian's representative and an enemy of Christianity, Margaret prays for a steadfast heart to endure the torments of death and to die on account of her love of Christ. Olibrius appears, sees Margaret tending sheep, and "anon riȝt in fole loue · is herte to hure drou" (293/44). Olibrius decides to "take" her for his wife if she is of noble blood, and if she is not free, he wants to "buy" her in order to hold her, as the *South English Legendary* author notes, "in sunne of lecherie" (293/50). She immediately cries out to God to protect her body from harm and defilement—proclaiming that she commits her body and soul to Christ and lamenting that she is surrounded by evil men from whom she cannot flee.

In this narrative, Margaret does not struggle (*pace* Robertson) with sexual temptation.[10] As the *South English Legendary* author narrates this tale, there is no ambiguity here: this is a story of female fear at the advances of a male aggressor. She does not fear for her life, because dying on behalf of Jesus is admirable, but fears that her virginity, which physically represents her spiritual commitment to the Divine, will be violated. In hagiographical dramatizations of the struggle between good and evil, the external physical and social world often parallels the internal spiritual world. The spiritual state of the holy person is mirrored in the physical state of the holy person; that is, the body and soul reflect one another. Virginity, the preservation of which symbolizes Margaret's inviolability by her oppressors, often functions in martyrdom texts as a critical way of naming the essential integrity of the saint and as a physical sign of spiritual purity. In a universe charged with literal and spiritual correspondences and parallels, an untouched body signals a soul unviolated by "worldly" alliances.[11]

Margaret's bodily identity is at the center of this narrative, and through it, her relationship to the Christian God is made visible. This ascription of power to the body is characteristic of the medieval confidence in the powers of the body when guided by the soul. When disordered, the body opposes the soul, but "if it keeps itself pure and intact, it is a very good friend to us and gives us help as a faithful servant. For in it and through it, maiden, you earn the right to be the equal of angels in the eternal bliss of heaven . . . when you lead their life in your frail flesh without unchastity."[12] While this implies an unflattering picture of sexual relations and childbirth and downgrades the familial experience of the majority of medieval women and men, corporeal identity nevertheless functions in this text and others like it to render visible the saint's status as a medium for divine presence. Far from being denied or denigrated, the body becomes the battleground where the war between good and evil is waged and where victory is won by the saint whose powers are evident through her marvelous deeds of physical endurance.[13]

Margaret is initially depicted in this narrative as the object of the male gaze.[14] The story begins with her being *seen* by Olibrius, the personification of evil, as a sexual being and potential concubine. She is threatened with sexual violence, not tempted by sexual invitation. The audience knows from the start that Margaret will not succumb to her persecutor's threatening overtures, whether they be for sex, marriage, wealth, or even the preservation of her life. Thus the tension in this text is not about whether Margaret will be beguiled by her persecutor but

rather about how, in resisting his advances, her commitment to Christ will manifest itself as she suffers the inevitable torment that her oppressor will inflict upon
her. She seeks to avenge Christ's death and clings tenaciously to him even as she
is inevitably subjected to the fate of all martyrs for Jesus: torture. The central
issue in martyr narratives such as Margaret's therefore is not "temptation" (though
temptation does appear in saints' lives infrequently in a very stylized form) but
rather the question of how the Divine will become manifest in and through the
saint's life and death. In viewing and hearing these theatrical renderings of the
contest between good and evil, it is quite clear that Margaret will not bow to
the demands of her persecutor. The audience knows that although the heroic
figure will die, in the cosmic struggle between good and evil physical death does
not signal spiritual defeat, just as Jesus' death on the cross was only a prelude to
the victory which lay ahead.

    After casting aspersions on her "false" God who was slain on a tree, Olibrius
leers at Margaret and says that her body is more fit to be clasped in his arms
than to honor a false God. Margaret replies that although Jesus' killers had not
intended it, Jesus' death aided his followers. This mirrors her own experience,
because even if Olibrius kills her, he cannot control the meaning and effects of
her death. Olibrius responds with fury and orders her thrown into a dark prison
in an attempt to terrify her into cohabiting with him in his palace and into sac-
rificing to his gods. Olibrius wants power over Margaret—to dictate the lean-
ings of her heart. If he cannot do that, he wants at least to control her public
actions, to sever the body/soul alliance so significant to her. The meaning of his
sexual interest, his desire to control or possess Margaret, emerges when her rejection of him and the worship of his gods intensifies his fury. Thus, his threats
change; in light of her nobility and her "faire" body, he now suggests that she
should worship only his gods rather than die. Again, his instilling of fear and
threats of violence, not sexual temptation, underlie this suggestion. Margaret may
choose to worship his gods to "preserve" her body from death, or she may choose
to die to preserve her body (and by association her *self*) from becoming the possession of evil. She chooses death in imitation of Christ who forsook the world's
joy to "bringe us out of pine" (295/106). Upon hearing this, the maleficent
Olibrius's fury reaches a fever pitch because he cannot control Margaret's spirit.
In an act that recalls the fate of Jesus as decreed by Pontius Pilate, Olibrius orders that Margaret be publicly hanged on a nearby tree and tortured so much
that he should her "gottes ise[o]" (295/112).

    Margaret's torture evokes the image of the suffering Jesus, and her alliance
with Christ is sealed through this torment. In a paroxysm of violence echoing
medieval portrayals of the suffering of Jesus, her tormenters strip her and scourge
her so that blood streams from her body (295/120). Although some historians
seem to suggest that the torture of saints was perceived as erotic by viewers, we
might wonder in what sense it was erotic to read or hear about a victim being

beaten so viciously that her bones could be seen and that her guts were visible because her captors had ripped open her "wombe" with hooks.[15] They tore apart her limbs, so that even Olibrius was horrified and hid his eyes.[16] This excruciating disembowelment leads onlookers to beg Margaret to accede to his demands to preserve her body from the appalling torment. But as Job sent away his evil counselors, so Margaret rebuffs those who try to make her recant her commitment.

As she endures this torture and her body is bloodied and torn by the wrath of Olibrius, who cruelly attempts to impose his will upon her, Margaret becomes, in imitation of Jesus, a bearer of the sin of the world. The hate and anger of Jesus' enemies are imprinted on Margaret's body. She becomes an allegorical embodiment of the carnage wreaked by evil in this world insofar as her suffering and pain manifest the alienation of humankind from the Divine. But her suffering has a double valence: in addition to being an inscription of the hatred and evil of her persecutors, it also re-presents Jesus to the world because Margaret's willingness to endure the torture stems from her identification with Jesus Christ's Passion. Her suffering is suffering borne of her alliance with Christ as she joins herself with his opposition to his own persecutors and with his willingness to take upon himself the sins of the world. Her association with Christ provides her with the motivation to suffer as she does; she imitates Jesus in her suffering, and Jesus becomes visible in the imprinting of agony and pain on her body.

Olibrius, looking at her bloodied body, covers his eyes "for reuþe and deol" (296/139). This is not true pity and distress, for he says that if she will renounce her belief she will lead the best life among the women he knows. She silences him and reminds him that although he can do what he wills with her body, he cannot touch her soul. Transformed through her imitative suffering with Christ, Margaret shares his power. Though she is imprisoned, angels comfort her, and she prays to see the devil that torments her. The devil appears in the form of a dragon that swallows her, but she makes the sign of the cross and the devil bursts into pieces while she emerges unscathed.[17] The devil then appears in the form of a man; boldly Margaret grabs him, throws him to the ground, and places her right foot on his neck. Now, she literally controls evil.[18] Olibrius asks again whether she has changed her mind, but she replies that she has not. Furious, he orders that she be stripped and thrown into a fire, but the fire does not burn her. Overcome with wrath, he has her hands and feet bound and throws her upside down into deep water. Yet the bonds break and she emerges from the water. In response, he throws Margaret into a seething cauldron, but the earth begins to shake, terrifying the spectators, and Margaret emerges unharmed from the boiling water. Five thousand people who witness the events convert to Christianity and praise Christ, acknowledging the source of the wonders manifested by the events surrounding Margaret's extraordinary endurance of torture.[19]

Insofar as the power of good is manifested in her body, Margaret is the bearer of the Divine, representing Jesus to the world in carrying on the Christ-defined struggle of good against evil. In this part of the narrative, sense perception is the operative means of transformation. The five thousand spectators are led from seeing how impervious Margaret's body is to the elements of water and fire and from feeling the shaking of the earth to the *source* of this imperviousness to pain and of this power to move the earth—to Jesus Christ. Perceiving the Divine through the spectacle of Margaret's supernatural endurance, the five thousand observers see Christ and are transformed.

The obstinate Olibrius, chagrined and humiliated by the proceedings, orders that the five thousand onlookers and Margaret be beheaded. Before her death, Margaret prays to Jesus Christ "þat boȝtest me on þe rode" (301/269). She thanks Christ for taking her out of the world without her body having been blemished (referring to her virginity) and prays that Christ should grant mercy and grace to any person who lights candles on her behalf or who is mindful of her life or suffering. She adds that if any woman in childbirth who has read the Life of Margaret cries out, both mother and child should be safe "for loue of me" (301/287). Suddenly, thunder and lightning strike with such force that people fall down in terror. A dove comes down through the thunder to Margaret, saying to her, "Iblessed þou ert and hende / Oure [Louerd] granteþ þe þi bone · to þe worles ende" (301–302/295–296). The dove assures her that after her harsh suffering she will come to the joy of heaven. The dove returns "from whence" it came, indicating to readers that the spirit of God not only grants her request but also invites Margaret to heaven.

Through Margaret's life and suffering, divine mercy becomes visible and accessible to those who are mindful of it. Her own mimetic pain enables her to become a purveyor of divine presence as well as a broker of spiritual power because, by virtue of her love of God (manifest in her suffering), she so allies herself with Jesus Christ that she herself becomes invested with spiritual power. The result is that all who pray to her will be aided as if they were praying to Jesus Christ himself. She links herself with Jesus in suffering and thus obtains for those who pray to her the very benefits that Jesus' suffering made possible. In the medieval mind, Margaret's achievement is not identical with Christ's insofar as he made salvation possible and is the final arbiter of persons' ends. But she does provide temporal help and succor for those who appeal to her, even as she advocates for the salvation of those who remember her.

In the final scene, Margaret invites Maltus, the executioner appointed by Olibrius, to kill her. The text suggests that Maltus is powerless to kill her unless she permits him to. Maltus hesitates, saying he is ashamed to kill her and wants to die with her, but she tells him he must do the deed to participate with her in the life to come. Maltus asks forgiveness of God, beheads her, and then, miraculously, falls down and dies alongside her. As she dies, a white dove flies out of her headless body into heaven. The dove renders visible her spirit and signals the presence within her of the Holy Spirit, the dove that appeared earlier in this story.

The narrative concludes with an affirmation of her virtue and the advice to women who are bearing children to read Margaret's life and to petition her to help them attain the joy of heaven (302/320).

In the late medieval rendering of the fourth-century Margaret of Antioch's life, the body is the violent theater in which the cosmic struggle with evil is played out. The heroic martyr is so tortured that "blood ran down her body like water from a well" (295/120; my transliteration). Since the body becomes the battleground on which the war of good against evil is waged, figurations of torture, endurance, and death become, ironically, body-affirming events. In and through her body, the contest between good and evil is inscribed for all to see, and the text demonstrates that Margaret is the bearer of divine presence, a trope of divine power (64:65; 70:71). While these persecution texts, suffused with violent suffering, can be studied as revealing something of prevailing attitudes toward women as victims of tyrannical oppression, they are also stories about the *power* of spiritual women to mediate Jesus' appeal to believers and to advocate on behalf of the world to Jesus Christ.

Katherine of Alexandria and Eruptions of the Divine

In the life of Katherine of Alexandria, the second saint's life we consider here, the human relationship to the Divine is again displayed through the body of a woman who figures Christ to the world through mimetic suffering. The literary hero enters into the realities of Jesus' suffering to participate in healing the breach between God and humankind, summoning witnesses to heed the work of Christ and beseeching Christ to respond to the pleas of humankind.

The fourth-century Katherine, daughter of royal parents, is called to Alexandria to sacrifice to the gods. She goes to the city but boldly approaches the emperor and tries to persuade him to forsake the worship of idols and pursue the true wisdom found in following the Christian God. In this narrative, Katherine is figured as Wisdom—an erudite rhetor who is skilled in the liberal arts. The Divine becomes present through the speech of the saint who is depicted as the mouthpiece of the Holy Spirit. Although she does not succeed in persuading the proud emperor during this first encounter with him, he is nevertheless unable to refute her. As was the case with Margaret, the significance of the body in this story appears during her first discussion with the emperor. She urges the emperor to turn his thoughts from his created temple with its stone idols to ponder the heavens above—the moon, stars, and sun which traverse their course tirelessly—and to wonder about the creator of the universe. Katherine tells him that he is composed of body and soul and that the soul should lead and the body follow. She warns that it is "against nature" to reverse the order. As in the Margaret *vita*, the narrative of Katherine's life has as one of its guiding themes the emperor's attempt to persuade Katherine to place her attachment to her body before her commitment to Jesus Christ, who is described as the concern of her heart. The narrative throws into dramatic relief the contrast between the God-loving holy woman and the idol-bound miscreant.

Silenced by her arguments, the emperor summons fifty scholars to dispute with her. He answers their astonishment that they should be called to debate with a young woman by saying that she is "wisere þan ȝe wene" (536/79). Before the debate, an angel appears to Katherine and assures her that she will prevail so marvelously that she will inspire the scholars to love Christ even in the face of their own martyrdom. During the debate, one of her disputants challenges her belief in a God who suffered death on earth, arguing that one who dies cannot rise from the dead and suggesting that her claims are absurd. In response, she explains the Incarnation and the identity of Jesus Christ as human and divine. Her opponents, confounded by her reply, recognize the Holy Spirit's presence in her: "We seoþ þat þe Holi Gost is mid hire · & in hire mouþe" (537/133). The Divine speaks through Katherine; the Holy Spirit is present through her speech.

In this case, as in others to be considered in this chapter, the speech of medieval women is a bodily act, like weeping and praying, and in their own writings and in writings about them, the power of rhetorical excellence is often critical in the transformative process of which they are a part. Texts like the Margaret and Katherine *vitae* attest to the power of the body and the power of speech as a part of the relationship between God and the world.[20] Texts like the Katherine narrative, as well as martyr narratives in general, testify to the Incarnation—to the presence of the Divine in human flesh. They bear witness to the grandeur and goodness of the human body and suggest that when allied with a soul that loves God, the body symbolizes, voices, and manifests that love. As the body of Jesus Christ expressed God's love for humanity, the bodies and voices of human beings express their love of God.

Transformed by Katherine's rhetorical performance, the scholars convert to Christianity, and in response, the outraged emperor orders that they be burned to death. Ready to die for love of the Christian God, they make the sign of the cross and are cast into the fire. When the fire finally subsides, not only are their dead bodies unburned, but they have been purified by the flames, so that they are "whyttere & fairere in heu · þan hi euere were" (538/149–150). Again, the nature of the relationship to the Divine is displayed in and through the bodies of the characters in the drama. The sign of the cross each made before being burned signals their welcoming of death for the love of God and preserves their bodies from the flames. When guided by the love of God, the body becomes the companion of the soul and can symbolically express the state of the soul. The physical purity of the scholars' unburned bodies testifies to the holiness of their whole persons, bodies and souls.

Next, in a strange and perverse speech which characterizes his dialogue throughout this narrative, the emperor—whose discourse is always shadowed by the threat to kill Katherine if she does not worship his idols (an intention evident in his massacre of the scholars)—tells Katherine to take pity on her own body, and he invites her to live in great nobility, second only to his queen, if she will renounce her Christianity. He further offers to make a marvelous image of her that will be honored by all people. She refuses, reaffirming that she is God's spouse and that neither his flattery nor his torments will turn her heart from God.

Enraged by her refusal to succumb to his threats or to respond to his offer of worldly power, the emperor begins to torture Katherine. As in the scene of Margaret's passion, this description of the torment echoes descriptions of the suffering of Jesus: "Þemperour hire let strupe al naked · to a piler faste ibounde / & bete hire sore wiþ stronge scourges · & make hire harde wounde" (538/ 167–168). Through the suffering, Katherine's bond with Jesus becomes visible. Now not only is the Holy Spirit present through her voice, but Jesus Christ is manifest through her body. Despite this torment, she will not change her mind, so the emperor throws Katherine into a dark prison, commanding that no one feed her so that she will eventually starve to death. For twelve days and nights she remains in the prison, but a dove from heaven (the Holy Spirit) brings her food. While the emperor is away, the empress and her "priuei kniȝt," Porphyrius, come to visit her; the two see a great light and an angel anointing Katherine's wounds. They ask Katherine to teach them. She preaches to them and to a gathering crowd about God and Mary (539/190) so persuasively that they and two hundred knights are baptized. The Divine becomes present in and through Katherine's public speaking; as her first converts said, "God is in her mouth." Jesus appears, explaining that she suffers on his behalf: "Ich hit am · for wham þu ert in payne" (539/194). He urges her to be steadfast in her torment, for she will dwell in heaven eventually. The juxtaposition of this appearance of Jesus Christ with the conversion of those who heard Katherine's speeches figures her as a special friend and intimate of God and confirms her suffering as a sign of her love of God.

When the emperor returns, he tries to punish the jailers for feeding her until Katherine reveals the source of her sustenance. Again, against the backdrop of his murderous destruction of those who do not follow his will, he invites her to be the empress's peer if she will reconsider her faith. She refuses, saying that she wants nothing so much as to give her flesh and blood for Christ's love "þat for me ȝaf his" (540/220). Then the emperor, infuriated by her reply, has the wheel of torture (the historic symbol of Katherine of Alexandria) built to torture her. An angel appears and—in a miraculous display of divine power reminiscent of the Hebrew Scripture contests between the Hebrew prophets and the pagans (cf. 1 Kings 18)—destroys the wheel with a sword so that four thousand bystanders are slain by the debris. Thus Katherine becomes a channel of sacred power, the occasion for the eruption of the Divine into the world. The empress then testifies to Katherine's goodness and announces that she too forsakes the emperor's idols. In his fury, the emperor realizes that he cannot change his wife's mind and demands that she be tortured and her breasts torn from her body with sharp hooks. The text repeats the cruel torment as it is carried out; her head is cut off and she is left for the dogs, unburied, until the knight Porphyrius buries the "holi body" (541/253). When the emperor discovers that her body is gone, Porphyrius discloses that he has buried the emperor's "holi wyf þat was Cristes make" and then announces that he, too, has fastened his heart on Jesus. The emperor laments that he has lost his wife and now Porphyrius to Christianity: "Þo gan þemperour for sorewe · alle his lymes to schake" (541/260). The knights appear and announce that they, too, have become Christians. The emperor, in a great show of histrionic grief, tears his hair and groans, lamenting that he is left alone. But his grief does not abate his anger toward those who will not follow him, and he orders Porphyrius and his knights to be beheaded. The emperor's grief, which does not shake his resolve or call him back from his path of sin and hate, stands in stark contrast to the power of grief to transform the truly penitent, as testified to by the medieval drama we considered in chapter 3. The emperor's sorrow is false, unaccompanied by the repentance and remorse associated with sorrow borne of compassion for Jesus and the recognition of the sinner's own complicity in "causing" Jesus' suffering.

The emperor calls Katherine once more and says that if she will change her mind he will forgive her and as empress she will rule with him. The ascending series of rewards the emperor offers her recalls Satan's temptation of Jesus in the desert, but the question here is not whether Katherine is likely to be persuaded to abandon Jesus. The emperor's schemes are more telling as indicators of his own distortions since he is so focused on worldly concerns and the power to control those around him that he would rather kill his companions, including his wife and his favorite knight, than reassess his own life.[21] In this grotesque caricature of the unrepentant sinner, the audience sees writ large the state of persons unmoved by the suffering Jesus and the lineage of those who died in identification with him. First, the emperor says that if Katherine relinquishes her spiritual commitments she will live in great nobility, second only to his queen. In addition, he will make a gilded image of her, which will win her the worship of the people. When she survives torture and his attempt to starve her into submission, the emperor invites her to be the queen's peer; and then, after Katherine has defeated the wheel of torture and the emperor has killed his own wife, he makes Katherine his last and, he thinks, most irresistible offer: he invites her to be empress to rule with him. All along she refuses his offers, asserting from the beginning that she is God's spouse and saying later that she wants nothing more than to give her flesh and blood for Christ's love, just as he gave his for her. She will never turn away from the one who "me deore iboʒt" (542/280). Her identification of Jesus Christ as her spouse is affirmed when Jesus appears to her and asks her to "com her forþ mi lemman · mi leoue spouse" (542/293). This narrative contrasts the earthly realities of the emperor's threat to her life and his offer of an earthly betrothal with the spiritual realities of a marriage to the Divine, which endures beyond the vagaries of temporal earthly existence. Twentieth-century readers often express horror at such narratives in which women willingly choose to suffer grotesque deaths for love of Christ. But the alternative posed by the text—marriage to the embodiment of evil—is often overlooked. In the one case, Katherine may accept the twisted offer of marriage to the one who threatened to kill her; in the other, she dies in defense of her spousehood with the Divine One. In keeping with the Christian paradox of Jesus' death bringing life, God becomes accessible to her only after her death: death brings life.

When she refuses the terms of his offer of life, the emperor commands that she be beheaded, and again the theme of Katherine's imitative alliance with the suffering Jesus is announced. The connection between God and suffering is made early on in this text when the disputants first ask Katherine how the "almighty" God could have suffered death. Although she tells the emperor that even his torments will not change her mind, he tortures her, and her union with Jesus is enacted in the very torture which recalls the injuries Christ's tormentors inflicted on him. Christ appears the first time to tell her to be steadfast in her torment and to proclaim publicly that he is the one for whom she suffers. Her endurance of suffering and the miraculous happenings surrounding the torture reveal that Katherine is a conduit of divine power; through her, the Divine becomes visible in the preservation of her body from torture and in her voice and teaching which transform her hearers. Later she says that just as Christ gave his flesh and blood for her, so she wants mimetically to give her flesh and blood for love of Christ (540/220). And, finally, as she prays just before she knows she is going to die, echoing the meaning for her of Jesus' Passion, she prays that her passion should be of help to those who are in need and remember her story. As Jesus' death had functioned to enable him to appeal for God's mercy on humanity's behalf, so Katherine's suffering here transforms her into an advocate for those who need divine assistance.

Jesus Christ appears and assures her that her prayers will be answered, and he invites his beloved to heaven (542/293). She is beheaded, and in a miracle signaling both her identification with Jesus and her offer of sustenance to those who invoke her name, milk, not blood, comes from the wound.[22] An angel comes and carries the body to Sinai—the place where the author of the *South English Legendary* adds that her bones are still buried and her tomb is still a source of holy oil, as well as a place where the sick are brought to be cured.

In this narrative, as in the Margaret story, the struggle between the emperor and Katherine renders visible the power of loyalty to Christ in the face of the world's relentless opposition to him. Joseph Wittig has shown that in the writings of some medievals, including Rhabanus Maurus, the tortures endured by martyrs are "presented as having been endured by the church in the age of martyrs, not by one individual."[23] In keeping with John 16:21, in which the suffering woman is the early church in times of persecution and danger,[24] Katherine's *vita* symbolically figures the whole church in its trials and tribulations. Katherine personifies and dramatizes the persistence of the church universal in the face of its persecutors and its detractors.

In this hyperbolic drama of the perduring presence of God in the world, Katherine signals the ongoing struggle of the church in the face of persecutors. She also makes visible one of the underlying tenets of the medieval Christian belief systems, namely, that saints, as literary constructs, figure for the world the dynamic relationship between the Divine and humans. The inscription of the divine suffering on Katherine's body allies her with Jesus even as her macabre torture reminds her viewers of Jesus' endurance of violence and pain on their behalf. As I indicated in the chapter on medieval drama, the authors of these narratives are not interested in answering the theological question of *how* Jesus' suffering attains salvation for believers; their focus is rather on the *salvific power* of the alliance between God and humans forged by the Crucifixion. As the wonders that accompanied Jesus' death signaled his divine status (Luke 23:44–45; Mt. 27:51–53), so in the Katherine narrative and in martyrdom tales in general, the miraculous events surrounding the death of the saint, such as the feedings in prison and the breaking of the wheel, are magnificent displays of divine power that appear to the world through the voice, body, and in connection with the preservation of the saint's life.

And yet, as in the Jesus story, death is not averted, although in a hermeneutical continuance of the Jesus story, death only happens when the saint permits it, and, in turn, death is always the prelude to eternal life. The martyrdom stories do suggest that the powers of evil, and even death, will *appear* to have the last word. But the Katherine narrative makes clear that this appearance is fundamentally misleading—the saintly hero gains spiritual power by the love of God expressed in her willingness, even in death, to identify mimetically with Christ. This imitative bonding enables the saint to share in the distribution of spiritual power gained by the Crucifixion, death, and Resurrection of Jesus. In the speeches which empower her listeners to risk death by declaring their ties to Christ and in the dramatic acts of preservation in response to attempts to kill her, God's presence is made visible through Katherine. Through her feats of endurance, Katherine, as did all the saints, attains the status of advocate for humanity to the Divine. As an active participant in the sacred world, she now becomes a source to whom those in need may appeal. Indeed, her own exploits in identification with Jesus assure other believers, who are mindful of her life and death, that they too will achieve God's assistance in their times of trouble and misfortune.

An Athlete of the Passion of Christ: Elizabeth of Spalbeek

Mimesis and the Liturgical Hours

The tradition of mimetic suffering as a characteristic of holy people's spiritual lives continues beyond the telling and retelling of early Christian martyrdom narratives. Recent work of scholars like Caroline Walker Bynum demonstrates the centrality of suffering in the *vitae* of thirteenth-, fourteenth-, and fifteenth-century female saints.[25] I consider one example here, the Middle English translation of the Latin life of the thirteenth-century German holy woman, Elizabeth of Spalbeek.[26] The life of Elizabeth of Spalbeek represents a type of extreme hagiography told and heard by Christians in late medieval England. Although it centers on a more literal imitation of Christ's Passion than most saints' legends, in keeping with what we have observed in the Katherine and Margaret *vitae*, this narrative also demonstrates that mimetic identification with Jesus elevates the holy person to the status of advocate on behalf of humanity by refiguring the saint as a symbol of Christ who shares in divine power. But now the ritual imitative process is portrayed not only as a parable of divine summons and as a source of intercessory power but also (as seen in the previous two case studies) as an act of personal spiritual devotion. The spectacular, dramatic exploits recorded in this *vita* manifest the devotional impact of the liturgical hours we considered in the discussion of Books of Hours in chapter 2. Through stunning feats of self-inflicted torture, displays of acrobatic agility, and paroxysms of extravagant suffering, Elizabeth of Spalbeek physically reactualizes the Passion of Christ as a means of worship for herself and as an inspiration to devotion and an act of spiritual advocacy for those who witness and hear about her performances.

In the language of her biographer, Philip of Clairvaux, Elizabeth "figures" the suffering Christ so that in her "oure mercyful lorde haþ shewed merueilous miracles of his blissed passyone, þat maye stir alle cristen pepil to deuocyone" (107). She is the figurative embodiment of Christ crucified, but also, as martyrs often were in stories like those of Katherine and Margaret, she is "þe figuratif body of Cryste, þat is holy chirche" (118). Elizabeth performs an elaborate, ritualized enactment of the liturgical hours associated with Christ's suffering. Her performance roughly correlates with the common association in Books of Hours (as discussed in chapter 2) between the Hours and the stages of Jesus Christ's Passion, death, and Resurrection. Recited at daybreak (or at midnight, as in this text), matins are often associated with the Agony in the Garden, and lauds with the Betrayal; prime (at 6:00 A.M.) with Christ's appearance before Pilate; terce (at 9:00 A.M.) with the Flagellation; sext (at noon) with the Carrying of the Cross; none (at 3:00 P.M.) with the Crucifixion; vespers (at sunset) with the Deposition; and compline (in the evening) with the Entombment. Throughout Philip's narrative, Elizabeth is invested with a double signification: she is alternately the rep-

resentation of sinful humankind and the figure of the sinless Jesus who sacrificed himself on behalf of humanity. As she "stands in" for all persons impli-
cated in persecuting Christ, she also actually "becomes" Jesus Christ insofar as
she reenacts for her viewers the horrors of his suffering. Jesus becomes visible as
his agony is written on Elizabeth's body; like Margaret and Katherine, she is a
text of flesh, a carnal parable of Jesus' love for a sinful and suffering world. She
is simultaneously a testimony to the sinfulness of human persons, a goad to stir
up compassion in her viewers and readers, a witness to the power of God, a symbol of the intimacy possible between humans and Jesus Christ, and an intercessor on behalf of humanity.

At midnight, the hour of matins, Elizabeth is "rauesched," utterly absorbed
in spiritual reflection and oblivious to her earthly surroundings.[27] Philip draws a
sharp contrast between Elizabeth's powers before and after the ravishing. Elizabeth begins matins weak and "vnmyghty" (108) because, according to Philip of
Clairvaux, from age five to age twenty this virgin so mortified her flesh that she
is physically weak. Yet after the ravishing, she arises "merueylously stronge to
suffre labour and peyne" (108). Philip repeatedly insists that the marvels of strength
and endurance in this narrative come not from Elizabeth's own strength but "of
a priue vertue of god" (108). In seeking to magnify divine power in describing
Elizabeth, Philip asserts that on her own Elizabeth is feeble and weak: the exu-
berant feats of spiritual theater she performs are possible only "by a synguler
prerogatyfe of loue" (107). All of the energy, endurance, and magnificence she
displays comes from God (111); the torments and ecstasies she experiences are
initiated by God as manifestations of divine love. Philip's deflection of attention
from Elizabeth as the origin of her own special christological theater signals his
construction of Elizabeth as an almost passive testimony to the grandeur of the
Divine One whose power is manifest through her. We see, then, that within the
confines of the ecclesiastical and male world, female saints are the repositories
not just of divine power but of their biographers' social and political interests.
Philip's constant reminders that Elizabeth is "weak" and that God is the source
of her performances suggest that he wanted to keep his audience from attributing to Elizabeth enormous spiritual power based on her mimetic association with
the Divine. Nevertheless, from the beginning Elizabeth is figured as a messenger
from the Deity to an audience that even Philip acknowledges would recognize
the tactile, palpable presence of God in her.[28]

At matins, she grabs hold of her clothes at her chest and drags herself first to
the left, then to the right, as if she is being pulled along by force "representynge
oure lorde Jhesu wordes . . . 'ȝee come to take me as a þefe with swerdys and
battys'" (108). She reenacts the parts of both Jesus and his tormentors, playing
the role of the one who receives the blows and of the one who inflicts the blows,
first brandishing her fists, then hitting herself, and finally falling down and banging
her head on the ground (108). Philip comments that through this frenzy of beat-

ing and being beaten "in a newe and vnherde maner sche schewith in her-selfe booþ þe persone of Criste suffrynge and þe persone of þe enmye turmentynge" (109). As she beats herself on the face, head, neck, and shoulders, she inflicts on herself the sin of the world. Her violent outbursts expose the alienation of humanity from God—as she figures the tormentors of Jesus, she becomes an expression of the hatred and blindness that underlie such malevolent treatment of persons. At the same time, as she pulls herself backward and forward, beating and pummeling herself, hitting her face, pulling her hair, and poking at her eyes, the medieval viewer confronts the agony and trauma of Jesus and is stirred to compassionate identification with the innocent sufferer.

Elizabeth's entering into the Passion of Christ becomes a way of carrying on Christ's work. As she drinks deeply of his agonies and pains, her dramatization figures both the Passion of Jesus and her own compassionate response. Crucial to Elizabeth's function in this spiritual drama is the evocation of compassion in her audience in order to move them to renewed faith. Through her, the mechanism of transformation we have noted in sermons, art, and drama is evident once more: compassion is cast as the response to the pathos of the suffering Jesus. This compassion awakens viewers to their own spiritual turpitude, now not in a context that condemns them for their iniquities but in a place where God in Christ is vividly depicted as advocating mercy toward sinners and loving attentiveness toward the neighbor. Elizabeth figures the Passion of Christ to her viewers, and she also models the appropriate response to that Passion: "She schewith in weymentacyouns & turmentʒ hir owne compassyone boþ of herte and of body" (113). In rendering visible the horror and pathos of Jesus' Passion to those who gather around her, Elizabeth becomes a healer as those who watch her performance are stirred to devotion and sympathetic response.

After this self-tormenting at matins, Elizabeth lies down on the ground on her back to rest, and she goes "in spirite unto god" (109).[29] Elizabeth is portrayed in this text as the instrument of Christ, so that after some time, Christ "restorith hir aʒeyn to lyfe" (109), and she exhibits "schameful gladnesse of cheer" caused by spiritual joy (109–110). The hours continue with a cyclical repetition of ravishing during which she seems not to feel anything (she neither moves nor breathes [109]), followed by dramatic reenactment of the Divine Passion. This spiraling of action and contemplation is Elizabeth's worship. As Philip portrays her, she is not simply an instrument of transformation for the outside world; she is also an intimate of the Divine, a spiritual virtuoso who experiences the delights of those beloved by God.

As I suggested in the discussion of Julian of Norwich and Margery Kempe in chapter 1, suffering is not an end in itself in medieval spiritual life. The life of Elizabeth of Spalbeek further demonstrates this point. Although I focus on Elizabeth's identification with the Passion of Jesus, the pain and anguish associated with her appropriation of the suffering Jesus are always complemented by the great joy she experiences in her figuring of Christ's Ascension. In this text, as well as in other medieval sources such as Julian's *Showings*, the bliss and joy of the divine life are accessible only through an appropriation of the suffering Jesus. Though this text does not explicitly say this, the silence that surrounds Elizabeth's trances, in which her experience of the Divine is not expressed in words but primarily by bodily stillness, evokes Margery Kempe's affirmation that believers are led from the more dramatic and visible experiencing of Christ's humanity to the more subtle and less easily expressed understanding of Christ's divinity.[30] Elizabeth is an athlete of the Passion who is taken up "in spirite unto god" (109). In these trances, she does not see or feel anything of the world around her but is utterly absorbed in spiritual joy and gladness (though Philip says little about her experience during the ravishings as a way of emphasizing her complete absence from the world her observers inhabit). The marvels of Elizabeth's actions figure to the world the possibilities of the intimacies of human interaction with the Divine.

The connection between spiritual joy and the Passion of Jesus becomes visible as Elizabeth takes up a tablet depicting the crucified Jesus. She addresses the image as "sweet lord" and "wiþ hire clene virgyn-lippys," she kisses the feet of the image (110); she sighs and whispers, and then, looking at the image "with alle þe intente of her mynde" (110), she tastes the "vnspekabil swetnesse of his passyone" (110) and is ravished, still kissing the feet of the crucifix.[31] Her entrancement is so deep and she is so united with the image that it cannot be removed from her hands; if the tablet moves, her body moves along with it (110). With matins and lauds ended, she spends the time until prime in joy, savoring the delights she had experienced.

As was the case for many medieval mystics, such as Mechthild of Magdeburg and Catherine of Siena, the receiving of the Eucharist is a potent occasion of spiritual intimacy in which the pain of Jesus' suffering and the joy of what the suffering has accomplished are fundamentally linked.[32] Philip records that from Elizabeth's room, and even her bed, she can see the altar that is separated from her chamber by a small door. He describes her activity at mass "whan sche maye haue a preste; to whom sche gyueþ entente wiþ study of wonder deuocyone, sighynge & coueitynge wiþ hyჳ desyres þe sighte of oure lordes body" (115). At the point of the elevation of the Host, Elizabeth evokes the figure of Christ by stretching her arms out and making a cross of herself (115). She remains perfectly still for the duration of the mass, staring up at the altar "as if sche byhelde allewey þe sacramente þurgh þe myddes of the dore" (115). When she receives the Host from the priest, "she metiþ oure lorde with alle her spirite" (115). Again, while the cross is the central symbol, suffering is not the last word here, and after receiving the Eucharist, she is "delityd wiþ heuenly and goostly swetnesse of oure lorde" (115). As in the narratives of Margaret and Katherine, the inward purity of the saint is mirrored in Elizabeth's external "cleanness": she speaks no evil and so "fro hir mouþe comeþ neiþer spotel ne spittynge nor no maner of moisture or mater of vnclennes fro hir nese-þirles" (118). She eats and drinks sparingly. All of these details contribute to Philip's hagiography of the saint who lives as much in the spiritual world of her spouse, Jesus Christ, as she does in the material world of the society around her. Elizabeth's feats of extreme physical endurance and sanguinary extravagance portray the possibilities of human interaction with the Divine, on the one hand, and provide the means by which she spiritually experiences her own relationship with Jesus, on the other. Through her raptures and displays of mimetic suffering, Elizabeth physically demonstrates that she is the spouse of God, an intimate with the Divine, and a parable of Jesus to the world.

At prime, she enacts the common English association of prime with the appearance of Jesus before Pilate by walking around with her hands intertwined behind her back as if bound by her captors; she walks back and forth, enacting the journey from Annas to Caiaphas, to Pilate, to Herod, and back to Pilate again. Again she lies on the ground and rests "in a rauischynge," then beats herself with such vigor and strength that Philip wonders "how o persone maye booþ smyte and soffre so many, soo swifte and heuy strokes" (111). He reports again that he is astonished at the strength and endurance of this "febil and freel creature" (111) but attributes the events to God. Similar to the miraculous endurance of saints like Margaret and Katherine, Philip describes Elizabeth's performance as a testimony to the marvels and power of the Divine. Anguish and grief follow; once again she is ravished, after which she looks at the image of the crucified Jesus Christ which brings her solace and gladness (112). Jesus is both the source of her pain and the source of her comfort and ecstatic joy.

At terce, the customary time for recollecting the flagellation, Elizabeth acts out Jesus' being bound to the pillar and scourged. At sext, none, and evensong, the usual times for recalling the carrying of the cross, the Crucifixion, and the deposition, respectively, she enacts a series of events surrounding the torture, Crucifixion, and Deposition of Christ. Each reenactment is preceded by a "rauischynge," a trance-like state of absorption into the Divine. In actions that resemble liturgical dance, she performatively exhibits the wounds (the stigmata) in her hands and feet, and, stretching out her arms, she stands in the form of the cross. Then she bends backward and forward, swoons, and lies on the floor as if on a cross, beating herself with both hands. Later she reenacts Christ's Crucifixion, standing on one foot and bowing to the side, and she positions her body in a hanging posture as if it is Christ's body on the cross. She enacts the crucified Jesus and the tortured Virgin Mother and prays aloud. Then, in the manner of Jesus, pale and bloodless, after sobbing and lamentation, she "yields the ghost," and her head falls to her right shoulder (113).

The viewers see Jesus Christ through her actions: "Þese worschypful signes of the crosse are schewyd in the body & lymmes of þe Innocente virgyn þoos þree oures in þe whiche, as byleue is, oure lorde Jhesu henge on þe rood" (113). Next,

Elizabeth dramatizes the Deposition, and, here again, the author points to the power of God to effect these marvelous feats. At compline she enacts the entombment, and at matins she manifests the "gladnes of þe resurrexione and fruyte of the passyone" (113). The Passion is not the last word: Elizabeth's "text of flesh" points beyond the cross to the Resurrection, but the meaning of the Resurrection is accessible only to those who first travel the path toward understanding the Crucifixion.

Saint as Visage of Christ to the World

One of the more dramatic and compelling aspects of Elizabeth's christological theater is her capacity to bleed on demand at the places in her body and during the times of the day and night that most vividly signify Christ's Passion and death. At midnight and at other hours, blood flows from her eyes and soaks her linen garment. The stigmata bleed on Fridays at noon, and blood streams from her eyes, her hands and feet, and under her fingernails, and water and blood gush from a hole in her coat near her breast (114). In this liquid mixture of mimetic suffering, the boundaries between Jesus and Elizabeth blur as she mimes self-crucifixion and bleeds from wounds that are fleshy replicas of Jesus' wounds: "And wee sawe not alloonly þe vttir cloþe þat toucheþ þe maydens flesche, þat is to saye handes, feet and syde, sprenkelyd & dyed wiþ blood, but also hir pappys were alle defuyled wiþ blood rennynge fro hire eyȝen" (114). Although it has been quite clear from the start that she is imitating Jesus, the presence of the profusely bleeding stigmata imprinted on her body attests to the intensity of her special identification with Christ. The stigmata testify to Elizabeth's union with the blood-soaked Jesus and to a profound loss of distinction between the Crucified One and the one who reactualizes the Crucifixion through self-directed liturgical violence.

Elizabeth's authority, derived from her identification with the anguished Christ, is evidenced in part by her activity as a spiritual counselor. Elizabeth had observed the therapeutic role in the life of her cosufferer, Mary of Flanders, a woman she had never seen in person but with whom she often miraculously "conversed" while they were ravished. Elizabeth, who maintains that Mary's sufferings were much greater than her own, describes Mary as a "ful wyse mayden & þat sche hadde þe spirit of wisdome and cownseyle" (117). Like Mary of Flanders and Katherine of Alexandria, Elizabeth's alliance with Christ renders her a spokesperson for the Divine and an advocate for humans to God. Crowds gathered to gain strength and renewal by witnessing her actions; they were encouraged by her evident spiritual power and appealed to her to pray for them. Philip tells the story of the keeper of his horse, who asks Elizabeth to pray for him and his companions. She replies that if he will follow her advice and go to confession and do penance she will pray for him—otherwise "I schulde trauel in veyne" (116). Three days later, the keeper of the horse appears again. This time she confronts him, demanding to know why he has not been to confession and warning him that he cannot predict the hour of his death. He is ashamed and the next morning confesses to a friar "þat hadde Popes powere" (117). Here Elizabeth prays to God on behalf of the horse-keeper. In another case which displays her power of discernment (as well as Philip's religious allegiances), she advises a young man to become a Cistercian. After following her advice, the man comes to be known for his religious devotion. By warning the horse-keeper to confess his sins and advising the young man about his calling to the Cistercians, Elizabeth is similar to Margaret of Antioch and Katherine of Alexandria insofar as she is a spokesperson for and representative to God on behalf of individual Christians.

This holy woman who strikes herself, bleeds profusely, weeps, sings, and performs an elaborate dance of worshipful reenactment of the Passion of Jesus Christ is portrayed by Philip as an instrument of Divine power who makes Jesus present to believers. In a manner analogous to the function of medieval art, but now as that art is imitated in this saintly *vita*, Elizabeth re-presents the suffering Jesus to her viewers. The community's wonder at the dramatic mimesis enacted by her is attributed by Philip to the power of God to act through this "feeble" woman. But no number of reminders of the source of Elizabeth's powers masks the marvel at the heart of this text: Christ is present in a female body and in a woman's voice. Through Elizabeth, the transformative powers of the crucifix are accessible to the medieval audience. The viewers are urged to see Jesus Christ in her and to witness the customs of the church by remembering Christ's suffering throughout the liturgical day. The point is that Elizabeth's extravagant suffering is a window onto the *via dolorosa* of Jesus; viewers respond to Elizabeth as they would respond to the crucified Jesus himself.

Even her own death is symbolically brought into the interpretive world of the suffering Christ—not only does Jesus Christ become visible through her, but her experiences are interpreted through the events of Jesus' life. Philip reports that in the year of her death, on Good Friday, at a time when she usually rested—a time between two hours "whan she hadde reste fro peynes" (117)—her head began to ache and roll back and forth on the pillow. Wondering at this, her mother and sisters lighted candles, observed her closely, and perceived spots of blood around her head "in þe maner of a gerlonde, figurynge the corowne of þornes of oure lorde" (117). Once again, Christ becomes visible by inscribing his suffering on Elizabeth's body; her unusual suffering (between two hours, usually a time of rest) is christomorphized through the signs of her bloody identification with Jesus.

Elizabeth's christological performances—her many ravishings, her joyful singing, her visage of gladness and joy, and the marvelous feats she performs in imitation of Jesus' Passion and in expectation of the Eucharist—enact with extravagance and abandon the possibilities of human intimacy with the Divine. Elizabeth is larger than life, empowered, as Philip emphasizes repeatedly, by the power of

God; viewers, hearers, and readers perceive a glimpse of the joy wrought by Christ's work in the world and are offered a taste of the sorrow and pain which must be endured in the course of spiritual transformation. In dramatizing the events of Jesus' Passion, Elizabeth makes Christ visible by entering into the realities of his suffering and joy as her own spiritual practice. Literally, Elizabeth bodies forth salvation history: in the sacred time of the liturgical hours that enshrine her dramaturgy and in the sacred space of the church that surrounds her actions, Elizabeth's spectacle of divine presence offers forgiveness and transformation to her audience.

꒰ ꒱

As much as the events narrated here magnify the spiritual powers of Margaret of Antioch, Katherine of Alexandria, and Elizabeth of Spalbeek, these tales of gothic spirituality are told not for their own sakes but for their readers and hearers. These women's dramatizations re-present Jesus Christ's suffering to a broken and needy world. As I have suggested, the suffering of Jesus is the primary manifestation of God's love for creation, and witnessing the spectacles of suffering and joy conveyed through the literary figure of the saint's body testifies to the ongoing divine invitation to respond to the love offered in Jesus' Passion. Such suffering constitutes a means of appeal to the reader/audience to be renewed and transformed through the saints' imitation of Jesus. By imitating the suffering of Jesus, these holy women intercede with the Divine on behalf of all Christians and offer them the promise of healing and new life.

The Body as Parable of Divine Sorrow: Margery Kempe

Margery Kempe and the Medieval Milieu

While the role of the suffering woman in the lives of the saints is often that of a literary figure (far removed from the lives of historical women), the next example suggests how widespread mimetic suffering is in writings by women, as well as in guide books for women.

The hagiographical material considered in the previous sections dramatizes association with Christ in a grandiose manner that magnifies the identification between Christ and the saint by the imprinting of Christ-like wounds on the holy person's body. In the narrative of Margaret of Antioch, the experiencing of pain is presumed, but the actual sensation of pain is in the background, as indicated by the appearance of an angel to salve Margaret's wounds, as well as by the text's emphasis on Margaret's impassive endurance of suffering. Although the context of suffering is crucial to martyrs' narratives, records of martyrs' deaths do not generally focus on the experiences of suffering; rather, texts highlight the martyrs' obliviousness to pain and complete absorption in preparing for the world to come. Martyrs are frequently referred to as "regaining the bloom of youth" or as expressing joy and tranquillity in what must have been situations of agonizing pain.[33] Narratives about martyrs evoke a sense of the awesomeness of the martyrs' determination by suggesting its power to render suffering impotent. Nevertheless, it is their suffering that links them with Jesus Christ.

In the *vita* of Elizabeth of Spalbeek, the recording of the actual experience of suffering moves to the fore as Philip describes Elizabeth's sobbing, aching, and anguish. In the vivid portrayal of suffering in the fifteenth-century *Book of Margery Kempe*, readers observe the pain of a woman who, like Elizabeth, figures Christ himself and also the pain of one who suffers in compassionate solidarity with Christ, now as if she is one of the witnesses present at Jesus' Passion.

> Whan þei cam vp on-to þe Mownt of Caluarye, sche fel down þat sche mygth not stondyn ne knelyn but walwyd & wrestyd wyth hir body, spredyng hir armys a-brode, & cryed wyth a lowde voys as þow hir hert xulde a brostyn a-sundyr, for in þe cite of hir sowle sche saw veryly & freschly how owyr Lord was crucifyed . . . & sche had so gret compassyon & so gret peyn to se owyr Lordys peyn þat sche myt not kepe hir-self fro krying & roryng þow sche xuld a be ded þerfor. (68)[34]

During her lifetime, Margery Kempe was well known for her boisterous crying, which was triggered by anything that reminded her of Christ. She wept at the sight of crucifixes, images of Christ, and animals being beaten by their owners and even at the sight of small boys with their mothers. Her loud and public sobbing in the street or in the midst of sermons not only led many of her contemporaries to dismiss her as crazy but also has led many present-day scholars to view her spirituality with skepticism.[35] Be that as it may, I will suggest here that although she was more dramatic than some of her contemporaries, Margery Kempe's identification with the suffering Jesus represents a phenomenon common to fourteenth- and fifteenth-century spirituality.[36]

The life of this fifteenth-century English laywoman illustrates that for many medieval viewers the suffering of Jesus was perceived as an invitation to become an integral part of the Divine's ongoing work in the world. Far from encouraging a privatized religious experience or subduing or silencing people, the figure of the suffering Jesus led the faithful to a praxic relationship with the God of love, and it prompted them to act in a public way as representatives of Christ so that they could become an integral part of the Divine's ongoing cultivation of the spiritual well-being of the world. This is certainly the case for women like Margery Kempe, Catherine of Siena, Bridget of Sweden, Elizabeth of Spalbeek, and Mechtild of Magdeburg, all of whom were brokers of spiritual power and purveyors of the divine presence. Their lives and writings are filled with what seems to us to be extravagant desire for the welfare of the Other.[37] They were convinced of their power not only to stir their contemporaries to action but, even more, to prevail upon God to be merciful to the world. We can understand the social function of these female religious leaders only when we address the magnitude of their claims to be spiritual instruments of the Divine and to be intercessors on behalf of humanity.

In portraying herself as a holy person, a special friend of God, Kempe identifies not only with St. Paul and St. John but also with the cloud of female witnesses that surrounds her on her spiritual journey. These witnesses include her contemporary, Bridget of Sweden (d. 1373), mother of eight children, founder of the Brigittine Order, and political and religious reformer; the early Christian martyrs Katherine of Alexandria and Margaret of Antioch discussed in the previous sections; Mary Magdalene; and, not least of all, the Virgin Mary. She envisions herself as part of a long tradition of women saints who inspire her, deepen her spirituality, and offer legitimacy for her lifestyle of preaching and traveling in connection with her faith.[38]

Mary, Mother of Jesus Christ, presents herself to Margery as Margery's spiritual mother (175) and also as a teacher: "Dowtyr, I am thy modyr, þi lady, and thy maystres for to teche þe in al wyse how þu shalt plese God best" (50). She guides Margery in the spiritual life and, along with Mary Magdalene, provides a model for Margery's commitment to crying and weeping in response to the suffering of Jesus Christ. As Margery relives Christ's suffering and death, she watches with Mary and focuses on the dynamics of her relationship with Jesus, the quintessential expression of love between humans and God. Mary is the primary exemplar for her own work of sorrowing for Christ: "Lady, I wil sorwe for ȝou, for ȝowr sorwe is my sorwe" (193). Mary reminds Kempe that Mary Magdalene was not ashamed to cry: "And þerfor, dowtyr, ȝyf þu wylt be partabyl in owyr joye, þu must be partabil in owyr sorwe" (73).

Kempe's longing to be with Christ is expressed by her spiritual "contemplation" at the tomb with the mourning Mary Magdalene. Kempe marvels that Mary Magdalene left the tomb joyfully to tell Jesus' followers that he had risen. She observes that if Christ had said to her, "Touch me not," as he said to Mary Magdalene, she could never have been joyful. But she writes that "the creatur [Margery's moniker in the *Book*] had so gret swem & heuynes in þat word þat, euyr whan sche herd it in any sermown, as sche dede many tymys, sche wept, sorwyd, & cryid as sche xulde a deyd for lofe & desir þat sche had to ben wyth owr Lord" (197).

Mary Magdalene may seem a likely person for Margery to appeal to because Margery, like the Magdalene, perceives herself as a sinner raised by Christ from the pit of sin who has become a devoted follower of Jesus. But there were undoubtedly other reasons as well. Medieval stories about the Magdalene went far beyond any present-day harmonizing of the gospel narratives by recording that Mary was the sister of Martha and Lazarus, the woman from whom Christ exorcised seven devils, and the woman who anointed Jesus' head. The tenth-century

legend widely circulated in late medieval England (a legend that was appropriated, it appears, by Margery) painted a much fuller picture of the Magdalene as
a person of wealthy and powerful lineage who descended into the sin of lechery
not long after receiving her inheritance, until, upon receiving Christ's forgiveness, she became his devoted follower. After Christ's death, Mary and her companions were cast into a ship by their persecutors and put out to sea. They were
guided to Marseilles, where Mary preached to the heathens, converted a princess
and prince, later raised the princess from the dead, nourished the princess's child,
and led the princess on a pilgrimage. What we find in this medieval hagiography
is not simply Mary Magdalene the sinner but also Magdalene the holy woman,
spiritual pilgrim, biblical preacher, and nurturing healer. Mary Magdalene was a
perfect exemplar for Margery, who also crafted her identity in terms of being a
preacher, prophet, pilgrim, and healer.[39]

Margery describes herself as part of a long tradition of female saints. After
she explains her lineage to the mayor of Leicester, he retorts, "A, . . . Seynt Kateryn
telde what kynred sche cam of & ȝet ar ȝe not lyche, for þu art a fals strumpet,
a fals loller, & a fals deceyuer of þe pepyl, & þerfor I xal haue þe in preson"
(111–112). The protestations of her detractors notwithstanding, Kempe's self-
portrayal as spouse of God is in keeping with a celebrated tradition of holy women
like the Beguine Mary of Oignies (d. 1213) and Bridget of Sweden, who also understood themselves as Brides of Christ—often in a climate of opprobrium and
hostility.

Female saints such as Katherine, as well as male saints such as Peter and Paul,
appear as Kempe's teachers (39). Legitimation for her work of weeping comes
not only from the writings of male religious like the Pseudo-Bonaventure and
Richard Rolle but also from writings by and about women like Mary Magdalene
(154). The priest who eventually wrote down Kempe's dictation had himself
doubted her legitimacy after a preaching friar had denounced her from the pulpit. But after reading about St. Mary of Oignies "& of þe plentyuows teerys þat
sche wept" (153) and about Elizabeth of Hungary who "cryed wyth lowde voys"
(154), he was persuaded of Margery's sincerity.

The association with Mary of Oignies is particularly significant to Margery
Kempe's depiction of herself. As Margery's scribe specifically raises Mary of
Oignies's name in connection with the legitimation of Margery's weeping, so we
notice a number of connections between Mary of Oignies's life and Margery's
Book. Mary persuaded her husband, John, to take a vow of chastity with her, just
as Margery finally persuaded her husband, John, to live in a chaste marriage with
her (after the birth of fourteen children).[40] Mary was a great supporter of preaching and was devoted to sermons (163–164), even as Margery Kempe enthusiastically attended the sermons of the renowned preachers of her day. Yet the similarities to Margery are probably most apparent in respect to Mary's devotion to
the Passion of Jesus. Mary of Oignies swooned when she saw a cross or heard

people talking about Christ's Passion; and confession of any sin, no matter how small, evoked tears, anguish, and loud crying (139). When Mary tried to restrain her weeping, she only cried harder (137), and she carried linen cloth to soak up the tears (138). Mary called the tears her refreshment, a special gift from God— a sort of spiritual sustenance that fed her soul and her mind (138). Just as Margery Kempe did, Mary warned people who were in danger, cared for the needy, and comforted the afflicted and downtrodden. Thus, the *Book* reveals a series of intertextual affinities between Mary of Oignies and Margery Kempe in terms of prodigious weeping, vows of chastity, and devotion to the Passion of Christ. These affinities suggest that Mary of Oignies modeled and empowered Margery's witness to Christ in the world.

Kempe also maintains a mimetic relationship with her near contemporary, Bridget of Sweden, as both competitor and ally. In some respects, her experience explicitly supersedes that of Bridget. Margery writes that no book other than her own, including Walter Hilton's *Scale of Perfection*, Richard Rolle's work, or Bridget's *Revelations*, "spak so hyly of lofe of God" (39). When she sees a host and chalice flicker at the Consecration, Christ tells Margery that Bridget "say me neuyr in þis wyse" (47). But while superseding Bridget's experiences in some respects (for example, Margery avers that she has more intense experiences of the Divine than Bridget had and claims that she has fourteen children whereas Bridget had only eight), Kempe carries on and actively promotes the work of Bridget in other respects. In Kempe's *Book*, Christ says, "I telle þe trewly it is trewe, euery word þat is wretyn in Brides boke, & be þe it xal be knowyn for very trewth" (47). In Rome she visits the place where Bridget had died, and she speaks with Bridget's attendant and others who knew her. She says that while she was there tremendous storms disturbed the area, and she interprets them as a sign that God wanted recognition of Bridget's saint's day and increased devotion to her.[41]

Margery's connections to Bridget are also evident in the nature of Margery's *Book*. Christ and Mary speak to Bridget throughout her *Revelations*, just as they do to Margery Kempe throughout her *Book*. Although the tone and style of the works is quite different, the two authors share common themes: a focus on the spiritual meaning of scripture, an interest in imaginatively reexperiencing the historical events of Christ's life as a way of grasping the significance of the events, and a concern to reform the priesthood and rejuvenate believers' faith and commitment to love God. Kempe's references to Bridget's *Revelations*, her measuring of her own experiences in relation to Bridget's, and her encouraging devotion to Bridget all suggest how significant this near contemporary female saint was to her own process of self-representation. Margery's work is not a repetition of themes found in Bridget's *Revelations*, but she clearly styles her self-presentation in keeping with Bridget's model.[42]

The number and consistency of references to female saints set Kempe's autobiography apart from those of her male contemporaries. Her association with a

tradition of holy women who share features similar to those which characterize
her own life provides categories for naming her experiences and models for shaping
her religious life. In most cases, the examples of religious women Kempe draws
on are part of the popular culture of medieval piety. For example, as I pointed
out in a previous section, depictions of St. Katherine of Alexandria and St. Margaret of Antioch commonly adorned the walls of even the smallest country
churches in fourteenth- and fifteenth-century England.[43] These images, like those
of Mary, Mother of Jesus, and Mary Magdalene, functioned not to inculcate
religious subservience or cultural docility in women like Margery Kempe but rather
to inspire and legitimize a socially active and at times controversial witness to
the living Word of God.

In what follows, in keeping with the discussion of the function of mimetic
identification with the suffering Christ in saints' lives, I consider two central
aspects of Margery Kempe's public response to the invitation of the suffering
Christ: her role as an agent of reform in the spiritual lives of her contemporaries
and her status as a representative of humanity to God. Here Margery Kempe
advocates on humans' behalf and urges God to deal mercifully with the unrepentant living and the contrite dead. I focus on this second aspect of response in
which women like Margery Kempe act as *intercessors*, because it is here that we
can recognize the depth of medieval women's claims to be arbiters of religious
authority and influence in medieval society. To illustrate my point, I look at the
prominent place of purgatory in Kempe's work (representative of its prominence
in late medieval women's religious writing generally), and I discuss the significance of works of prayer and weeping that are central to her ministry.

Margery Kempe: Representative of God to Humanity

Like the biblical prophets, Kempe perceives herself as God's spokesperson, personally charged to deliver God's offer of mercy and compassion, to preach the
dangers of spiritual lassitude, and to exhort believers to reform their lives and
renew their spiritual vigor.[44] The prevalence of Jesus Christ's suffering in Margery
Kempe's life is intimately linked with her self-understanding as an agent of religious transformation. Through her storytelling, journeys, and identification with
spiritual women, Kempe embodies in her own life and ministry the Passion and
death of Christ. Christ tells her, "I haue ordeynd þe to be a merowr amongys
hem for to han gret sorwe þat þei xulde takyn exampil by þe for to haue sum litil
sorwe in her hertys for her synnys þat þei myth þerthorw be sauyd" (186). As a
living reminder of Christ's suffering, she weeps and wails in imaginative recollection of the Passion; through her preaching, storytelling, and caregiving, her
audience is called to compassionate sorrow and contrition for their forgetful-
ness of God's love and mercy. Her teaching, weeping, and praying for the world

convey the underlying and deep-rooted experience that motivated Margery Kempe's work: the merciful God loves all people and calls them to abandon sin through repentance and to respond with love of God and the world.

Her unwavering, vociferous, and demonstrative affirmation of her religious experiences (which often took the distinctive form of shouting or weeping loudly in the midst of sermons) resulted in continual conflict with church authorities and frequent charges of heresy. Nevertheless, she was an influential reformer of laypeople and religious leaders. In the face of heckling crowds, abandonment by followers, and denunciations from the religious community, this Jeremiah of medieval England dedicated her life to fulfilling the responsibility that arose from her personal religious experience of a merciful and loving God.[45]

Kempe's continual trials and tribulations and her emotional dialogues with God provide visual, dramatic, and embodied manifestations of the religious experiences she wants to convey. Domestic and familial language, the feeding of Christ, acting as a maid for Mary, self-descriptions as daughter, mother, or sister to Christ and the people to whom she speaks—all of this imagery runs throughout the *Book*, and portrays a woman unrelentingly committed to her work in representing Jesus to the world yet thoroughly human and involved in the daily life of common people struggling for spiritual assurance and maturity. One's senses are quickened by a tale so rich in colorful imagery: sounds of the sweet melodies of heaven, tastes of food, heavenly perfumes, the touch of Jesus, and the sight of Jesus crucified. Vignettes about weeping and shame, loud shoutings and crying out, control of the weather, and the sharing of meals are all woven into the variegated tapestry of the narrative. In this way, the *Book* conveys that Kempe was chosen by Christ and relates the turbulent events of her ministry: the calling of the world to repentance and recognition of a merciful God.

As discussed in chapter 1, after suffering through contrition in the face of her own sin and distance from God, Kempe begins to experience the suffering of Jesus. The process of cultivating compassion for Jesus' work awakens her to Christ's love for humanity—but the process does not stop there. Like Julian, as Margery experiences the suffering of Jesus, she comes to recognize Christ's love for humanity, and this leads her to testify publicly to that love in the world.[46] Margery participates in the ongoing work of Christ in the world by calling wayward sinners back to the spiritually nourishing path, strengthening the faith of the weak and deepening the faith of her peers. Margery Kempe carries out her work through her body: her tears and sorrow are a public visage of divine suffering for the world. The public expression of sorrow in the body plays a central place in Margery's enacting of her relationship to God through her interaction with the world.

Jesus says to her that at times he gives her "gret cryis and roryngys for to makyn þe pepil a-ferd wyth þe grace þat I putte in þe in-to a tokyn þat I wil þat my

Modrys sorwe be knowyn by þe þat men & women myth haue þe mor compassyon of hir sorwe þat sche suffyrd for me" (183). Her weeping and crying are directed toward awakening people to their spiritual condition. Christ tells her that any people who have as much sorrow for their sins as she does will be saved, as will anyone, no matter how sinful at first, who will "takyn exampil of thy leuyng & werkyn sumwhat þeraftyr" (183).

Like biblical prophets such as Jeremiah, Ezekiel, and Isaiah, Margery rebels against her mission. She says that she does not want to weep and cry out at sermons anymore (181) and bitterly laments the pain of her compassion for Christ's suffering. This work of weeping pains Margery to the point that she shouts out to God, "Lord, I am not þi modir. Take a-wey þis peyn fro me, for I may not beryn it" (164). Christ tells her not to pray in this manner because her desire will not be fulfilled; he then explains to her how her weeping will benefit the world (181–184). He tells her that the suffering she experiences on earth in weeping will be the reason she will feel no pain in the world to come: "For þu hast so gret compassyon of my flesche I must nede haue compassyon of þi flesch" (183).

As that of the preachers discussed in chapter 1, Kempe's work is intended to evoke contrition in her listeners: "Ʒyf I myth as wel, Lorde, ʒeuyn þe pepyl contricyon & wepyng as þu ʒuyst me for myn owyn synnes & oþer mennys synnys also & as wel as I myth ʒeuyn a peny owt of my purse, sone xulde I fulfille mennys hertys wyth contricyon þat þei myth sesyn of her synne" (141). When the Archbishop of York says he has heard that she is a wicked woman, she cautions him, "Ser, so I her seyn þat ʒe arn a wikkyd man. And, ʒyf ʒe ben as wikkyd as men seyn, ʒe xal neuyr come in Heuyn les þan ʒe amende ʒow whil ʒe ben her" (125).[47] Like the biblical women and men of judgment, Margery Kempe warns people about the consequences of continuing in their current course. She warns a widow that her husband is in purgatory and will be there for another 30 years unless, through almsgiving, the woman provides him with better support on earth. The widow pays no attention, and Jesus later tells Margery that she never changed her ways (46–47). Kempe's usual message, however, is that God will be merciful to those willing to change the direction of their lives. She recites to a priest details of his sinful life—his swearing, gluttony, lechery, and inattentive mass saying—and warns him that unless he reforms he will be damned. He takes her words to heart and begs for her forgiveness and prayers (126–128).

Kempe preaches not despair but undaunted hope, testifying to a God who suffered on humans' behalf and who extends mercy and compassion to even the most unrelenting of sinners. In a society that believed that right-standing before God at death was critical for one's well-being in the world to come, Kempe's effort to call people to attend to their status before the Divine and awaken them to compassionate identification with the suffering Christ was a work of immense responsibility.

Margery Kempe: Representative of Humanity to God

I have suggested that Margery's work is to remind the world of the God of mercy and justice and, even more, to implore God to be merciful to the public, for whom she is God's minister and representative. The immensity of the spiritual power she wields is manifest in her claims to transform the state of souls in purgatory.

Kempe's work is a good example of the concern with purgatory that has a prominent place in the writings and spiritual practices of late medieval women in general. In her impressive study of medieval women's purgatorial piety, Barbara Newman points to the prevalence of references to purgatory in sermons preached to Beguines in the thirteenth century. In sermons, and even in community rules, Beguines were urged to pray for "the dead who await mercy, that God may relieve their torment and hasten their glory."[48] Thomas of Cantimpré, the thirteenth-century Lutgard of Aywières's biographer, describes Lutgard as "specializing in liberating souls from purgatory."[49] Bynum, arguing that "suffering is service" for medieval women, records the claims of Lidwina of Schiedam's (d. 1433) hagiographers, who explain that "the fevers [Lidwina] suffered almost daily for many years before her death released souls from Purgatory."[50] Accounts of the miraculous "death" and "resurrection" of Catherine of Siena say that "she agreed to continue living only because the Virgin Mary promised that God would free souls from Purgatory because of her pain."[51] Bynum points to the "immoderate" nature of Mechthild of Magdeburg's confidence that her "suffering with Christ saves 70,000 souls from purgatory."[52] Immoderate though this claim may be, it is extremely common in stories about and writings by medieval women.

In describing the process of spiritual development, the twelfth-century Augustinian, Richard of St. Victor, pointed out that the fourth and final stage of spiritual growth is not withdrawal from the world but rather service within the world.[53] As he and figures like Margery Kempe and Julian of Norwich convey so clearly, the spiritually mature person desperately longs to be with God but remains on earth for the sake of others. The centrality of purgatory in the lives of the twelfth-century Christina the Astonishing and the fourteenth-century Catherine of Siena appears in Margery Kempe's text also. When she is still young, Christina dies, and God tells her that she can either remain in heaven or be separated from the Divine by returning to earth, where she can work to free others from purgatory.[54] Margery Kempe's situation is not quite as dramatic, but when she protests against being ridiculed and scorned by her contemporaries and expresses her desire to be with God, Christ reminds her of her critical work in liberating souls from purgatory. The work of freeing souls from purgatory runs throughout the writings of many religious women and is a theme critical to understanding the manner in which holy women participate in Jesus Christ's work in the world.[55]

It was generally agreed in the late Middle Ages that purgatory housed "elect souls, destined ultimately to be saved."[56] If only contrition or confession but not penance had occurred during the believer's life, then the punishment must be completed in purgatory. Further, the purgatorial system from its earliest forms (which medieval thinkers located in the Second Book of Maccabees) allowed that "a soul then may win reprieve or early release from punishment, not by virtue of its own conduct but thanks to outside intervention [in the form of suffering]."[57] In 1274, the Council of Lyons articulated the worldview that lay behind what motivated Margery Kempe to act in the world as an advocate for those in purgatory. In an appendix to the constitution *Cum sacrosancta*, the council affirmed

> that if, truly penitent, they die in charity before having by worthy fruits of penance rendered satisfaction for what they have done by commission or omission, their souls, as brother John has explained to us, are purged after their death by purgatorial or purifactory penalties, and that, for the alleviation of these penalties, they are served by the suffrages of the living faithful, to wit, the sacrifice of the mass, prayers, alms, and other works of piety that the faithful customarily offer on behalf of others of the faithful according to the institutions of the Church.[58]

In other words, without seeking to unseat the claims of God's justice by asking that those already dead and headed for damnation be spared, Margery and other religious like her seek to evoke divine mercy on behalf of those not dead who have time to repent and those in purgatory whose time of purgation may be shortened.[59] Like most of her Christian contemporaries, she believes that the works of piety suggested by the Council of Lyons—which she says include praying, thinking, weeping, going on pilgrimage, fasting, and speaking good words—benefit not only herself but also the world (20–21). Prayer and weeping are two of the good works that have particular prominence among other suffrages, such as almsgiving and the Eucharist, which can be carried out on the neighbor's behalf.

We cannot underestimate the importance of prayer in the medieval context. At times we forget, for example, how utterly dependent the fifth- through tenth-century medieval religious system was on the symbiotic relationship between monasteries, whose raison d'être was prayer, and the society outside the monasteries that provided both a need for prayer and financial support in return for prayer. As new options for men's public religious life emerged in the twelfth through fourteenth centuries in the growing number of mendicants whose presence became more public and sermonic, it is easy to lose sight of the continuing role of prayer in stabilizing and contributing to the God-human relationship. In the same vein, it is easy to lose sight of how public a work prayer is in the lives of medieval women.

Margery encourages relatives to pray for family members in purgatory (an emerging feature of twelfth-century practices relating to purgatory), but religious women like Margery Kempe seek much more magnificent and extravagant goals.[60]

She works not only on behalf of one or another individual but also on behalf of the whole world. At one point, when Kempe languishes in love in her desire to be "delyueryd owt of þis wretchyd world" (20), Jesus Christ charges her to work in the world, saying that he has "ordeyned" her to pray for all the world. He assures her that her prayers will be effective and will save many hundreds of thousands of souls (20).

Prayer is quite common in the medieval context, but for Margery Kempe, weeping takes a central place in the category of works that alleviate the penalties of those in purgatory. Weeping has a long and prominent history as a work of value in the Christian tradition, but it appears with renewed vigor from the late twelfth century on. Julian of Norwich cites the authority of Jerome to Margery Kempe, telling her that tears torment the devil more than the pains of hell (43). Later, Jerome himself appears to Kempe to say that she shall be saved by her weeping for people's sins and that her tears are a "synguler & a specyal ʒyft" from God (99). Margery cites the tradition of Jerome to legitimize her seeming innovation; she calls weeping a gift and says it is as effective as almsgiving or pilgrimages in benefiting those for whom she weeps. She receives further legitimation when Jesus tells her that she is his sister when she weeps for other people's sins and adversities (31). Her weeping becomes such an integral part of her vocation that she tells Christ that if he wants her to cease weeping he should take her "owt of þis world" (142).

Margery weeps on the world's behalf. She cries for her own sins, for the sins of the people, for the souls in purgatory, and for persons in poverty and disease. She desires to comfort them all (20). She relates that on Good Friday she weeps an hour for the sins of the people (140). Sometimes she weeps "an-oþer owr for þe sowlys in Purgatory; an-oþer owr for hem þat weryn in myschefe, in pouerte, er in any disese; an-oþer owr for Iewys, Saraʒinys, & alle fals heretikys þat God for hys gret goodnes xulde puttyn a-wey her blyndnes þat þei myth thorw hys grace be turnyd to þe feyth of Holy Chirche & ben children of saluacyon" (140–141).

It is in the context of this medieval milieu, with its consuming attention to the post-mortem condition of the person and its recognition of the power of acts of piety to affect that situation, that we can understand the significance of Christ's repeatedly telling Margery that "many thowsand sowlys xal be sauyd thorw þi preyerys, & sum þat lyn in poynt of deth xal han grace thorw þi merytys & þi preyerys for þi terys & þi preyerys arn ful swet & acceptabil un-to me" (186). What is implicit in the statements of the Council of Lyons now becomes explicit in the conversations between God and Margery Kempe. Over and over again, the *Book* asserts that Margery's work influences God. At one point, Jesus tells her that if she could see humanity's sins as he does, she would be amazed at his patience. In this way, her tears serve to hold God back from taking vengeance on the humans' souls. "Dowtyr, ʒyf þu sey þe wikkydnes þat is wrowt in þe werld as

I do, þu schuldist haue gret wondyr þat I take not vttyr veniawns on hem. But, dowtyr, I spar for thy lofe. Þu wepist so euery day for mercy þat I must nedys grawnt it þe" (158). Margery's advocacy succeeds in assuring the spiritual well-being of the world. Jesus thanks her for her love and for her desire that all people should love God (160).

Margery Kempe's extraordinary claims are not unusual and characterize the religious self-understanding of female religious leaders in the Middle Ages. Women like Kempe wept publicly to make the suffering of Jesus present to their viewers and to urge their observers to avail themselves of the mercy of God. Although at first glance, Margery Kempe's claims to be both an agent of spiritual transformation for the faithful in this life and an advocate for divine mercy for souls in the next may seem extravagant, such claims are quite common in writings of medieval women and must be accounted for if we are to grasp the integrity and self-understanding of female religious leaders. Women like Kempe function as agents of reform insofar as they teach and weep to warn the world of the dangers of neglecting God. Trusting in the mercy manifest in the figure of the suffering Jesus, they weep and pray to blunt the wrath of God that has been directed against sin and to mitigate the pains of souls confined to purgatory. Thus they live as advocates for divine mercy and as brokers of spiritual power by securing the well-being of the unrepentant living and the contrite dead.

❧ ❧

In conclusion, then, the examples I discuss in this chapter call attention to the place of Christ-identified suffering in texts by and about medieval women. Attention to genre suggests that we be cautious when we draw conclusions about historical women from hagiographical texts. But these texts are important because they show how the body functions as the theater where the Divine-human relationship is dramatized in a most extravagant manner. As the examples of Margaret of Antioch, Katherine of Alexandria, and Elizabeth of Spalbeek illustrate, the female body, as well as the male body, figures Christ to the world. The examples of Elizabeth of Spalbeek and Margery Kempe indicate that spiritual life, while suffused with joy at times (often overlooked in our analyses of medieval texts), is also beset with pain—though pain is never pursued for its own sake but is a by-product of, and even a catalyst in, the difficult process of spiritual transformation. Suffering has a significant public function in the matrix of spiritual growth: Elizabeth of Spalbeek and Margery Kempe are the pathos of Christ in a world that cries out for spiritual ablution. In keeping with the charge of Mark 13:9–13 to preach the gospel in the face of betrayal and torment and the precept of Romans 8:17 "to suffer with Christ in order [to be] glorified with him," the women of medieval literature, such as Katherine, Margaret, Elizabeth of Spalbeek, and Margery Kempe, become purveyors of divine power, advocates for humanity's well-being, and intimates with God through their entry into the world of the Passion of Jesus. We may dismiss these texts as denigrating the female body, or we may observe that, in a world far removed from our own but at a time not unlike our own when women were associated both medically and theologically with "the body," women of medieval spiritual literature functioned in and through their bodies to become Christ to the world.[61] Of course, many other forms of suffering appear in these religious texts, but this chapter's taxonomy of the body in pain illustrates how women, in and through their bodies, are parables of divine suffering in the world of late medieval England.

Conclusion

This study of medieval literature and iconography has explored the transformative power of Jesus' *wounded* body as it manifests divine presence and evokes compassionate response on the part of viewers. My analysis of artistic and literary images of the bleeding Savior suggests that late medieval iconography, homilies, and guidance literature construct a world in which readers and listeners are brought to new understandings of their relationships to God and neighbor by encountering the living flesh of the wounded Jesus. The Jesus Christ of late medieval England is the enfleshed body of God, and it is in engaged relationship to this bleeding and tormented body that believers meet the medieval God of Love. In a theologically and emotionally sophisticated manner, medieval art, drama, sermons, and devotional literature project a common spiritual cosmos in which the person is transformed from being a sinner to being an intimate of the Divine in the encounter with the suffering Jesus. Through the media of manuscript illuminations and church wall paintings, as well as on the stages of the mystery plays, portrayals of the suffering Jesus reconfigure space and time and invite viewers and readers to be participants in the ongoing narrative of divine mercy and love. Confession, compassion, and mimetic identification with the bloody Jesus remake believers in their relationships with God.

Jesus' suffering is a somatization of divine love insofar as the intensified enfleshment of the suffering body becomes the very source of the manifestation of divine presence to humanity. In medieval drama, for example, this suffering is conveyed to viewers through an elaborate interweaving of prefiguration, prophecy, event, and recollection of the torment endured by Christ. Dramatic foretelling, enacting, and recalling of the agony suffered by Jesus testify to how the wounded body scripts the divine offer of healing and forgiveness. The dramatic performances of persuasion invite viewers to participate in the world in which Jesus' body effects the salvation of humanity. This manifestation of the Divine through the flesh extends beyond medieval portrayals of Jesus Christ to portrayals of the Eucharist which, understood in terms of transubstantiation, is the very body and blood of Jesus Christ. Furthermore, the enfleshment of the Divine is graphically displayed in artistic renditions of the Crucifixion in which the blood flows from the crucified Jesus' wounds into chalices and, in some cases, into the mouths of those who witness his suffering. In their encounters with the wounded Jesus—the bleeding Savior who nurtures, feeds, and heals people—believers encounter God.

In the system of salvation portrayed by medieval literature and art, persons are called upon to respond to the divine offer of love and mercy expressed in the Passion and death of Jesus Christ. The art, literature, and drama considered in this book are unified by their participation in the rhetoric of transformation that persuades viewers and listeners to respond to the events they observe. In particular, the textual and artistic sources demonstrate the integral place of Jesus' pain and anguish in evoking both repentance and compassion in the process of persons' spiritual transformation. Compassion, the initial root of repentance, arises in the viewers and readers who witness the excruciating suffering of Jesus. Manuscript illuminations, sermons, wall paintings, and devotional literature emphasize the details of Jesus' suffering to foster empathy in the witnesses to this suffering.

From compassionate response to Jesus' anguish, spectators are led to sorrowful recognition of their own implication in the sins for which Jesus suffers. Jesus' body is a text of flesh inscribed by the bloody marks of human transgressions: "Swete Ihesu, þi bodi is lijk a book writen wiþ reed enke: so is þi bodi al writen wiþ rede woundis."[1] In interpreting Jesus' body as the medium of relationship between persons and the Divine, believers both acknowledge their participation in causing the suffering Jesus endured and confront their alienation from God. The intensified corporeality of the wounded Jesus transforms hearers and spectators and moves them to repentance.

The spiritual guide, Richard Rolle, begs to be bathed in the blood of Jesus so that his compassion may be awakened: "Lord, I wele in my thouȝt þe rode foot take in my armys . . . þennes wyl I not ryse . . . tyl I be with þi precyous blood bycome al reed, tyl I be markyd þere-with os on of þine owne, & softyd in þat swete bath . . . so may it falle . . . þat myn herd harte may opene þere-with, þat is now hard os ston, bycomen al nesche and quyckenen in þi felyng."[2] In his mind's eye, Rolle clings to the foot of the cross, unwilling to rise until he is showered by the healing blood of Jesus, which will melt the hardness of his heart and engender empathy and compassion toward the suffering Christ. Rolle's devotion to Jesus' blood expresses a central spiritual passion of late medieval England: the extravagant desire to be bathed in the sacred blood that flows from the body of God. The red rain of Jesus' Passion melts the hardened heart of the unrepentant believer and inspires the acceptance of the offer of mercy. After provoking the believer's repentance, the bath washes and purifies the sinful body and soul.

Drama, art, and sermons direct the acknowledgment of individual responsibility for Jesus' suffering toward penitence in confession. In the late medieval sacramental system, confession cultivated not only discipline but also consolation in believers so that their sorrow was indispensable to the process of healing.[3] Although sin signals humanity's alienation from the Divine, the focus in medieval texts is not on the presence of sin but rather on the process by which persons repent and open themselves to the divine offer of mercy. As indicated in sermon stories, for example, Jesus Christ offers mercy, but persons must respond to that offer by asking for the mercy and accepting it when it is offered. Refusal to seek forgiveness is of much more significance than is the presence of sin itself. The repentant sinner may even be closer to the Divine than the believer who does not sin.

The transformative process does not end with compassion toward Jesus and sacramental confession: sorrow and repentance lead spectators to imitate Jesus' merciful action toward others. The suffering Jesus awakens empathy in those who witness the agony he suffers out of compassion for sinful humanity. This awareness of the suffering Jesus' compassion is united with the pathos awakened by meditation on Jesus' suffering and stirs believers to a Jesus-like compassion for the world. In the medieval schema described here, imitating Jesus' love for humankind by loving the world serves as the primary way for persons to express their ongoing love of the God who suffered on their behalf. Response to the bloody wounds, the visible signs of divine mercy, becomes the very measure of human response to God. Thus, persons' eternal state is determined by whether or not they are merciful in their interactions with their neighbors. This taxonomy of salvation, with the ethical imitation of Jesus at its center, is depicted in wall paintings such as the one at Trotten in which Christ in Judgment is pictured as rejecting the sinner surrounded by symbols of sins such as gluttony and welcoming the saved person encircled by the symbols of works of mercy. As Eamon Duffy aptly expresses it: "Into what appears to be a simple affective devotion to the Passion, there was compressed the essence of the practical soteriology of late medieval religion."[4]

This general observation about the process of transformation is instantiated in the writings of individual authors like Julian of Norwich and Margery Kempe. Rather than understanding these authors as anomalies, as some scholars have suggested, I understand them as articulate representatives of a common medieval outlook. Julian's and Margery's writings focus on three types of personal suffering: the suffering caused by their awareness of their own complicity in the death of Jesus, the suffering of compassionate identification with Jesus, and the suffering of longing to be with Jesus. Meditation on the details of Jesus' Passion initiates the personal suffering described here, just as it awakens Julian of Norwich to the magnitude of divine love expressed in the suffering. For Julian, the central meaning of Jesus' Passion is the theopaschite affirmation that "the one who suffered is God." Julian's insight stands at the heart of medieval piety and is reflected in artistic images of the triune Godhead in which the Second Person of the Trinity is pictured as the bloodied and wounded Savior nailed to the cross.

In some contexts, compassionate response to the Passion of Jesus leads beyond ethical imitation of Jesus to mimetic identification with the crucified Savior. I argue that there is a basic affinity between saints' lives, martyrs' narratives, and the self-authored works of medieval women like Margery Kempe. Attention to the presence of the suffering Jesus in medieval women's lives, whether legendary or real, alerts us to the dynamics of female public religious authority in the late medieval world. Women used their theological, biological, and social identification with the body to express religious meaning and spiritual authority. In mimetic identification with Jesus, women manifest the ongoing presence of the Divine through their own bodies. Women's Jesus-identified suffering signals the intimacy of their personal relationships with the Divine. Moreover, Jesus becomes visible to the world through imprinting his suffering on the holy woman's body. In their mimetic identification with Christ, women function publicly to promote the spiritual growth of humanity; like Jesus' body, their suffering bodies are marked by the sin of the world and function as reminders of humanity's separation from the Divine. As the original witnesses to the crucified Jesus were awakened to compassionate response, so the medieval witnesses to the suffering of their contemporary female imitators of Christ are also called to compassion. Furthermore, women's mimetic identification signals their power of intercession with the Divine; just as the suffering Jesus functioned as a healer, mending the breach between humans and God, so these women, in their Christ-marked bodies, offer healing and transformation to the world. The spiritual authority gained through their imitation of the enfleshed God enables them to function as powerful advocates for sinful humanity seeking divine mercy.

Although this extraordinary suffering may seem bizarre and unhealthy to many of us now, I nevertheless urge us to attend to the function and meaning of this suffering in its medieval context. The ritualized identification of holy women with the suffering Jesus, in a world far removed from our own, did not foment a self-denigrating, silencing, private agony in religious women but rather enabled them to function as public embodiments of the Divine. In their personal devotion, suffering erased the boundaries between the Divine and humans and invested medieval women with the transformative power expressed by Christ himself. It is not the Jesus who is the male hierarch of a vengeful God, however, who inspired this mimetic suffering, but rather it is the doubly-gendered Jesus, the literal embodiment of divine mercy reconciled with justice, who functions as the definitive paradigm of God's love for humankind. The doubly-gendered Jesus who lactates, bleeds, nurtures, heals, and feeds the world with his body becomes the root metaphor for an entire epoch.

Late medieval English artistic, literary, and dramatic portrayals of the suffering Jesus invite believers to experience for themselves the theological promises of medieval Christianity. Much of medieval theology is *affective theology* which begins with the premise that God is love and then urges believers to *experience* that love. Depictions of the suffering Jesus in late medieval English sources are not random and haphazard presentations but are focused on evoking the theologically expressive and emotionally transformative experiences of loving kinship with Jesus Christ.[5]

In discussing Corpus Christi imagery, Eamon Duffy makes a distinction between trinitarian-focused images in which "the sufferings of Christ are revealed not to evoke pity or compunction for sins but as a theological statement," on the one hand, and images of "our Lady of Pity," on the other hand, which have the affective intent of evoking "repentance and compassion with the suffering of Christ" and are not intended as theological statements.[6] I do not think, however, that the distinction between the theological and the affective can be consistently sustained on the basis of the evidence I have examined here. On the contrary, I argue that both types of art have affective and theological dimensions, and that these dimensions—trinitarian, Marian, and christological—cannot be separated from one another. The theological message of mercy conveyed through the trinitarian depiction of Christ operates in both emotional and propositional registers. That is, as Duffy suggests, the trinitarian images which include a suffering Jesus are certainly making a theological statement (about the doctrine of the person of Jesus Christ and the nature of the Resurrection, for example), but these portrayals also contain an important affective dimension as well: the trinitarian images which include the crucified Jesus Christ appeal directly to human emotions because these images are inseparable from the medieval portrayal of the Jesus of Compassion. Such christological images are part of the widespread invitation to experience the meaning of the theological affirmation that God is love through meditating on the Passion of Jesus.

The Marian images Duffy studies are integral to the spiritual process that stirs spectators' compassion in reponse to the suffering endured by Mary. In studying late medieval art, James Marrow observes that just as late medieval devotional writers "place new emphasis upon addressing their audience and instructing them about appropriate displays of emotion," artists like Roger van der Weyden "provide their viewers with figures who visualize the kinds of responses they should cultivate and experience."[7] Images of Mary carry out precisely this function. After recounting Mary's agony at watching Jesus suffer, Richard Rolle implores Mary to let him share in her lamentation. He asks her for "a drope of þat ruþe þat þou haddist . . . I axe . . . woundis of ruþe, of peyne and of cumpassioun of swete Ihesu my lordis passioun is al my desire."[8] These images are moving, heartfelt figurations of a mother's love for her son, but they also function as discursive articulations of the theological claim that the love of God is expressed in the incarnation of Jesus Christ through the *Theotokos*.

This book analyzes critically the central dimensions of late medieval devotion to the suffering Jesus. I agree with Duffy, who finds little support for the claims that the late medieval period is characterized by a growing division between individual and official religion and who argues instead for a "homogeneity" of religious sensibilities and a shared religious culture in medieval society.[9] Medieval "popular religion," the "elite piety of the devout," and the "official liturgy of the church" are much more closely related than many historians have assumed.[10] I am not suggesting, however, that we can find an absolute uniformity of belief and practice in the religion-saturated culture of medieval England. As Sarah Beckwith has convincingly demonstrated, much of fifteenth-century England was divided over competing doctrinal and liturgical appropriations of the meaning of the body of Christ.[11] The Lollards' rejection of the doctrine of transubstantiation, for example, signals the extent to which the understandings of the body of Christ were contested in the theology and religious life of the medieval church. Yet the fact that the struggles were so often centered around the meaning of Jesus' *body* highlights the centrality of the wounded Jesus in medieval religious life. Although the religious vision of Christ I have articulated here was not without its medieval detractors, my thesis is that the body-identified devotion to Jesus practiced during this period was an extraordinarily fecund and widespread form of transformative spirituality.

In the preceding chapters, I have isolated some of the identifiable patterns in literature and art that illustrate key features of bodily devotion to Jesus Christ. This pervasive body-centered religiosity is replete with images of the flowing, bleeding, feeding, and crucified Jesus who offers transformation to those who avail themselves of the palpable and liquid signs of love he offers. The bleeding christological body simultaneously signals death and life. Yet this spirituality is no maudlin sentimentality obsessed with the death of a crucified Jesus and with fear for the post-mortem fate of an unrepentant humanity. The bleeding Jesus is a dying figure whose visage reminds witnesses that they will be held accountable for that death unless they acknowledge their guilt in his torture and murder and respond with empathy to Jesus' suffering and with compassion for the rest of the world. Duffy is right to suggest that although "the cult of the dead was ubiquitous" in medieval culture, this attentiveness to death and dying does not reveal a culture morbidly obsessed with death.[12] Rather, acute awareness of responsibility for the anguish of the tormented and crucified Jesus Christ spurs believers to repentance—that is, toward the possibility of eternal life. Awareness of the possible states of persons after death urges believers to attend to their spiritual well-being before they die. Moreover, the message of medieval piety is that believers can influence the status of the repentant dead. This is evident in the above discussions of women's roles as mediators of divine power in affecting the situation of souls in purgatory. Rather than signaling an unproductive morbidity, medieval interaction with the dead in general, as well as with the dying Jesus Christ in particular, reveals the hope for transformation that undergirded medieval culture.[13] The boundaries between life and death were much more fluid in medieval times than they are in our own.

In art, sermons, and devotional literature, the blood flowing from the crucified Christ also signals life. The blood flowing from Jesus' wounds, the "wells of mercy," pours itself out onto persons. It is to be tasted and swallowed and can temper, bathe, and purify those in its liquid path. Like the pelican restoring life to its young by feeding them its blood, the flow of blood from the wounded Jesus offers healing and nourishment for all God's children: "I aske . . . þat he wole to my dede herte laien his holi woundes to restore me to life."[14] Believers come to know and experience God through the wounds of Jesus: "Thorow þe blodi woundes of his flesh entre in-to the ioie of his godhede."[15]

Twentieth-century readers of this material often wonder why, if the divinity of Jesus Christ is at the heart of medieval religiosity (as I have argued here), the Resurrection is not the most prominent portrayal of Jesus in this piety. Affirmation of the Resurrection does underlie medieval religion; after all, the Christ of Judgment, the one who separates the saved from the damned according to their merciful actions in the world, is the resurrected Christ. However, it was not Jesus Christ's rising from the dead that this culture found so remarkable; it was the miracle that God became embodied in order to suffer on behalf of humanity that captivated the imagination of medieval Christians. God bled and wept and suffered on the cross to draw persons to Godself; God bled and wept and suffered on the cross to manifest the boundless mercy of divine compassion. The blood of Jesus *is* the love of God literally poured out onto the witnesses of this suffering. Believers who bathe in this blood and drink the life fluids of this wounded God find themselves, in devotion and Eucharist, transformed into compassionate friends and lovers of God.

The medieval valorization of bodily pain may seem to be a self-abnegating and pernicious model to many of us in the West in the late twentieth century, but the study of history is not always about seeking comfortable life-models. Rather, the goal of the study of history is to *understand* a world that came before ours, a world which, contrasted with our world, may have something to teach us about our own cultural fears and abjections. In our own time, for example, when the AIDS crisis and anxiety about bodies, especially women's bodies, shape the cultural discourse of our age, we may better understand our own culture by reflecting on a period in which the fascination with blood and bodies had a very different cultural meaning. When we ask how people experience relationships and even unity with the Divine, we may be intrigued and challenged by the power and integrity of this medieval world in which suffering manifested divine presence and, at times, erased the boundaries between Divine and human in empowering women and men to become agents of God in the world.

Notes

INTRODUCTION

1. This is not to suggest that the image of the suffering Jesus did not appear until the twelfth century. Barbara Raw's *Anglo-Saxon Crucifixion Iconography and the Art of Monastic Revival* (Cambridge: Cambridge University Press, 1990) provides a superb analysis of Anglo-Saxon Crucifixion iconography and demonstrates the centrality of "love" in Anglo-Saxon depictions of the Crucifixion. She suggests that "the meditative prayer of the late Anglo-Saxon period was much closer to that of the time of Anselm and Aelred than the texts would suggest" (66). I am pointing out a matter of emphasis and prevalence here. On the shift in artistic depictions of the Crucifixion, see, for example, Hans Belting, *Likeness and Presence: A History of the Image before the Era of Art*, trans. Edmund Jephcott (Chicago: University of Chicago Press, 1994), and Emile Mâle, *Religious Art in France: The Late Middle Ages: A Study of Its Iconography and Its Sources*, trans. Marthiel Mathews (Princeton: Princeton University Press, 1986), 83, chap. 3.

2. On the Passion of Jesus in liturgical drama, see Rosemary Woolf, *The English Mystery Plays* (London: Routledge and Kegan Paul, 1972), chap. 11. On the association between liturgical drama and church architecture, see M. D. Anderson, *Drama and Imagery in English Medieval Churches* (Cambridge: Cambridge University Press, 1963), and on the association between liturgical drama and art, see Otto Pächt, *The Rise of Pictorial Narrative in Twelfth-Century England* (Oxford: Clarendon Press, 1962), chap. 3. On Passion imagery in late medieval poetry, see Rosemary Woolf, *The English Religious Lyric in the Middle Ages* (Oxford: Clarendon Press, 1968), chap. 6, and Douglas Gray, *Themes and Images in the Medieval English Religious Lyric* (London: Routledge and Kegan Paul, 1972), chap. 7.

3. G. R. Owst, *Preaching in Medieval England: An Introduction to Sermon Manuscripts of the Period 1350–1450* (New York: Russell and Russell, 1965), 349.

4. On the importance of visualization in medieval culture, see Margaret Miles, *Image as Insight: Visual Understanding in Western Christianity and Secular Culture* (Boston: Beacon Press, 1985), esp. chaps. 2 and 4.

5. O. Elfrida Saunders, *A History of English Art in the Middle Ages* (Oxford: Clarendon Press, 1932), 173–74.

6. Richard Kieckhefer, *Unquiet Souls: Fourteenth-Century Saints and Their Religious Milieu* (Chicago: University of Chicago Press, 1984), chap. 4, esp. 110–14. See also Jaroslav Pelikan, *Jesus through the Centuries* (New York: Harper and Row, 1985), chaps. 6–11; Mâle, *Religious Art in France*, 118–24; Johanna Ziegler, *Sculpture of Compassion: The Pietà and the Beguines in the Southern Low Countries, c. 1300–c. 1600* (Rome: Academia Belgica, 1992); and Gertrud Schiller, *Ikonographie der christlichen Kunst*, 4 vols. (Gütersloh: Humphries, 1971–72), 2:98–176, for a pictorial representation of this transition. For English examples of the transition, see Tancred Borenius and E. W. Tristram, *English Medieval Painting* (New York: Hacker Art Books, 1976).

7. G. R. Owst, *Literature and Pulpit in Medieval England: A Neglected Chapter in the History of English Letters and of the English People* (Cambridge: Cambridge University Press, 1933), 142.

8. An interpretation akin to Jean Delumeau's leads in this direction: "In addition to the 'fear,' the 'dread,' the 'terror,' and the 'fright' occasioned by exterior pulls of all kinds (natural or human), Western civilization was affected by two supplementary and equally oppressive causes for alarm: the 'horror' of sin and the 'obsession' of damnation" (Jean Delumeau, *Sin and Fear: The Emergence of a Western Guilt Culture, 13th–18th Centuries*, trans. Eric Nicholson [New York: St. Martin's Press, 1990], 3).

9. "For the spirit which this art denotes is the same one which was pointed out in religious life: a spirit rather decadent than primitive, a spirit involving the utmost elaboration, and even decomposition, of religious thought through the imagination" (Johan Huizinga, *The Waning of the Middle Ages: A Study of the Forms of Life, Thought and Art in France and the Netherlands in the XIVth and XVth Centuries* [London: E. Arnold, 1924], 241).

10. See Delumeau, *Sin and Fear*, 410–21.

11. For a discussion of the theological development of interpretations of the Atonement, see Gustaf Aulén, *Christus Victor: An Historical Study of the Three Main Types of the Atonement* (New York: Macmillan, 1969), esp. chaps. 3, 4, 5; Jaroslav Pelikan, *The Growth of Medieval Theology (600–1300)*, vol. 3, *The Christian Tradition: A History of the Development of Doctrine* (Chicago: University of Chicago Press, 1978), 129–57; and idem, *The Reformation of Church and Dogma (1300–1700)*, vol. 4, *The Christian Tradition: A History of the Development of Doctrine* (Chicago: University of Chicago Press, 1984), 22–38.

12. See Huizinga, *Waning of the Middle Ages*, 173–81.

13. Aron Gurevich, *Medieval Popular Culture: Problems of Belief and Perception* (Cambridge: Cambridge University Press, 1988), 174.

14. Thomas Tentler, *Sin and Confession on the Eve of the Reformation* (New Jersey: Princeton University Press, 1977), 233–63.

15. For further consideration of the social function of Eucharist-related practices, see Miri Rubin's excellent study, *Corpus Christi: The Eucharist in Late Medieval Culture* (Cambridge: Cambridge University Press, 1992). On the body of Christ as a symbolic center for late medieval English debates about "sacrality," see Sarah Beckwith's thought-provoking and insightful book, *Christ's Body: Identity, Culture, and Society in Late Medieval Writings* (New York: Routledge, 1993).

16. Caroline Walker Bynum, in her excellent book on medieval women's spirituality,

Holy Feast and Holy Fast: The Religious Significance of Food to Medieval Women (Berkeley: University of California Press, 1987), and Richard Kieckhefer in *Unquiet Souls* have recently noted the pervasiveness of suffering in medieval spirituality. Without systematically developing it, Kieckhefer and Bynum point to what I consider to be critical. Kieckhefer remarks on the progression from comprehension of Christ's humanity to understanding of his divinity but does not discuss the mechanism of the progression (*Unquiet Souls*, esp. chap. 4). Bynum also notes the progressive tendency in the texts she considers. Although she gives an example of how the progression might work in the case of the fourteenth-century Dominican, Catherine of Siena—in which Catherine explains that the more we taste of God, the more we crave of God and thus are drawn along the path toward understanding the fullness of God—Bynum does not explore how the process of suffering in *imitatio Christi* works (*Holy Feast and Holy Fast*, 176–80). Scholars like Bynum and Kieckhefer have seen that for most late medieval authors spiritual growth does not end at recognition of the humanity of Jesus, but they do not develop this point.

17. Among recent studies of late medieval religion and culture, Eamon Duffy's excellent book, *The Stripping of the Altars: Traditional Religion in England c. 1400–c. 1580* (New Haven: Yale University Press, 1992), stands out. Eamon Duffy explores "the character and range of late medieval English Catholicism, indicating something of the richness and complexity of the religious system by which men and women structured their experience of the world, and their hopes and aspirations within and beyond it" (1). He also details the sixteenth-century's "dismantling and destruction of that symbolic world" (1). In the first half of his book, Duffy considers some of the same material that I do, although he does not focus on christological issues in particular. Nevertheless, our views of the late medieval world, and, in particular, our views of the sophistication of lay piety, are similar.

18. Raw, *Anglo-Saxon Crucifixion Iconography*, esp. chap. 8.

19. Caroline Walker Bynum, *Fragmentation and Redemption: Essays on Gender and the Human Body in Medieval Religion* (New York: Zone Books, 1991), 102–8.

20. Walter Hilton, *The Scale of Perfection*, trans. John P. H. Clark and Rosemary Dorward (New York: Paulist Press, 1991), 116.

21. For a discussion of clerical religious education of the laity, see Jonathan Hughes, *Pastors and Visionaries: Religion and Secular Life in Late Medieval Yorkshire* (Woodbridge, Suffolk: Boydell Press, 1988), esp. 143–61.

22. Tentler, *Sin and Confession*, 345. While Tentler does attend to issues of social control connected with the sacrament of penance, he is also rightly concerned with addressing how the sacrament functioned to comfort and console believers.

23. MS Harley 635, fol. 11, quoted in Owst, *Preaching in Medieval England*, 333.

24. John Bellamy, *Crime and Public Order in England in the Late Middle Ages* (Toronto: University of Toronto Press, 1973), 37, chap. 2.

25. Sanford B. Meech and Hope E. Allen, eds., *The Book of Margery Kempe*, vol. 212 of Early English Text Society (New York: Oxford University Press, 1940), 125.

CHAPTER ONE

1. John Mirk, *Mirk's Festial: A Collection of Homilies*, ed. Theodor Erbe, vol. 96 of Early English Text Society, extra series (London: Kegan Paul, Trench, Trübner, 1905), 93–94. For helpful introductions to the variety of sources for medieval devotional literature and

sermons, see Jonathan Hughes, *Pastors and Visionaries: Religion and Secular Life in Late Medieval Yorkshire* (Woodbridge, Suffolk: Boydell Press, 1988), chaps. 3–5; Eamon Duffy, *The Stripping of the Altars: Traditional Religion in England, 1400–1580* (New Haven: Yale University Press, 1992), chap. 2; H. Leith Spencer, *English Preaching in the Late Middle Ages* (Oxford: Clarendon Press, 1993); W. A. Pantin, *The English Church in the Fourteenth Century* (Cambridge: Cambridge University Press, 1955); G. R. Owst, *Literature and Pulpit in Medieval England: A Neglected Chapter in the History of English Letters and of the English People* (Cambridge: Cambridge University Press, 1933); and idem, *Preaching in Medieval England: An Introduction to Sermon Manuscripts of the Period c. 1350–1450* (New York: Russell and Russell, 1965).

2. We will also observe this struggle in medieval liturgical cycle plays. On the theological and thematic affinity between sermons and religious drama, see Marianne G. Briscoe, "Preaching and Medieval English Drama," in *Contexts for Early English Drama*, ed. Marianne Briscoe and John Coldewey (Bloomington: Indiana University Press, 1989), 150–72. On later medieval English prose styles in general, see Janel Mueller, *The Native Tongue and the Word: Developments in English Prose Style, 1380–1580* (Chicago: University of Chicago Press, 1984), chap. 3.

3. Woodburn O. Ross, *Middle English Sermons*, vol. 209 of Early English Text Society, o.s. (New York: Oxford University Press, 1960), 44. (This sermon does not refer to Peace, the usual fourth counselor in medieval portrayals of God's decision to respond to humanity's pleas for assistance.)

4. Ross, *Sermons*, 45.

5. Ross, *Sermons*, 45.

6. Mirk, *Festial*, 172.

7. Mirk, *Festial*, 172.

8. Edward H. Weatherly, ed., *Speculum Sacerdotale*, vol. 200 of Early English Text Society, o.s. (London: Oxford University Press, 1936), 124. The *Speculum Sacerdotale* was written sometime in the late fourteenth century as a vernacular guidebook for priests; drawing heavily on Belethus's *Rationale* and Jacobus de Voragine's *Legenda Aurea*, it provided homilies and instructive exposition to aid parish priests in their pastoral work.

9. Henry E. Nolloth, ed., *The Layfolk's Catechism, or Archbishop Thoresby's Instructions for the People*, vol. 118 of Early English Text Society, o.s. (London: Early English Text Society, 1901), 30.

10. Nolloth, *Layfolk's Catechism*, 30.

11. For a discussion of this point in late medieval drama, see Friedrich Ohly, *The Damned and the Elect: Guilt in Western Culture*, trans. Linda Archibald (Cambridge: Cambridge University Press, 1992), 76–78.

12. Ross, *Sermons*, 45.

13. Mirk, *Festial*, 171. On Lollard attitudes toward images, see Margaret Aston, *Lollards and Reformers: Images and Literacy in Late Medieval Religion* (London: Hambledon Press, 1984), 135–92.

14. Mirk, *Festial*, 172.

15. MS Linc. Cath. Lib. A.6.2, fols. 130–31, quoted in Owst, *Preaching in Medieval England*, 347–48. See also W. A. Pantin, "The Monk-Solitary of Farne: A Fourteenth-Century English Mystic," *English Historical Review* 59 (1944): 168.

16. Ross, *Sermons*, 271–73.

17. Mirk, *Festial*, 113.

18. Mirk, *Festial*, 118.

19. Ross, *Sermons*, 27.

20. These stories begin to appear in increasing numbers from the twelfth century onward (Marcia Kupfer, *Romanesque Wall Painting in Central France: The Politics of Narrative* [New Haven: Yale University Press, 1993], 136).

21. Mirk, *Festial*, 173. Stories of this type usually end with the return of the bleeding flesh to the form of bread and wine. In this case, Gregory asked people to pray again that Christ's body turn once more into the form of bread, which it did; he then administered it to Lasma.

22. Mirk, *Festial*, 171.

23. These stories are part of a general category of the "coming alive" of images which converts witnesses. But as a subcategory, they work with the same literalizing of the wounded presence as described in the eucharistic examples above.

24. Mirk, *Festial*, 145–46.

25. In this story (Mirk, *Festial*, 252), as in many others we have considered, the miraculous appearance of blood is of critical importance in achieving a transformation of humans. These stories reflect the anti-Semitism present in much medieval literature, which assumes that Jews were responsible for Jesus' death and that medieval Jews continued the hostilities attributed to their forebears at the time of the Crucifixion. See Gavin L. Langmuir, "Historiographic Crucifixion," in *Les Juifs au regard de l'histoire: melanges en l'honneur de Bernhard Blumenkranz*, ed. Gilbert Dahan (Paris: Picard, 1985), 109–27, and idem, *Toward a Definition of Antisemitism* (Berkeley and Los Angeles: University of California Press, 1990), chap. 13, "Medieval Antisemitism."

26. Mirk, *Festial*, 114.

27. Mirk, *Festial*, 114.

28. For discussion of medieval images of Jesus' body as a parchment or page, see Mary Caroline Spalding, "The Middle English Charters of Christ," Ph.D. diss., Bryn Mawr, 1914, cited in Sarah Beckwith, *Christ's Body: Identity, Culture, and Society in Late Medieval Writings* (New York: Routledge, 1993), 152 n. 78.

29. Mirk, *Festial*, 26.

30. Pantin, *Church in the Fourteenth Century*, 191. For the pronouncement, see J. D. Mansi, *Sacrorum Conciliorum: Nova et Amplissima Collecto* (Venice: Antonio Zatta, n.d.), 2: 1010. On attitudes toward sin and confession in late medieval culture in general, see Thomas N. Tentler, *Sin and Confession on the Eve of the Reformation* (Princeton: Princeton University Press, 1977). On the place of confession in medieval English literature, see Mary F. Braswell, *The Medieval Sinner: Characterization and Confession in the Literature of the English Middle Ages* (Toronto: Associated University Press, 1983).

31. Owst, *Preaching in Medieval England*. See also Alan J. Fletcher, "The Sermon Booklets of Friar Nicholas Philip," *Medium Aevum* 55 (1986): 188–202.

32. Kieckhefer, *Unquiet Souls*, 124–35; Tentler, *Sin and Confession*, 76–79, 156–62.

33. Kieckhefer, *Unquiet Souls*, 126.

34. Kieckhefer, *Unquiet Souls*, 126–28.

35. Ross, *Sermons*, 67.

36. Ross, *Sermons*, 277.

37. MS. Add. 37677, fol. 60b, from a sermon by Richard Alkerton, quoted in Owst, *Literature and Pulpit*, 522.

38. For example, Ross, *Sermons*, 24.

39. Ross, *Sermons*, 182 (my transliteration).

40. Ross, *Sermons*, 241.

41. MS Harley 2398, fol. 186b, quoted in Owst, *Literature and Pulpit*, 508.

42. Ross, *Sermons*, 216–17 (my transliteration).

43. Ross, *Sermons*, 217 (my transliteration).

44. Weatherly, *Speculum Sacerdotale*, 65.

45. Nolloth, *Layfolk's Catechism*, 64–66.

46. Weatherly, *Speculum Sacerdotale*, 73.

47. Weatherly, *Speculum Sacerdotale*, 74.

48. Weatherly, *Speculum Sacerdotale*, 63.

49. John Mirk's *Instructions for Parish Priests*, vol. 31 of Early English Text Society, o.s. (London: Trübner, 1868), written not later than 1450, is a translation (and adaptation) of the earlier *Pars Oculi*. Like the *Layfolk's Catechism*, it covers the basics of Christian education, exhorting the priest to preach the pater noster and the creed two or three times a year to the whole parish, to teach the articles of faith, to inquire about the Ten Commandments, to make certain that parishoners understand that it is God's own body that the priest gives, and to inquire about works of mercy performed by believers.

50. Mirk, *Instructions*, 50.

51. Mirk, *Instructions*, 54.

52. Mirk, *Instructions*, 54.

53. Mirk, *Instructions*, 51.

54. Mirk, *Instructions*, 55.

55. The devil is thwarted by the cross, and Christians are invited into heaven by it. Meditation on the breadth of the cross stirs up reflection on the works of mercy (Weatherly, *Speculum Sacerdotale*, 111). As Thomas Bestul points out, one of the six causes of contrition listed in Chaucer's "Parson's Tale" is an addition to the list found in Chaucer's main source, Pennaforte's *Summa de poenitentia*: "Remembrance of the passioun that oure Lord Jhesu Crist suffred for oure synnes" ("Chaucer's Parson's Tale and the Late-Medieval Tradition of Religious Meditation," *Speculum* 64 [1989]: 607).

56. Weatherly, *Speculum Sacerdotale*, 112.

57. Mirk, *Festial*, 154.

58. Mirk, *Festial*, 187.

59. I am grateful to an anonymous reader from Oxford University Press for pointing out to me that this story of Peter's healing abilities through the falling of his shadow upon the afflicted is based on a reading of Acts 5:15.

60. Mirk, *Festial*, 75.

61. Mirk, *Festial*, 152.

62. Ross, *Sermons*, 45. For an excellent study of the christological impetus to social action, see Miri Rubin, *Charity and Community in Medieval Cambridge* (Cambridge: Cambridge University Press, 1987), 86–93.

63. Weatherly, *Speculum Sacerdotale*, 112.

64. Weatherly, *Speculum Sacerdotale*, 113.

65. Nolloth, *Layfolk's Catechism*, 70.

66. Ross, *Sermons*, 19.

67. Nolloth, *Layfolk's Catechism*, 76.

68. Nolloth, *Layfolk's Catechism*, 80.

69. Mirk, *Festial*, 123–24 (my transliteration). One manuscript omits the word "for" (124). On the origins and permutations of this tale, see Gordon H. Gerould, "The North English Homily Collection: A Study of the Manuscript Relations and the Sources in the Tales," bachelor of letters diss., Oxford University, 1902, 84–86.

70. Weatherly, *Speculum Sacerdotale*, 226.

71. Weatherly, *Speculum Sacerdotale*, 226. On the power of this-wordly actions to impact the dead in purgatory, see Hughes, *Pastors and Visionaries*, 58–59; Joel T. Rosenthal, *The Purchase of Paradise: Gift Giving and the Aristocracy, 1307–1485* (Toronto: University of Toronto Press, 1972), 11–30; and Duffy, *The Stripping of the Altars*, chap. 10.

72. Weatherly, *Speculum Sacerdotale*, 225.

73. Ross, *Sermons*, 78 (my transliteration).

74. "For þe beholding of other m(a)nnes synne, it makyth as it were a thyck myst afore þe eye of þe soule, and we may nott for þe tyme se the feyerhede of god, but yf we may beholde them with contrycion with him, with compassion on hym, and with holy desyr to god for hym" (Julian of Norwich, *A Book of Showings to the Anchoress Julian of Norwich*, ed. Edmund Colledge and James Walsh, in *Studies and Texts* 35, 2 parts [Toronto: Pontifical Institute of Medieval Studies, 1978], 686). For a translation of this text, see Julian of Norwich, *Showings*, trans. Edmund Colledge and James Walsh (New York: Paulist Press, 1978).

75. Sanford B. Meech and Hope E. Allen, eds., *The Book of Margery Kempe*, vol. 212 of Early English Text Society (New York: Oxford University Press, 1940), 31. Page number references for subsequent quotations are given in parentheses to this critical edition. For a translation of this text, see *The Book of Margery Kempe*, ed. W. Butler-Bowden (New York: Devin-Adair, 1944).

76. On the social role of anchoresses like Julian, see Ann K. Warren, *Anchorites and Their Patrons in Medieval England* (Los Angeles and Berkeley: University of California Press, 1985).

77. For a fascinating and persuasive argument about the dating of Julian's *Showings*, see Nicholas Watson, "The Composition of Julian of Norwich's *Revelation of Love*," *Speculum* 68 (1993): 637–83.

78. See Janet Coleman, *Medieval Readers and Writers 1350–1400* (New York: Columbia University Press, 1981).

79. An enlightening comparison with the fourteenth- and fifteenth-century context discussed here can be found in Ulrike Wiethaus's article on the transformative nature of suffering in the thirteenth-century Mechthild of Magdeburg; see Ulrike Wiethaus, "Suffering, Love, and Transformation in Mechthild of Magdeburg," *Listening* 22 (1987): 139–50.

80. Julian of Norwich, *Showings*, 375. All subsequent quotations are from the Long Text and subsequent references are given in parentheses to page numbers in vol 2 of Colledge and Walsh, *A Book of Showings*.

81. For example, Margery Kempe was a mother of fourteen, yet she rarely mentions

her children except to talk about the late conversion of one of her sons. She speaks often of herself as a mother but almost always as a spiritual mother to religious figures.

82. Kempe, *Book*, 21–22.

83. Julian of Norwich, *Showings*, 244.

84. "Sche had a thyng in conscyens whech sche had neuyr schewyd be-forn þat tyme in alle hyr lyfe . . . for dreed sche had of dampnacyon on þe to syde & hys [her confessor's] scharp repreuyng on þat oþer syde, þis creatur went owt of hir mende & was wondyrlye vexid & labowryd wyth spyritys half ʒer viij wekys & odde days" (Kempe, *Book*, 6–7).

85. Aelred of Rievaulx, *Aelredi Rievallensis Opera Omnia*, in Corpus Christianorum, Continuatio Medievalis 1, ed. A. Hoste and C. H. Talbot (Turnhout: Brepols, 1971), 663–73. See also John Hirsch, "Prayer and Meditation in Late Medieval England: MS Bodley 789," *Medium Aevum* 48 (1979): 55–66.

86. Hirsch, "Prayer and Meditation in Late Medieval England," 60. The Passion of Christ, and particularly the Crucifixion, is the theme of vast numbers of medieval devotions and lyrics. See Rosemary Woolf, *The English Religious Lyric in the Middle Ages* (Oxford: Clarendon Press, 1968), esp. chaps. 2 and 6. See also Douglas Gray, *Themes and Images in the Medieval English Religious Lyrics* (Boston: Routledge and Kegan Paul, 1972), esp. chap. 7. In accord with what I am suggesting is the case for the mystics considered here, Gray notes that the Passion is portrayed as the supreme expression of Christ's love and calls for a response of love from humanity (123). Many of the lyrics are "poems of meditation" (126) designed to make the worshiper present at the events surrounding Christ's Crucifixion.

87. "The loue that made hym to suffer it passith as far alle his paynes as hevyn is aboue erth; for the payne was a noble precious and wurschypfulle dede done in a tyme by the workyng of loue. And loue was without begynnyng, is and shall be without ende" (Julian of Norwich, *Showings*, 386–387). And "he shewyd to my vnderstandynge in part the blyssydfulle godhede as farforth as he wolde that tyme, strengthyng the pour soule for to understande as it may be sayde, that is to mene the endlesse loue that was without begynnyng and is and shal be evyr" (Julian of Norwich, *Showings*, 395).

88. "Thus I saw how Crist hath compassyon on vs for the cause of synne; and ryght as I was before in the passion of Crist fulfyllyd with payne and compassion, lyke in thys I was in party fulfylled with compassion of alle my evyn cristen" (Julian of Norwich, *Showings*, 408).

89. Kempe, *Book*, 62. Again, this is not without parallel in the lives of other religious figures. See, for example, the work of Henry Suso (Kieckhefer, *Unquiet Souls*, 107).

90. Hirsch, "Prayer and Meditation," 64.

91. Kempe, *Book*, 183.

92. On Jesus' spiritual thirst, see Richard Rolle, "Meditations on the Passion," in *Yorkshire Writers: Richard Rolle of Hampole and His Followers*, ed. Carl Horstmann (London: Swan Sonneschein, 1895), 101.

CHAPTER TWO

1. For background on the history of images of the suffering Jesus, see Hans Belting, *The Image and Its Public in the Middle Ages: Form and Function of Early Paintings of the Passion*, trans. Mark Bartusis and Raymond Meyer (New Rochelle, N.Y.: A. D. Caratzas, 1990). Belting

finds, for example, the source of the "Imago Pietatis" in eastern icons (7). See also Hans Belting, *Likeness and Presence: A History of the Image before the Era of Art*, trans. Edmund Jephcott (Chicago: University of Chicago Press, 1994).

2. James H. Marrow, *Passion Iconography in Northern European Art of the Late Middle Ages and Early Renaissance* (Kortrijk, Belgium: Van Ghemmert Publishing, 1979); Jeffrey Hamburger, *The Rothschild Canticles: Art and Mysticism in Flanders and the Rhineland circa 1300* (New Haven: Yale University Press, 1990), esp. chap. 5.

3. F. Harrison, *Treasures of Illumination: English Manuscripts of the Fourteenth Century (c. 1250–c. 1400)* (London: The Studio, 1937), 15.

4. "That the Tree of Jesse may be regarded as a Tree of Salvation is shown by its occasional connection with the iconography of the Tree of the Cross" (Ernest William Tristram, *English Wall Painting of the Fourteenth Century*, ed. Eileen Tristram [London: Routledge and Kegan Paul, 1955], 76). See Emile Mâle, *The Gothic Image: Religious Art in France of the Thirteenth Century*, trans. Dora Nussey (New York: Harper, 1958), 208, and Gertrud Schiller, *Iconography of Christian Art*, trans. Janet Seligman (Greenwich, Conn.: New York Graphic Society, 1971), 1: 15–22.

5. Lambeth Palace Library MS 233, f. 15 (1300–1310).

6. British Library MS Add. 49622, f. 8 (c. 1310–c. 1320).

7. See also Lambeth Palace Library MS 233, f. 15.

8. British Library Yates Thompson 14, f. 120 (c. 1325–1330, and early fifteenth century). As we shall see, this Psalm is often illustrated with an image of the Trinity.

9. Bodleian Library MS Douce 366, f. 55 (c. 1310–1325). The link between the Psalms and interpretation of the New Testament itself is enacted in the elaborate N-Town dramatization of Jesus' refusal to speak when he is brought before Pilate (see chap. 4).

10. Roger S. Wieck, *Time Sanctified: The Book of Hours in Medieval Art and Life* (New York: George Braziller, 1988), 27. On Books of Hours, also see L. M. J. Delaisse, "The Importance of Books of Hours for the History of the Medieval Book," in *Gatherings in Honor of Dorothy E. Miner*, ed. Ursula E. McCracken, Lillian Randall, and Richard Randall, Jr. (Baltimore: Walters Art Gallery, 1974), esp. 203–210; and John Harthan, *The Book of Hours* (New York: Thomas Y. Crowell, 1977).

11. "The Mirror of St. Edmund," in *Yorkshire Writers: Richard Rolle of Hampole*, ed. Carl Horstmann (New York: Macmillan, 1895), 254.

12. The Visitation occurs at lauds; the Nativity at prime; the coming of the Shepherds at terce; the coming of the Magi at sext; the Presentation at none; the Flight to Egypt at vespers; and the Coronation of the Virgin, the Flight into Egypt, or the Massacre of the Innocents at compline (Janet Backhouse, *Books of Hours* [London: The British Library, 1985], 15; Harthan, *Book of Hours*, 26).

13. Wieck, *Time Sanctified*, 66; Robert G. Calkins, *Illuminated Books of the Middle Ages* (Ithaca, N.Y.: Cornell University Press, 1983), 248.

14. Cambridge University Library MS Dd. 8.2, f. 27v–f. 37v (c. 1300–1310).

15. Cambridge University Library MS Dd. 8.2, f. 27v. For an interpretation of an archer and victim in a mural painting at Brinay, see Marcia Kupfer, *Romanesque Wall Painting in Central France: The Politics of Narrative* (New Haven: Yale University Press, 1993), 114. On marginal art, see Michael Camille, *Image on the Edge: The Margins of Medieval Art* (Cambridge: Harvard University Press, 1992), esp. chap. 1.

16. Lucy Freeman Sandler, *Gothic Manuscripts: 1285–1385*, 2 vols., vol. 5 of *A Survey of Manuscripts Illuminated in the British Isles* (London: Harvey Miller, 1986), 35.

17. Matins was sometimes held at midnight or 2:30 A.M., and lauds at 3:00 or 5:00 A.M. (Calkins, *Illuminated Books*, 207).

18. Wieck, *Time Sanctified*, 28; Virginia Reinburg, "Prayer and the Book of Hours," in *Time Sanctified*, 42.

19. On the significance of readings which emerge from the pairing of depictions, see Ursula Nilgren's argument about the eucharistic meanings of portrayals of the Adoration of the Magi. Among other examples, she finds the Adoration of the Magi on the lintel of a church portal situated between the Annunciation and the Crucifixion, and she notes the association between these scenes and the scene of the Last Supper which fills the typanum above. A depiction of the Man of Sorrows, which Nilgren interprets as "the essence of both the sacrifice on the Cross and the offering of the Mass" (313), stands just below a portrayal of the Adoration of the Magi in a lunette in the cloister at Brixen (Ursula Nilgen, "The Epiphany and the Eucharist: On the Interpretation of Eucharistic Motifs in Medieval Epiphany Scenes," *Art Bulletin* 49 [1967]: 311–16).

20. Wieck, *Time Sanctified*, 89.

21. British Library MS Add. 16968 (c. 1380–1390) (Sandler, *Gothic Manuscripts*, 167–69).

22. British Library MS Add. 16968, f. 19 (Sandler, *Gothic Manuscripts*, 167).

23. British Library MS Add. 16968, f. 20 (Sandler, *Gothic Manuscripts*, 168).

24. British Library MS Add. 16968, f. 21 (Sandler, *Gothic Manuscripts*, 168). This same pairing is apparent, for example, in the fourteenth-century mural Life of Christ sequence by "Barna" de Siena in the right aisle of the Collegiata, San Gimignano, where the Massacre of the Innocents is artistically and architecturally paired with the Crucifixion. Borsook argues that the Flight into Egypt "was even shifted out of chronological order" so that the Massacre of the Innocents could be paired with the Crucifixion (Borsook, *Mural Painters of Tuscany*, 45 [and plate 54]).

25. Cambridge University Library MS Dd. 4.17, f. 11v–12 (c. 1320–1324); Corpus Christi College MS 53, ff. 15v–16 (early fourteenth century).

26. Cambridge University Library MS Dd. 4.17, f. 12.

27. On gestures in medieval art, see Moshe Barasch, *Gestures of Despair in Medieval and Early Renaissance Art* (New York: New York University Press, 1976), and idem, *Giotto and the Language of Gesture* (Cambridge: Cambridge University Press, 1987).

28. Cambridge University Library MS Dd. 4.17, f. 11v.

29. Westminster Abbey MS 37 (1383–1384), f. 120.

30. Trinity College Library MS B.10.15 (c. 1370–1385), f. 33v. See also the depiction of the First and Second Persons of the Trinity in Bodleian Library MS Rawlinson G. 185, f. 236 (1348–1374).

31. Fitzwilliam Museum, MS 242, f. 28, (c. 1300–1308).

32. Bodleian Library MS Digby 227, f. 113v (1461). As Martin Kauffmann has pointed out in conversation, this illumination may portray a literal rendering of Luke 23:46: "Father, into thy hands I commend my spirit!," but I would add, significantly, that through the medium of art the creator of this image interprets Jesus' exclamation to be an expression of trinitarian unity.

33. Westminster Abbey MS 37, f. 156v.

34. Pierpont Morgan Library M. 107, f. 142 (1311–1332) (Sandler, *Gothic Manuscripts*, 84–86). For a helpful discussion of the medieval mass, see Duffy, *Stripping of the Altars*, chap. 3, which also emphasizes the "physical realism" so central to medieval religiosity.

35. Bodleian Library MS Digby 227, ff. 113v–114.

36. Westminster Abbey MS 37, f. 156v, 157.

37. Trinity College Library MS B.11.3, f. 123 (c. 1380–c. 1400).

38. See, for example, M. R. James, "Pictor in Carmine," *Archaeologia* 94 (1951): 161.

39. Westminster Abbey MS 37, f. 156v; British Library MS Arundel 83 II (c. 1308 and c. 1339), f. 132; British Library MS Yates Thompson 13, f. 122v (c. 1325–c. 1335).

40. Bodleian Library MS Laud Misc. 165, f. 548 (c. 1350–before 1375).

41. Siegfried Wenzel, ed. and trans., *Fasciculus Morum: A Fourteenth-Century Preacher's Handbook* (University Park: Pennsylvania State University Press, 1989), 209. "[Pelicanus], post compassione motus corpus suum usque ad cor rostro perforat, ex cuius sanguine aspersi reviviscunt" (206–208).

42. Wenzel, *Fasciculus Morum*, 209. "Reversa sic peccatores spiritualiter mortuos Dei offencione per compassionem tamen motus, quia non vult mortem peccatoris, effundendo sanguinem cordis sui benedicti ad vitam gracie reconciliavit" (208).

43. British Library MS Arundel 83 II, f. 125v; Westminster Abbey MS 37, f. 156v.

44. British Library MS Add. 47682, f. 3v (c. 1320–c. 1330).

45. British Library MS Add. 49622, f. 7.

46. British Library MS Yates Thompson 13, f. 122v.

47. Bodleian Library MS Gough liturg. 8, f. 61v (c. 1300–c. 1310).

48. Trinity College Library MS O.4.16, f. 113v (mid- and late thirteenth and early fourteenth centuries) (Sandler, *Gothic Manuscripts*, 34–35).

49. British Library MS Add. 16968, f. 22v.

50. Glasgow University Library Hunter 231, p. 62 (c. 1325–c. 1335).

51. Glasgow University Library Hunter 231, p. 89.

52. See Nancy G. Saraisi, *Medieval and Early Renaissance Medicine: An Introduction to Knowledge and Practice* (Chicago: University of Chicago Press, 1990), 105. On the feeding imagery associated with medieval iconography of Jesus, see Caroline Walker Bynum, *Fragmentation and Redemption: Essays on Gender and the Human Body in Medieval Religion* (New York: Zone Books, 1991), 117–38.

53. Fitzwilliam Museum MS 259, f. 3v (c. 1350–c. 1360); Trinity College Library B.10.15, f. 7v.

54. Wenzel, *Fasciculus Morum*, 221. "Et adverte: Caro enim hominis est tenerior quam caro bruti animalis, et inter homines caro femine tenerior est quam masculi, et inter feminas tenerior est caro virginis quam corrupte. Set caro Christi fuit de purissimis sanguinibus Virginis Benedicte assumpta et propagata, et ipsemet in purissima virginitate usque ad mortem permansit" (220).

55. Trinity College Library MS O.4.16, f. 113v. See also British Library MS Arundel 83 II, f. 116v and British Library MS Add. 47682, f. 32v.

56. British Library MS Yates Thompson 13, f. 122v.

57. Wenzel, *Fasciculus Morum*, 255. "Et nota quod Christus . . . venit in terris . . . ut medicus bonus ad nos sanandum, secundo venit ut pia mater ad nos pascendum, tercio venit ut fortis miles ad nos salvandum" (254).

58. Bodleian Library MS Auct. D.4.4, f. 209 (c. 1380).

59. Bodleian Library MS Digby 227, f. 113v.

60. Glasgow University Library Hunter 231, p. 53.

61. Bonaventure, "The Privity of the Passion," in Horstmann, *Yorkshire Writers*, 204.

62. Bodleian Library MS Auct. D.4.4, f. 169.

63. British Library MS Royal 6.E.VI–6.VII, f. 14 (c. 1360); British Library MS Yates Thompson 14, f. 120.

64. Wenzel, *Fasciculus Morum*, 209. "Set timeo michi quod est de multis sicut de filio frenetico, qui quanto plus pia mater eius infirmitatem deplorat, tanto magis ipse in risum et cachinnaciones prorumpit nichil matri compaciendo. Reversa sic Christo pro peccatoribus lacrimas fundente et sanguinem [minuente], ipse non tantum sicut ingrati sue passionis obliti, verum eciam tamquam frenetici ipsum derident et blasphemant. . . . Non sic, karissimi, set cum universis creaturis passioni sue compati debemus. Sol enim sibi compaciens in sua morte radios suos retraxit, terra mota est, petre scisse sunt, monumenta aperiebantur, et ob compassionem [corpora] sanctorum surrexerunt" (208).

65. John Phillips, *The Reformation of Images: Destruction of Art in England, 1535–1660* (Berkeley and Los Angeles: University of California Press, 1973), 21–26.

66. M. D. Anderson, *Drama and Imagery in English Medieval Churches* (Cambridge: Cambridge University Press, 1963).

67. Phillips, *Reformation of Images*, 27.

68. Tristram, *Fourteenth Century*, 11.

69. Phillips, *Reformation of Images*, 27.

70. Tristram notes that there are relatively few scenes from Christ's ministry (Tristram, *Fourteenth Century*, 81). (This is also the case in Books of Hours and Psalters, alerting scholars to possible connections between book illumination themes and mural themes.)

71. Wenzel, *Fasciculus Morum*, 201. "Ista ergo passio quam pro nobis sustinuit ad perfectam caritatem reducet" (200).

72. The narration of these stories in pictures was much more readily accessible to the majority of believers than was the Latin Mass during which they were often advised to pray the Pater Noster and the Ave Maria. But seeing the stories in pictures also influenced the way the preaching and readings were heard. As Kupfer and Michael Camille have demonstrated, "Medieval images privilege the informed and especially the literate viewer" (Kupfer, *Romanesque Wall Paintings*, 15). In the medieval context, though, we need to consider the varieties of literacy in the culture; we must not, for example, underestimate the educative functions of sermons and readings which were heard by medieval congregations. As Camille observes, "Medieval pictures cannot be separated from what is a total experience of communication involving sight, sound, action, and physical expression" (Michael Camille, "Seeing and Reading: Some Visual Implications of Medieval Literacy and Illiteracy," *Art History* 43 [1985]: 26–49). See also the article by Lawrence Duggan, "Was Art Really the 'Book of the Illiterate,'" to note the importance of word-laden contexts for conveying the meaning of art (*Word and Image* 5 [1989]: 227–51).

73. Wenzel, *Fasciculus Morum*, 201. "Unde notandum quod maximum remedium est eius sanguinis effusio eo quod inducit peccatorem ad dolorem contricionis, ad pudorem confessionis, et ad laborem satisfactionis" (200).

74. Marilyn Aronberg Lavin, *The Place of Narrative: Mural Decoration in Italian Churches,*

431–1600 (Chicago: University of Chicago Press, 1990), 4–5. This excellent study of patterns in cycles of monumental wall paintings explores the means by which mural narratives go beyond being narratives of well-known biblical stories to address also issues of "dogma, morality, and political power" (6). Kupfer also explores strategies by which painters carried out their construction of narrative cycles (*Romanesque Wall Paintings*, chap. 4, esp. 61–66). Like Lavin, Kupfer argues that wall paintings are not "passive surface decorations" but rather carefully choreographed presentations integrally linked with their architectural settings (Marcia Kupfer, "Spiritual Passage and Pictorial Strategy in the Romanesque Frescoes at Vicq," *Art Bulletin* 68 [1986]: 52). See also Eve Borsook, *The Mural Painters of Tuscany: From Cimabue to Andrea Del Sarto*, 2d ed. (Oxford: Clarendon Press, 1980), xxiii, xxx.

75. A. Caiger-Smith, *English Medieval Mural Paintings* (Oxford: Clarendon Press, 1963), 18; Tristram, *Fourteenth Century*.

76. On this practice, see Lavin, *Place of Narrative*, 48, 61, 139, and Schiller, *Iconography*, 1:37, 48.

77. In discussing monumental painting cycles, Kupfer observes, "Such works, by framing their viewers' present in relation to a common past and future, make their audience into a community" (*Romanesque Wall Painting*, 16). An analogy here can be made to the common fourteenth-century practice of decorating refectories with murals of the Last Supper (Borsook, *Mural Painters of Tuscany*, 87). Through the artistic construction of their eating area, monks and nuns are invited into the company of the friends and disciples of Jesus at the Last Supper.

78. Lavin, *The Place of Narrative*, 75. Kupfer points out that the left-to-right reading order of mural paintings (such as this series at Chalgrove) indicates the primacy of the word even in artistic presentation (*Romanesque Wall Painting*, 16). (It is important to note, though, that we find this left-to-right order only in some, and certainly not in all, mural painting cycles.)

79. Kupfer, *Romanesque Wall Paintings*, 135. See also note 19.

80. Tristram, *Fourteenth Century*, 154.

81. Tristram, *Fourteenth Century*, 155.

82. R. W. Heath-Whyte, "Brochure of St. Mary-the-Virgin, Chalgrove," n.p.

83. Lavin notes the same symbolic upward movement from the Entombment to the Descent into Limbo and then upward to the Resurrection and Ascension at the Collegiata, San Gimignano (Lavin, *The Place of Narrative*, 77).

84. Tristram, *Fourteenth Century*, 154.

85. The feast days of these two saints were frequently celebrated together on June 24, though in some contexts the celebrations were separated and the feast of John the Evangelist was celebrated on December 27 and that of John the Baptist on June 24.

86. Hans Belting notes the correspondence between the calendar cycle of feast days and the image cycles in churches (Belting, *Likeness and Presence*, 174).

87. Ross, *Sermons*, 228. On the recognition of royalty portrayed in Adoration of Magi scenes, see Kupfer, *Romanesque Wall Painting*, 111.

88. Mirk, *Festial*, 49.

89. See note 24. Lavin points to the identification in the Upper Church of San Francesco in Assisi of St. Francis with Christ, communicated by the placing of a mural

Crucifixion scene directly above a depiction of Francis's death and apotheosis (Lavin, *The Place of Narrative*, 39).

90. In discussing the scenes of the Adoration of the Magi, the Baptism of Christ, and the Wedding at Cana in French Romanesque murals, Kupfer also recognizes the affirmations of divinity present in these scenes: "Led to a manger by the Star, the Magi recognized and adored the incarnate God in a human infant. In the waters of the Jordan, Christ revealed himself as the Son within the Trinity. At Cana, Christ demonstrated that he was God" (Kupfer, *Romanesque Wall Painting*, 108).

91. St. Pega's brochure, no author, n.d.

92. Tristram, *Fourteenth Century*, 234.

93. Tristram, *Fourteenth Century*, 234.

94. Tristram, *Fourteenth Century*, 235.

95. Tristram, *Fourteenth Century*, 160.

96. Tristram, *Fourteenth Century*, 161.

97. Tristram, *Fourteenth Century*, 161.

98. St. Peter Ad Vincula houses a number of other fourteenth-century paintings including an elaborate Standing Virgin and Child at the eastern end of the north wall (fig. 2.35).

99. Tristram, *Fourteenth Century*, 78. Tristram says this with some degree of speculation since, as he points out, most retables were destroyed.

100. In the tomb of Duke Humphreys at St. Albans Abbey, there are faint remains of a large Crucifixion scene in which angels collect Jesus' flowing blood in chalices. (My thanks to Peter Moore and J. J. Brookes for making it possible for me to see this painting.)

101. Tristram, *Fourteenth Century*, 79.

102. Tristram, *Fourteenth Century*, 25.

103. Tristram, *Fourteenth Century*, 80, 188.

104. Tristram, *Fourteenth Century*, 175.

105. Tristram notes that with one exception at Bradwell in Essex (where the depiction is in a window splay "at the eastern end of the chancel, below an abbreviated Last Judgment on the soffit"), images of the Trinity "are located on the east wall, whether of a church or of a chantry chapel" (*Fourteenth Century*, 81).

106. Tristram, *Fourteenth Century*, 67.

107. A similar scene is visible in the Abbey Church of St. Peter and St. Paul in Dorchester, where a painted Crucifixion is visible above the altar in what was the fourteenth-century part of the church. This painting was extensively restored in the nineteenth century, as the recently repainted blessing posture of Jesus' left hand suggests, although the general tone of the painting, with the presence of the sun and the moon, indicates the cosmic significance of Jesus' suffering and death and, along with the Mary and John figures (although in the case of John the hand posture is reversed at All Saints, Turvey), evokes the type of painting evident in churches like Turvey. There is further evidence of contemporary wall painting in this church but little indication of the precise nature of the scenes.

108. Caiger-Smith, *Mural Paintings*, 31.

109. Caiger-Smith, *Mural Paintings*, 32.

110. Wenzel, *Fasciculus Morum*, 205.

111. Wenzel, *Fasciculus Morum*, 205, 207. "Set certe hoc non obstante ipse tamquam gratissimus et fidelissimus cessare pulsando non desistit et clamare, ['Beholde myn woundes,' etc.] O igitur, anima humana, erubesce, et . . . '[a]perite' . . . anime affectiones erga Deum et eius beneficia, que tam fortiter per peccatum sunt serate, et hoc per claves contricionis, confessionis, caritatis, et amoris" (204, 206).

112. Caiger-Smith, *Mural Paintings*, 53.

113. Caiger-Smith, *Mural Paintings*, 53.

114. Wenzel, *Fasciculus Morum*, 193. " . . . Dilectio et caritas erga proximum in <necessariorum> supportacione est. . . . Et si queras que est illa, respondeo quod modo mortuos sepelire, modo infirmos pascere et curare, sicut fecit Thobias; modo eciam pauperes hospitare, sicut fecit beata Martha; modo nudos vestire, sicut fecit beatus Martinus, et cetera huiusmodi. Et ista dicuntur opera misericordie. . . . Qui subvenerit proximo indigenti, modo dando, modo accomodando, modo remittendo, certe perfecta [caritas] manet in illo, sicut habetur secundum Iohannem <canonica> ubi supra: 'Deus caritas est, et qui manet in caritate, in Deo manet et Deus in eo'" (192). (Note: Wenzel's use of angle brackets signals variations among the manuscripts he considers.)

115. Caiger-Smith, *Mural Paintings*, 54.

116. Caiger-Smith, *Mural Paintings*, 55.

117. While the role of the Virgin is not a focus of my study here, it is clear to me that the figure of the Virgin and the many depictions of the Annunciation (of which there are almost as many as of the Crucifixion), along with the many narratives about the Virgin's life, must have influenced and been influenced by the presence of the images of saints. In the earlier sections of this chapter, we have seen how images of the suffering Jesus must have impacted viewers. I would suggest that something similar obtains in the case of Mary, but I will not explore the nature of the rhetorical appeal of Marian images here. On Mary and medieval piety, see Eamon Duffy, "Mater Dolorosa, Mater Misericordiae," *New Blackfriars* 69 (1988): 210–27.

CHAPTER THREE

1. Arthur F. Leach, "Some English Plays and Players," in *An English Miscellany Presented to Dr. Furnivall in Honour of His Seventy-Fifth Birthday*, ed. W. P. Ker, A. S. Napier, and W. W. Skeat (Oxford: Clarendon Press, 1901), 205–34. As the text list suggests, and as Leach points out, there was often a correspondence between the event dramatized in the plays and the nature of the work of the performers. For example, the cooks performed the Harrowing of Hell "because they were in the habit of taking things out of the fire" (219). Often the wealthiest guilds, the Mercers and Goldsmiths in many places, dramatized the sumptuous play of the three Magi (219).

2. See Marianne G. Briscoe, "Preaching and Medieval Drama," in *Contexts for Early English Drama*, ed. M. Briscoe and J. Coldewey (Bloomington: Indiana University Press, 1989), 150–72, on the difficulty of determining the authorship of the plays. Lawrence M. Clopper's "Florescence in the North's Tradition of Drama and Ceremony," *Fifteenth Century Studies* 9 (1986): 249–55, suggests that there is "little evidence of clerical presence in the development of the drama" (253) but acknowledges that scholars stand on both sides

of this issue. He suggests O. B. Hardison, Jr., *Christian Rite and Christian Drama in the Middle Ages* (Baltimore: Johns Hopkins University Press, 1965), as support of independent development and E. Catherine Dunn, "Popular Devotion in the Vernacular Drama of Medieval England," *Medievalia and Humanistica* 4 (1973): 3–76. On the connection between the English cycle plays and Continental cycle plays, see Robert Potter, "The Unity of Medieval Drama: European Contexts for Early English Dramatic Traditions," in Briscoe, ed., *Contexts of Early English Drama*, 41–55.

3. Rosemary Woolf, *The English Mystery Plays* (Berkeley: University of California Press, 1972); Martin Stevens, *Four Middle English Mystery Cycles* (Princeton: Princeton University Press, 1987). See also Clifford Davidson, *From Creation to Doom: The York Cycle of Mystery Plays* (New York: AMS Press, 1984), for an astute analysis of the mystery cycles and insightful linkage of them with medieval iconography. At the other extreme, Alexander Franklin's *Seven Miracle Plays* (New York: Oxford University Press, 1963) states, "They [the plays] are not so much dramatized versions of Bible stories as imaginative interpretations of them, and a simple, unsophisticated view of the Bible they reveal, too" (15).

4. Middle English citations are from K. S. Block, ed., *Ludus Coventriae; or, The Plaie Called Corpus Christi*, vol. 120 of Early English Text Society, extra series (London: Oxford University Press, 1922). References are given first by the initial N to the N-Town cycle and then to page and line numbers in Block (N 262/907–908; 263/935; 943–944). Modern English translations and spellings may be found in R. T. Davies, *The Corpus Christi Play of the English Middle Ages* (Towota, N.J.: Rowman and Littlefield, 1972). Middle English citations from the York Mystery Cycle are from Richard Beadle, ed., *The York Plays* (London: E. Arnold, 1982). References are given first by the initial Y to the York cycle and then to page and line numbers in Beadle.

5. Elaine Scarry, *The Body in Pain: The Making and Unmaking of the World* (New York: Oxford University Press, 1985), 212. Scarry generally speaks of "existence" being confirmed through bodies. Given the contexts of assumed belief in which many of the scriptural narratives are told, I think the dynamics are expressive of the oscillation between divine presence and divine absence rather than between belief and unbelief.

6. Scarry, *Body in Pain*, 194. Although Scarry does not cite Walter Brueggemann's *The Land: Place as Gift, Promise, and Challenge in Biblical Faith* (Philadelphia: Fortress Press, 1977), he provides an excellent example of expressions of divine presence and absence manifested through the land.

7. Scarry, *The Body in Pain*, 203.

8. Scarry, *The Body in Pain*, 183.

9. Scarry, *The Body in Pain*, 200.

10. Scarry, *The Body in Pain*, 209.

11. Scarry, *The Body in Pain*, 213.

12. Mark I. Wallace, *Fragments of the Spirit: Nature, Violence, and the Renewal of Creation* (New York: Continuum, 1996), 188. See also Graham Shaw, *The Cost of Authority: Manipulation and Freedom in the New Testament* (Philadelphia: Fortress Press, 1983).

13. Scarry, *The Body in Pain*, 214.

14. Scarry, *The Body in Pain*, 217.

15. Scarry, *The Body in Pain*, 215.

16. Woolf, *English Mystery Plays*, 65–66.

17. Woolf also notes the typological significance of the story, *English Mystery Plays*, 147.

18. N 45/57–58.

19. Erich Auerbach, *Scenes from the Drama of European Literature*, 2d ed. (Minneapolis: University of Minnesota Press, 1984), 53.

20. Auerbach, *Scenes from the Drama of European Literature*, 53.

21. Auerbach, *Scenes from the Drama of European Literature*, 58.

22. While the N-Town and York plays make great use of prefiguring to point to the suffering of Jesus (and York even more extensively than N-Town, as it includes the play of Moses and the Pharoah, for example), the N-Town relies more heavily on the Old Testment prophecies to describe explicitly the suffering of Jesus. The York play prophecies emphasize that Jesus Christ will be the king and Savior, and while New Testament figures like the shepherds and Simeon allude to Jesus' suffering, the detailed *prophetic* attention to suffering does not occur until Christ greets the prophets in the Harrowing of Hell play.

23. "Or he be borne in burgh hereby, / Balaham, brothir, me haue herde say. . . . And als the texte it tellis clerly / By witty lerned men or oure lay, / With his blissid bloode he shulde vs by" (Y 129/13–19).

24. See Norman Perrin, *The New Testament*, 2d ed. (New York: Harcourt Brace Jovanovich, 1982), 240.

25. Woolf, *English Mystery Plays*, 257. See V. A. Kolve, "The Passion and Resurrection in Play and Game," in *The Play Called Corpus Christi* (Stanford: Stanford University Press, 1966), chap. 8.

26. "The circumstances of Christ's death are to emphasize the brutality of the Jews in an age when Jews were persecuted as heretics" (Edelgard E. DuBruck, "The Death of Christ in French Passion Plays of the Late Middle Ages: Its Aspects and Sociological Implications," in *Dies Illa: Death in the Middle Ages*, ed. Jane H. M. Taylor [Liverpool: F. Cairns, 1984], 89). My thanks to Donald Duclow for pointing this article out to me. See also F. Heer, *The Medieval World* (New York: New American Library, 1963), chap. 13.

27. Clifford Davidson argues that the attention to detail in the plays is a strategy for establishing credibility (Clifford Davidson, "Northern Spirituality and the Late Medieval Drama of York," in *The Spirituality of Western Christendom*, ed. E. Rozanne Elder [Kalamazoo: Cistercian Publications, 1976], 129).

28. Woolf, *English Mystery Plays*, 261.

29. Y 316–317/49–60.

30. Woolf, *English Mystery Plays*, 261–62.

31. Kolve, *The Play Called Corpus Christi*, 190.

32. Kolve, *The Play Called Corpus Christi*, 199–200.

33. Stevens, *Four Middle English Mystery Cycles*, 30.

34. James, "Drama and Ritual," 20. Martin Stevens notes the use of anachronisms as another strategy for bringing the events dramatized in the plays into the medieval present (Stevens, *Four Middle English Mystery Cycles*, 77).

35. In the York cycle, one of the most vivid recountings is that of Thomas in the Assumption play (Y 392/1ff.). The centrality of Thomas in the plays is striking and correlates with the importance of the affirmation of Jesus Christ's physicality in the medieval drama.

36. "Þerfore all þis my sisteres hende, / Þat ȝe forth preche" (Y 351/262–263).

37. DuBruck, "The Death of Christ in French Passion Plays of the Late Middle Ages," 89.

38. Davidson, *Creation to Doom*, 124.

39. Although works like Gail McMurray Gibson, *The Theater of Devotion: East Anglian Drama and Society in the Late Middle Ages* (Chicago: University of Chicago Press, 1989), are not wrong in pointing to the centrality of the incarnation in the plays, their perception of the theological meaning of the cycle plays would be deepened by attention to the centrality of the medieval understanding of Jesus Christ as both human and divine.

40. Julian of Norwich, *Showings*, 375 (see discussion in chapter 1).

41. Y 209/134–140.

42. Y 215/365–375.

43. "Bothe god and man he doth hym calle" (N 246/445).

44. Woolf, *English Mystery Plays*, 167.

45. This struggle appears in the York cycle in the Harrowing of Hell play in which Satan tries to persuade Jesus that he contradicts the bidding of God and the words of the prophets by freeing the souls (Y 340/277ff.).

46. Gustaf Aulén, *Christus Victor: An Historical Study of the Three Main Types of the Idea of the Atonement* (New York: Macmillan Publishing, 1969). The following discussion draws from chaps. 3–5.

47. Aulén, *Christus Victor*, 50.

48. Aulén, *Christus Victor*, 52.

49. Aulén points out that the New Testament lends itself to ransom language in speaking of Christ as the one "Who gave Himself a ransom for all" (1 Timothy ii.6). He cites other examples as well, including Mark 10:45; Ephesians 1:7; I Peter 1:18 (*Christus Victor*, 73).

50. Again, Aulén suggests scriptural sources here, including the Epistle to the Hebrews 8:6 and 9:15ff. (*Christus Victor*, 77).

51. Aulén, *Christus Victor*, 82.

52. Aulén, *Christus Victor*, 83.

53. Anselm, "Why God Became Man," in *A Scholastic Miscellany: Anselm to Ockham*, ed. Eugene R. Fairweather (New York: Macmillan, 1970), 176.

54. "Now it seems to us that we have been justified by the blood of Christ and reconciled to God in this way: through this unique act of grace manifested to us—in that his Son has taken upon himself our nature and preserved therein in teaching us by word and example even unto death—he has more fully bound us to himself by love; with the result that our hearts should be enkindled by such a gift of divine grace, and true charity should not now shrink from enduring anything for him" (Peter Abelard, *Exposition of the Epistle to the Romans*, in Fairweather, *A Scholastic Miscellany*, 283). ("Nobis autem uidetur quod in hoc iustificati sumus in sanguine Christi et Deo reconciliati, quod per hanc singularem gratiam nobis exhibitam quod Filius suus nostram susceperit naturam et in ipsa nos tam uerbo quam exemplo instituendo usque ad mortem perstitit, nos sibi amplius per amorem adstrixit, ut tanto diuinae gratiae accensi beneficio, nihil iam tolerare propter ipsum uera reformidet caritas" [Peter Abelard, *Commentaria in Epistolam Pauli ad Romanos*, in Eligii M. Buytaert, ed., *Petri Abaelardi, Opera Theologica*, Corpus Christianorum, Continuatio Mediaevalis, 11 (Turnhout: Brepols, 1969), 117].)

55. DuBruck, "The Death of Christ," 88.

56. John R. Elliott, Jr., "Medieval Acting," in *Contexts for Early English Drama*, 242; see also 238–251.

57. The York Vinter's Play is missing, but I think it is reasonable to speculate that this play may have made some references to the sacrament of marriage. In what follows, I focus on the sacraments of penance and Eucharist, although the theme of baptism is closely connected with penance in the figure of John the Baptist, who in the N-Town cycle charges people to repent of their sins and reconcile themselves to God with contrition and penance. He assures his listeners that God is ready to grant mercy to those who seek it (N 192/147). The York Baptism play teaches the necessity of baptism for reconciliation with the Divine. Jesus announces that "Mankynde may noȝt vnbaptymde go / Te endles blys" (Y 183/90–91). In keeping with the portrayal of Jesus as an exemplar throughout the York cycle, Jesus describes himself in the Baptism play as a "myrroure" for people who should "haue my doyng in ther mynde" (Y 184/94); he himself receives baptism so that those who imitate him should do the same. Jesus institutes the sacrament of baptism and endows it with its ongoing power when he invests baptism with divine presence. "My will is þis, þat fro þis day / Þe vertue of my baptyme dwelle / In baptyme-watir euere and ay, / Mankynde to taste, / Thurgh my grace þerto to take alway / Þe haly gaste" (Y 184/100–104). This play introduces baptism as a sine qua non of the reconciliation between God and humans, a necessary component of the means by which persons avail themselves of the offer of reconciliation which God extends to them. Those who refuse to participate in the process are not welcomed into the heavenly world.

58. One of the reasons the Noah's Ark play may have appeared is that traditionally the Ark was understood as a prefiguration of the church (Auerbach, *Scenes from the Drama of European Literature*, 38).

59. Jean Delumeau, *Sin and Fear: The Emergence of a Western Guilt Culture, 13th–18th Centuries*, trans. Eric Nicholson (New York: St. Martin's Press, 1990).

60. For other examples of medieval texts which make this connection, see T. F. Simmons and H. E. Nolloth, eds., *The Layfolks' Catechism: Archbishop Thoresby's Instruction for the People*, vol. 118 of Early English Text Society, o.s. (London: Kegan Paul, Trench, Trübner, 1901), 58–59, 65–67; and John Mirk, *Instructions for Parish Priests*, vol. 31 of Early English Text Society, o.s. (London: Trübner, 1868), 24–29. Robert Potter, in *The English Morality Play: Origins, History and Influence of a Dramatic Tradition* (London: Routledge and Kegan Paul, 1975), suggests that medieval morality plays such as *Everyman, King of Life, Castle of Perseverance, Wisdom,* and *Mankind* are linked by the affirmation that although sin is inevitable, repentance is always possible. The plays focus on repentance: "why it is necessary, how it may be carried out and what it will accomplish" (16).

61. Tentler, *Sin and Confession*, 300.

62. Theresa Coletti, "Sacrament and Sacrifice in the N-Town Passion," *Mediaevalia* 7 (1981): 245.

63. Clifford Davidson, *Creation to Doom*, 105–106, sees Peter and Judas as prefiguring the two thieves on the crosses beside Jesus.

64. Eleanor Prosser argues that in general the cycle plays tend to "stress the commemorative nature of the feast as the last meal together" and to neglect what she sees as a focal point in the Hegge plays—namely, an emphasis on "the institution of the Sacrament, on Christ's love offering of his heart's blood for man's sins" (141). While Prosser sees the

centrality of repentance in the cycle plays, she overlooks the emphasis on love as the motivation for Jesus' suffering and as the source of the sacrament of the Eucharist, which I suggest is so central to the N-Town play (Eleanor Prosser, *Drama and Religion in the English Mystery Plays* [Stanford: Stanford University Press, 1966]).

65. Coletti, "Sacrament and Sacrifice," 257.

66. This theme of love of neighbor appears in the play alongside virulent anti-Semitism, suggesting a narrow interpretation of "neighbor." Some medieval thinkers such as Margery Kempe seem to have recognized the possibly wider implications of the idea of neighbor love although generally with the intention of "Christianizing" those who belonged to other religion traditions (see chapter 4). For an important discussion of Christian models for interacting with other religious traditions, see Richard Southern, *Western Views of Islam in the Middle Ages* (Cambridge: Harvard University Press, 1962). Although the Ten Commandments are significant in both the N-Town and York cycles, Jesus teaches a way of being in the world that centers on the first two commandments: "Þan schulde we God honnoure / With all oure myght and mayne, / And loue wele ilke a neghboure / Right as oureselfe, certayne" (Y 178/168). These commandments encapsulate the others and incorporate all believers need to learn to live in a fitting way in the world (Y 180/259–260).

67. N 376/79–90.

68. Kolve, *The Play Called Corpus Christi*, 239. Eamon Duffy also observes that it is not "professions of piety" but "actions toward the poor and weak" which distinguish the saved from the damned in the medieval schema of salvation (Duffy, *Stripping the Altars*, 357).

69. Tentler, *Sin and Confession*, 263.

70. Kolve, *The Play Called Corpus Christi*, 268.

71. Potter, *English Morality Play*, 10–11. The ritualistic role of these plays in creating Christian social unity illuminates their danger as well: at times these plays cultivated ecclesiastical unity at the expense of those, in particular Jews and Christian dissenters, who did not share the model of salvation projected by the plays.

72. "The art of late medieval drama is, in one sense, the art of objectifying universal ideas in the particularity of dramatic action" (Robert Potter, "Divine and Human Justice," in *Aspects of Early English Drama*, ed. Paula Neuss [Cambridge: D. S. Brewer, 1983], 129).

CHAPTER FOUR

1. From the *Ancrene Wisse*, in Bella Millett and Jocelyn Wogan-Browne, eds., *Medieval English Prose for Women: Selections from the Katherine Group and Ancrene Wisse* (New York: Oxford University Press, 1990), 117.

2. Although this chapter manifests my disgreement with Edith Wyschogrod's assertion that "self-renunciation to the point of effacement is the mark or trace of saintly labor," I find her notion of body as "text," or "surface of writing," to be helpful and important (Edith Wyschogrod, *Saints and Postmodernism: Revisioning Moral Philosophy* [Chicago: University of Chicago Press, 1990], 30, 96, 204).

3. For recent interesting discussions of sainthood, see Alison Goddard Elliot, *Roads to Paradise: Reading the Lives of the Early Saints* (Hanover, N.H.: University Press of New England, 1988); André Vauchez, *La Sainteté en Occident aux Derniers Siècles du Moyen Age: d'après les Procès de Canonisation et les Documents Hagiographiques* (Rome: École Française de Rome, 1988);

Phyllis Johnson and Brigitte Cazelles, *Le Vain Siecle Guerpir: A Literary Approach to Sainthood through Old French Hagiography of the Twelfth Century* (Chapel Hill: University of North Carolina Press, 1979); and Renate Blumenfeld-Kosinski and Timea Szell, eds., *Images of Sainthood in Medieval Europe* (Ithaca, N.Y.: Cornell University Press, 1991). See also the older but classic study, Hippolyte Delehaye, *The Legends of the Saints* (New York: Fordham University Press, 1962).

4. The significance of reciprocity between the saint and the worshiping community has been explored in Patrick Geary, "Humiliation of Saints," in *Saints and Their Cults: Studies in Religious Sociology, Folklore, and History*, ed. Stephen Wilson (New York: Cambridge University Press, 1983), 123–40, and Thomas Head, *Hagiography and the Cult of Saints: The Diocese of Orléans, 800–1200* (New York: Cambridge University Press, 1990).

5. The texts for the Life of St. Margaret and the Life of St. Katherine are taken from the *South English Legendary* (Charlotte D'Evelyn and Anna J. Mill, eds., *The South-English Legendary*, vol. 87 of Early English Text Society, 3 vols. [London: Oxford University Press, 1956, 1959]). References are given to page numbers and line numbers in this edition. On English traditions generally, see Gordon H. Gerould, *Saints' Legends* (Boston: Houghton Mifflin, 1916), and Theodor Wolpers, *Die Englische Heiligenlegende des Mittelalters* (Tübingen: Max Niemeyer Verlag, 1964).

6. For discussion of saints as friends and patrons, see Peter Brown, *The Cult of Saints: Its Rise and Function in Latin Christianity* (Chicago: University of Chicago Press, 1981), esp. chap. 3.

7. Millet and Wogan-Browne, *Middle English Prose for Women*, 101.

8. Eamon Duffy, "Holy Maydens, Holy Wyfes: The Cult of Women Saints in Fifteenth- and Sixteenth-Century England," in *Women in the Church*, ed. W. J. Sheils and Diana Wood (Oxford: Basil Blackwell, 1990), 175–96.

9. On the *South English Legendary* in general, see Annie Samson, "The South English Legendary: Constructing a Context," in *Thirteenth Century England I: Proceedings of the Newcastle upon Tyne Conference*, ed. P. R. Cross and S. D. Lloyd (Wolfeboro, N. H.: Boydell Press, 1986), 185–95. Forty-five surviving manuscripts dating from the late thirteenth through the late fifteenth century include all or parts of the *South English Legendary*. The original work is estimated to have been composed between 1260 and 1288 (Samson, 185). Samson, in the tradition of Manfred Görlach, argues that the influence of Jacobus de Voragine's *Legenda Aurea* on the *South English Legendary* is "only marginal" (189), and she maintains that the text probably did not have a liturgical use. Somewhat speculatively, noting the similarity to romance in some of the texts, Samson posits "the same kind of audience for the legendary as [Peter Coss] has for the romances. . . . We have a work written initially for gentry and perhaps secular clergy, and designed either for individual reading or for reading in the chamber, rather than as entertainment of the hall or public instruction in church" (194). In Klaus P. Jankofsky's, "National Characteristics in the Portrayal of English Saints in the South English Legendary," in *Images of Sainthood in Medieval Europe*, ed. Blumenfeld-Kosinski and Szell, he claims that "the collection's purpose was obviously the instruction of the laity in matters of the faith"; it was probably intended for "unlettered listeners, probably women" (83). The *Legendary* is distinguished by its "dramatization" of the narratives and by the compassion for its central characters (Jankofsky, 83). See also Wolpers, *Die englische Heiligenlegende des Mittelalters*, 209–58; Gordon H. Gerould, "A New Text of the

Passio S. Margaritae with Some Account of Its Latin and English Relations," *PMLA* 39 (1924): 525–56; and Elizabeth Francis, "A Hitherto Unprinted Version of the *Passio Sanctae Margaritae* with Some Observations on Vernacular Derivatives," *PMLA* 42 (1927): 87–105. For classification of Latin accounts, see *Catalogus codicum hagiographicorum Latinorum antiquiorum saeculo XVI qui asservantur in Biblioteca Nationali Parisiensi*, vol. 2 (Brussels: Polleunis, Ceuterick et Lefébure, 1889–93).

10. Elizabeth Robertson, "The Corporeality of Female Sanctity in *The Life of Saint Margaret*," in *Images of Sainthood in Medieval Europe*, ed. Blumenfeld-Kosinski and Szell, in which Robertson, while rightly pointing to the significance of corporeality, misconstrues, I think, the place of sexuality in this text: "Because a woman can never escape her body, her achievement of sanctity has to be through the body. Her temptation by the devil will be through the body and most probably will be sexual. She can overcome that sexual temptation only through her body, primarily by countering her physicality with the endurance of extreme physical torture" (269). And "it is certainly significant that most female saints' lives place at the center of their work the female saint's temptation to lose her virginity. . . . Physical suffering was the primary corrective to female sexual temptation" (271–72). The accent here is on the limitations imposed by the body and on the constraints the cultural association of physicality with women imposes on them. Although there is certainly ambiguity about the body expressed in medieval culture, I think the more appropriate starting point in reading these texts is with their affirmation of the positive character of the body in the light of the culture's belief in the incarnation or embodiment of the Divine in Christ. Christianity affirms the power of the body and the importance of physicality in the relationship between God and humanity. On this historical point, see Gedaliahu G. Stroumsa, "*Caro salutis cardo*: Shaping the Person in Early Christian Thought," *History of Religions* 30 (1990): 25–50.

11. Virginity is not only a sign pointing to something else. In the lives of medieval women, the historical and social possibilities for women who committed themselves to virginity gave them some degree of control over their bodies and some level of independence from men (see Eleanor McLaughlin, "Women, Power, and the Pursuit of Holiness," in *Women of Spirit: Female Leadership in the Jewish and Christian Traditions*, ed. Rosemary Ruether and Eleanor McLaughlin [New York: Simon and Schuster, 1979], 100–130). Even in the narrative context considered here, it may be that the listener's perceptions of Margaret's commitment to virginity evoked the aura of independence that contributes to whatever sense of "realism" or plausibility this narrative projects.

12. From *A Letter on Virginity* [*Hali Meidhad*], in Millett and Wogan-Browne, *Medieval English Prose for Women*, 13. Renunciation of physical desire by protecting virginity will be practiced "for a time in exchange for happiness which will last forever" (17). While denying and denigrating aspects of physical experience, these texts simultaneously affirm interaction with the body as a means of advancement in the Divine-human relationship. Medieval attention to body-related discipline, whether it be the preservation of virginity, fasting, physical exertions, or sleep deprivation, suggests how important interaction in and through the body is to medieval religious life. For an argument about the variety of ways of understanding virginity in the Middle Ages, see Clarissa W. Atkinson, "'Precious Balsam in a Fragile Glass': The Ideology of Virginity in the Later Middle Ages," *Journal of Family History* 8 (1983): 131–43.

13. This reading of the meaning of the body in these narratives may be better understood when the assembly of saints of which Margaret is a part is more clearly perceived. Eamon Duffy points to the frequent presence of the Holy Kin (including Mary, Anne, etc.) in church wall paintings, images which signaled the place of family in the Christian tradition, alongside images of virgin-saints such as Margaret and Katherine (Duffy, "Holy Maydens, Holy Wyfes," 191–96); see also Gail McMurray Gibson, "St. Anne and the Religion of Childbed: Some East Anglian Texts and Talismans," in *Interpreting Cultural Symbols: Saint Anne in Late Medieval Society* (Athens: University of Georgia Press, 1990), 95–110. Furthermore, the intercessory work of virgin-saints like Margaret is in part specifically associated with assisting women in the travails of childbirth, so the appearance of the virgin-saints is clearly not necessarily linked with the denial of the physical world of reproduction.

14. On women as the object of the male gaze, see Laura Mulvey, *Visual and Other Pleasures* (Bloomington: University of Indiana Press, 1989), and E. Ann Kaplan, "Is the Gaze Male?," in *Powers of Desire: The Politics of Sexuality*, ed. Ann Snitow, Christine Stansell, and Sharon Thompson (New York: Monthly Review Press, 1983), 309–27.

15. For a discussion of the "eroticization" of *vitae sanctarum*, see, for example, Thomas J. Heffernan, *Sacred Biography: Saints and Their Biographers in the Middle Ages* (New York: Oxford University Press, 1988), 272–92. Heffernan argues, for example, that "the stripping of the female's garments has clear erotic overtones lacking in Christ's disrobing. Indeed, none of the Gospels actually mentions the disrobing of Christ; they simply comment that his garments were divided among his tormentors" (279). Although he acknowledges the tradition of the disrobing of Christ in apocryphal traditions (although without conveying the extent of this tradition), Heffernan does not adequately explain the "clear erotic overtones" that obtain in the one case and not in the other.

16. See the discussion of the earlier Margaret legends in Kathryn Gravdal, *Ravishing Maidens: Writing Rape in Medieval French Literature and Law* (Philadelphia: University of Pennsylvania Press, 1991), 36–41. In discussing Wace's twelfth-century Old French version, Gravdal argues that Wace, a leader in the genre of romance, presents Olibrius as a "conflicted torturer-lover" (39). Gravdal argues that "in the central hagiographical tradition, the representation of the female saint in a sexual plot acts to feminize weakness and sexual transgression and to legitimize sexual violence as a test of the saintly female" (41). She continues that in "literary texts, the violence of the male is construed as an expression of conflicted love, the stuff of which romance is made" (41). In this *South English Legendary* version of the Margaret legend, I would argue that Olibrius is not so much the symbol of *conflicted* loves, as he is the model of *disordered* love. Medieval audiences, always presented with the good-versus-evil struggle, confronted in Olibrius the dangers of disordered love.

17. The author adds the caveat here: "Ac weþer it is soþ oþer it nis · inot noman þat wite" (297/166).

18. On Margaret's struggle with the dragon and the different versions of this scene in early medieval literature, see Jocelyn Price, "The Virgin and the Dragon: The Demonology of 'Seinte Margarete,'" *Leeds Studies in English* 16 (1985): 337–57.

19. In these narratives, it is often the case that the holy person's body resists the tortures that involve the participation of the elements. For example, boiling, fire, even the arrows that fly through the air can be stopped, but the saint's body does not resist piercing at close range or beheading.

20. Caroline Walker Bynum points out that "in such piety, body is not so much a hindrance to the soul's ascent as the opportunity for it" (*Fragmentation and Redemption: Essays on Gender and the Human Body in Medieval Religion* [New York: Zone Books, 1991], 194).

21. For a similar interesting analysis of protagonists as models of disordered desire, see Jocelyn G. Price's excellent study of the Juliana legend, "The *Liflade of Seinte Iuliene* and Hagiographic Convention," *Medievalia et Humanistica* 14 (1986): 37–58.

22. See chapter 2; also see Caroline Walker Bynum, *Holy Feast and Holy Fast: The Religious Significance of Food to Medieval Women* (Berkeley and Los Angeles: University of California Press, 1987), 273–75.

23. Joseph Wittig, "Figural Narrative in Cynewulf's *Juliana*," in *Anglo Saxon England* 4, ed. Peter Clemoes (Cambridge: Cambridge University Press, 1975), 50.

24. Wittig, "Figural Narrative in Cynewulf's *Juliana*," 50.

25. See Bynum, *Fragmentation and Redemption*, esp. 131–33, 145–46, 171–75, and chap. 6, and idem, *Holy Feast and Holy Fast,* esp. 153–86, 246–51, 294–96, even though Bynum does not often distinguish between saints' lives and other genres of medieval literature. See also Michael Goodich, "The Contours of Female Piety in Later Medieval Hagiography," *Church History* 50 (1981): 20–32; Ulrike Wiethaus, "Suffering, Love, and Transformation in Mechthild of Magdeburg," *Listening* 22 (1987): 139–50; and Kieckhefer, *Unquiet Souls*, chap. 4.

26. We have only one known copy of this Middle English text bundled in with translated lives of Mary of Oignies, Christina the Astonishing, and a letter concerning Catherine of Siena in a manuscript written in a late fourteenth-century hand (Carl Horstmann, "Prosalegenden: Die Legenden des ms. Douce 114," *Anglia: Zeitschrift fur Englische Philologie* 8 (1885): 107–118. Subsequent references to the Elizabeth of Spalbeek *vita* in the text are to page numbers in this edition. See also W. Simons and J. E. Ziegler, "Phenomenal Religion in the Thirteenth Century and Its Image: Elisabeth of Spalbeek and the Passion Cult," in *Women in the Church*, ed. W. J. Sheils and Diana Wood (Oxford: Basil Blackwell, 1990), 117–26. Elizabeth of Spalbeek was not a Cistercian, though she lived near Herkenrode, the important center of thirteenth-century women's Cistercian spirituality. For a general discussion of the type of Cistercian spirituality with which Elizabeth's biography has affinities, see Roger De Ganck, "The Cistercian Nuns of Belgium in the Thirteenth Century," *Cistercian Studies* 5 (1970): 169–87.

27. For a discussion related to the term "raueschynge," see Gravdal, *Ravishing Maidens*, 4–6. She notes the plurality of meanings associated with the classical Latin "rapere," including "to carry off or seize; to snatch, pluck, or drag off, to hurry, impel, hasten; to rob, plunder, and finally, to abduct (a virgin)" (4). She points to the thirteenth-century appearance of the French word "ravissement," which she argues at first named the action of "carrying off a woman." The meaning shifts by the fourteenth century to denote the spiritual "action of carrying a soul to heaven." In a fascinating study of the shifts in meaning associated with this word, she notes the fourteenth-century shift in which "ravissement" comes to mean "a state of exaltation" and then "the state of sexual pleasure or joy." She concludes, "The slippage or *glissement* from violent abduction to sexual pleasure is as breathtaking as it is telling" (5). In the Middle English text, "raueshynge" refers to Elizabeth's being taken up to the Divine, being lifted, as it were, outside herself.

28. For an initial discussion of some of the issues that may arise in considering the writings of male religious about female holy women, see John Coakley, "Gender and the

Authority of Friars: The Significance of Holy Women for Thirteenth-Century Franciscans and Dominicans," *Church History* 60 (1991): 445–60.

29. That Philip is not entirely unaware of the possibility of inappropriate responses to Elizabeth's dramatizations is evident when he asserts that there was no impropriety involved in her appearance: "In mouynges and berynges of body of þe forseyde virgin þere fallith no þinge unsemely no þinge þat may displese mannes syghte . . . couerde & becladde with hir own cloþes, nor no þinge apperith unsemely nor unhonest" (Horstmann, "Prosalegenden: Die legenden des ms. Douce 114," 114).

30. Sanford B. Meech and Hope E. Allen, *The Book of Margery Kempe*, vol. 212 of Early English Text Society (New York: Oxford University Press, 1940), 209. Subsequent page number references are to this critical edition. For a translation see *The Book of Margery Kempe*, ed. W. Butler-Bowden (New York: Devin-Adair, 1944).

31. On the place of images in medieval devotion, see Jeffrey Hamburger, "The Visual and the Visionary: The Image in Late Medieval Monastic Devotions," *Viator* 20 (1989): 161–82. The resemblance between Elizabeth's performances and religious art is striking. She dramatizes the scenes commonly depicted in Books of Hours, on church walls, and in other religious art. That this is the case is demonstrated in part by the nature of her actions and also by the events and characters she portrays. On a Friday, in keeping with many manuscript and wall painting depictions of the Crucifixion on Good Friday, Elizabeth dramatized how Christ's mother, Mary, stood beside the cross: she holds her left hand under her left cheek and leans her head and neck to the left side while holding her right hand under her right breast. In keeping with the usual depictions of the Crucifixion, she also enacted John the Evangelist bowing his head and holding his folded hands by his left side. Elizabeth re-creates the events the art of her day sought to evoke. As did the art, she sought to awaken her viewers to the meaning of what they saw and to stir their compassionate love for the suffering Savior.

32. For a discussion of the Eucharist in medieval women's spiritual life, see Caroline Walker Bynum, "Women Mystics and Eucharistic Devotion in the Thirteenth Century," in *Fragmentation and Redemption*, 119–50.

33. See Robin Lane Fox, *Pagans and Christians* (New York: Alfred A. Knopf, 1987), 438, and esp. chap. 9. See, for example, the life of Perpetua (martyred 203 A.D.): "Perpetua was tossed [into the arena] first, and fell on her loins. Sitting down she drew back her torn tunic from her side to cover her thighs, more mindful of her modesty than her suffering. . . . Then she rose, and seeing that Felicitas was bruised, approached, gave a hand to her, and lifted her up. And the two stood side by side, and the cruelty of the people being now appeased, they were recalled to the Gate of Life. There . . . being roused from what seemed like sleep, so completely had she been in the Spirit and in ecstasy, [she] began to look around her, and said to the amazement of all: 'When we are to be thrown to that heifer, I cannot tell.' When she heard what had already taken place, she refused to believe it till she had observed certain marks of ill-usage on her body and dress" ("The Passions of Saints Perpetua and Felicitas," in *Medieval Women's Visionary Literature*, ed. E. A. Petroff [New York: Oxford University Press, 1986], 76.)

34. See also Kempe, *Book*, 197.

35. Donald R. Howard, *Writers and Pilgrims: Medieval Pilgrimage Narratives and Their Posterity* (Berkeley: University of California Press, 1980), 35.

36. See Karma Lochrie, *Margery Kempe and Translations of the Flesh* (Philadelphia: University of Pennsylvania Press, 1991); Clarissa Atkinson, *Mystic and Pilgrim: The Book and World of Margery Kempe* (Ithaca, N.Y.: Cornell University Press, 1983); and Richard Kieckhefer, *Unquiet Souls: Fourteenth Century Saints and Their Religious Milieu* (Chicago: University of Chicago Press, 1984), on the normalcy of Kempe among fourteenth-century religious figures.

37. Edith Wyschogrod, *Saints and Postmodernism: Revisioning Moral Philosophy* (Chicago: University of Chicago Press, 1990), 256.

38. For a discussion of the female literary and spiritual milieu surrounding Kempe's *Book*, see Lochrie, *Translations of Flesh*, 76–88, and Atkinson, *Mystic and Pilgrim*, chap. 6.

39. Mary Serjeantson, ed., *Bokenham's Legendys of Hooly Wummen*, vol. 206 of Early English Text Society (Oxford: Oxford University Press, 1938), 157–60.

40. Horstmann, "Prosalegenden: Die Legenden des ms. Douce 114," 29. Subsequent references to the Mary of Oignies *vita* in the text are to page numbers in this edition.

41. Kempe seems to have been aware that there had been some controversy after the initial canonization of Bridget in 1391 (during the Great Schism). Hope Emily Allen estimates that Kempe was in Rome in 1414 during the time that the Council of Constance was considering Bridget's canonization (Kempe, *Book*, 304–305). For the Middle English translation of Bridget of Sweden's *Revelations*, see William P. Cumming, ed., *The Revelations of Saint Brigitta: Edited from the Fifteenth-Century MS in the Garrett Collection of Princeton University*, vol. 178 of Early English Text Society (London: Oxford University Press, 1929).

42. We might even ask the very speculative question of whether Kempe may have been writing her book to prepare for her own canonization process. She tells the priest, for example, not to make the book public until after her death and she insists, despite the difficulties involved, on making certain that the book is written.

43. E. W. Tristram, *English Wall Painting of the Fourteenth Century* (London: Routledge and Kegan Paul, 1955), 300–301.

44. Kempe is God's spokesperson: "And þei þat heryn þe þei heryn þe voys of God" (23). Images linking Kempe with the biblical prophets appear throughout her *Book*. See Ellen M. Ross, "Spiritual Experience and Women's Autobiography: The Rhetoric of Selfhood in 'The Book of Margery Kempe,'" *Journal of the American Academy of Religion* 59 (1991): 540–43.

45. The Gospels say that a prophet is not without honor except in his (or her) own country. In her dealings with the world, Margery is a laughingstock who is ridiculed by her family, mistreated by her friends, and slandered by her enemies. At times, she portrays herself as an outcast, subjected to scorn and shame by her own people, appreciated more by Muslims than by the Christians in her own country (75). Exasperated with her boisterous presence on one pilgrimage, her companions attempt to sneak off in the night and abandon her as they set out from one town to the next. Alerted to their intentions by a friend, she persuades them to let her stay with them. But her troubles do not end: "They cuttyd hir gown so schort þat it come but lytil be-nethyn hir kne & dedyn hir don on a whyte canwas in maner of a sekkyn gelle, for sche xuld ben holdyn a fool" (62). On another journey from Venice to Jerusalem, her companions lock up her clothes and a priest steals her bedsheet (67).

46. As I have suggested elsewhere ("Spiritual Experience and Women's Autobiography," 532–35), Margery's private biological and familial roles—as mother, daughter, sis-

ter, and wife—become the basis for her identification with Christ and for her work in the world. The general social significance of familial and relational connections is reflected in Kempe's *Book*, in which the constellation of categories of daughter, sister, wife, and mother at both a spiritual and literal level function as central identity markers in Kempe's portrayal of herself. While some have suggested a division between the private realm of women and the public realm of men, the example of Margery Kempe provides an interesting model for a situation in which a woman's private identification as a literal mother, sister, daughter, and spouse enables her to act in the public realm where the same categories, albeit now in a nonliteral or spiritual sense, locate and name one's activities. Far from limiting her to biological roles, Margery's status as "spiritual relative" transforms her world from one narrowly circumscribed by familial or marital ties to one extending to God and to the vast number of people—Christians, Jews, and Muslims—whom she meets and ministers to. The use of these categories extends her world beyond the narrow confines of a private setting to a broad public which includes the vast array of people who associate themselves with her during the course of her travels. Margery's work is a public witness to the presence of God in the world as she awakens her audiences' religious sensibilities and goads them to attentiveness to the God of justice and mercy.

47. For a thought-provoking, if not entirely unproblematic, analysis of the role of laughter in Kempe's *Book*, see Lochrie, *Translations of the Flesh*, 134–63.

48. Quoted from the French Beguine Rule, *La Règle des Fins Amans*, in Barbara Newman, *From Virile Woman to WomanChrist: Studies in Medieval Religion and Literature* (Philadelphia: University of Pennsylvania Press, 1995), 112. See also Jacques Le Goff, *The Birth of Purgatory*, trans. Alfred Goldhammer (Chicago: University of Chicago Press, 1981), 319. (For a critique of Le Goff, see Graham Robert Edwards, "Purgatory: 'Birth' or Evolution?," *Journal of Ecclesiastical History* 36 [1985]: 634–46.) On the history of purgatory and forms of religious practice associated with lessening the pains of purgatory in general, see R. R. Atwell, "From Augustine to Gregory the Great: An Evaluation of the Emergence of the Doctrine of Purgatory," *Journal of Ecclesiastical History* 38 (1987): 173–86; A. Michel and M. Jugie, "Purgatoire," in *Dictionnaire de Théologie Catholique*, XIII.i (Paris: Letouzey et Ané, 1936), cols. 1163–1357; and M. Louvet, *Purgatoire d'après les Révélations des Saints* (Albi: Imprimerie des Apprentis-Orphelins, 1899). For discussions of otherworldly visions which include visions of purgatory, see Peter Dinzelbacher, *Vision und Visionsliteratur im Mittelalter* (Stuttgart: Anton Hiersemann, 1981), and Howard R. Patch, *The Other World According to Descriptions in Medieval Literature* (Cambridge: Harvard University Press, 1950). For a discussions of the concept of purgatory in late medieval England, see Clive Burgess, "'By Quick and by Dead': Wills and Pious Provision in Late Medieval Bristol," *English Historical Review* 102 (1987): 837–58.

49. Le Goff, *Birth of Purgatory*, 324. Marie de France translated *St. Patrick's Purgatory*, a text calling people to repentance, at the end of the twelfth century. "I, Marie, have committed to writing the Book of the Purgatory in Romance, so that it may be intelligible and suitable for lay folk. Now let us pray God that by his grace he may purify us of our sins" (M. D. Legge, *Anglo-Norman Literature and Its Background* [Oxford: Clarendon Press, 1963], 204–5).

50. Bynum, *Holy Feast and Holy Fast*, 127.

51. Bynum, *Holy Feast and Holy Fast*, 171.

52. Bynum, *Holy Feast and Holy Fast*, 401 n. 81.

53. In *De quatuor gradibus caritatis*, Richard describes love of others as the highest kind of love possible and sets Christ as the exemplar for this love (Richard of St. Victor, *De quatuor gradibus caritatis*, ed. G. Dumiege [Paris: Vrin, 1967], 230; English translation in Richard of St. Victor, *Selected Writings on Contemplation*, trans. Claire Kirchberger [London: Faber & Faber, 1957], 171–73). In the fourth and highest degree of love, people are torn between being "dissolved and be[ing] with Christ which is far better" and remaining in the flesh, which the "charity of Christ compels" (*De quatuor gradibus*, 231; Kirchberger, *Selected Writings*, 173: "Caritatis enim Christi urget eum"). The final stage of charity attainable on earth is not one of separation from all humanity in contemplation; on the contrary, it entails active involvement in the community—activity necessitating the union of love and humility. "In the first [degree] she enters in by meditation; in the second she ascends by contemplation; in the third she is led into jubilation, in the fourth she goes out by compassion" (*De quatuor gradibus*, 224; Kirchberger, *Selected Writings*, 157: "In primo intrat meditatione, in secundo ascendit contemplatione, in tertio introducitur in jubilatione, in quarto egreditur ex compassione"). Margery Kempe's contemporary, Walter Hilton, reflects this perspective as well. For Hilton, charity refers not only to love of God but also to love of all Christians: "If you are wise, you shall not leave God, but you shall find him and possess him, have him and see him in your fellow-Christians just as well as in your prayer" (Walter Hilton, *The Scale of Perfection*, trans. J. P. H. Clark and Rosemary Dorward [New York: Paulist Press, 1991], 153). Hilton is not always explicit as to the identity of the neighbor, but he often speaks about love of "euen-cristens." Margery Kempe is generally more expansive in her definition of "neighbor" and prays regularly for "Muslims" and "Jews" as well as for Christians.

54. Horstmann, "Prosalegenden: Die legenden des ms. Douce 114," 120–21.

55. Unlike Margery, Hadewijch places purgatory on a continuum with final perdition. At one point, she blurs the general distinction between hell as the situation of the irrevocably damned and purgatory as a way station on a journey eventually leading to salvation. Nevertheless, Hadewijch does seem to be aware of the difference when she marvels that God miraculously and mercifully freed four hopeless souls condemned to hell after she had prayed for them, despite her ignorance of the hopelessness of their cause (Hadewijch, "Vision 5: Three Heavens and the Trinity," in *Hadewijch: The Complete Works*, trans. Mother Columba Hart [New York: Paulist Press, 1980], 276). Kempe, however, seems much more in keeping with the common practice of focusing one's attention on lessening the time contrite souls spend in purgatory and recognizing that one cannot affect souls who have been damned.

56. Le Goff, *The Birth of Purgatory*, 211. By the twelfth century, the theory of purgatory had become quite clear: "Guilt (culpa), which normally leads to damnation, can be pardoned through contrition and confession, while punishment (poena), or expiatory castigation, is effaced by satisfaction," that is, "by completing the penance ordered by the church" (Le Goff, *The Birth of Purgatory*, 224).

57. Le Goff, *The Birth of Purgatory*, 211.

58. Le Goff, *The Birth of Purgatory*, 285.

59. As Newman rightly puts it, "The aim of purgatorial piety was to reconcile justice with mercy, not override it" (Newman, *From Virile Woman to WomanChrist*, 119). See also Duffy, *Stripping of the Altars*, 345.

60. Le Goff, *The Birth of Purgatory*, 137; Newman, *From Virile Woman to WomanChrist*, esp. 108–22.

61. On medieval medical and religious views of women, see Vern L. Bullough, "Medieval Medical and Scientific Views of Women," *Viator* 4 (1973): 485–501; Jacqueline Murray, "Sexuality and Spirituality: The Intersection of Medieval Theology and Medicine," *Fides et Historia* 23 (1991): 20–36; Caroline Walker Bynum, *Holy Feast and Holy Fast*, chap. 9; and idem, *Fragmentation and Redemption*, 205–35. For a discussion of how association with the body "conditions" women's experience of the Divine, see Elizabeth Robertson, "Medieval Medical Views of Women and Female Spirituality in the 'Ancrene Wisse' and Julian of Norwich's 'Showings,'" in *Feminist Approaches to the Body in Medieval Literature*, ed. Linda Lomperis and Sarah Stanbury (Philadelphia: University of Pennsylvania Press, 1993), 142–67; and Karma Lochrie, *Translations of the Flesh*, 13–55.

CONCLUSION

1. Richard Rolle, "Meditations on the Passion," in *Yorkshire Writers: Richard Rolle of Hampole and His Followers*, ed. Carl Horstmann (London: Swan Sonnenschein, 1895), 97.

2. Rolle, "Meditations on the Passion," 90.

3. Thomas Tentler, *Sin and Confession on the Eve of the Reformation* (Princeton: Princeton University Press, 1977), esp. chap. 5.

4. Eamon Duffy, *The Stripping of the Altars: Traditional Religion in England, c. 1400–c. 1580* (New Haven: Yale University Press, 1992), 248.

5. Duffy also uses the term "kinship" (*Stripping of the Altars*, 236), which is even more apt for figures such as Margery Kempe, who speaks of her relationship to God as that of daughter, mother, sister, and spouse (see Ellen Ross, "Spiritual Experience and Women's Autobiography: The Rhetoric of Selfhood in 'The Book of Margery Kempe,'" *Journal of the American Academy of Religion* 59 [1991]: 532–35).

6. Duffy, *Stripping of the Altars*, 36.

7. James Marrow, "Symbol and Meaning in Northern European Art of the Late Middle Ages and the Early Renaissance," *Simiolus* 16 (1986): 156.

8. Rolle, "Meditations on the Passion," 98.

9. Duffy, *Stripping of the Altars*, 3, 254.

10. Duffy, *Stripping of the Altars*, 269.

11. Sarah Beckwith, *Christ's Body: Identity, Culture, and Society in Late Medieval Writings* (New York: Routledge, 1993), esp. chap. 2.

12. Duffy, *Stripping of the Altars*, 302.

13. Duffy, *Stripping of the Altars*, 306, 349.

14. Harold Kane, ed., *The Prickynge of Love*, Elizabethan and Renaissance Studies 92:10 (Salzburg: Universität Salzburg, 1983), 19.

15. Kane, *The Prickynge of Love*, 10.

Bibliography

Primary Sources

Manuscripts

CAMBRIDGE

Cambridge University Library	MS Dd. 4.17
	MS Dd. 8.2
Corpus Christi College Library	MS 53
Fitzwilliam Museum	M48
	M242
	MS 259
Trinity College Library	MS B.10.15
	MS B.11.3
	MS O.4.16

GLASGOW

Glasgow University Library	MS Hunter 231

LONDON

British Library	MS Add. 16968	MS Egerton 2781
	MS Add. 24686	MS Egerton 3277
	MS Add. 44949	MS Royal 2.B.VII
	MS Add. 47682	MS Royal 6.E.VI–6.VII

	MS Add. 49622	MS Yates Thompson 13
	MS Arundel 83 I	MS Yates Thompson 14
	MS Arundel 83 II	
Lambeth Palace Library	MS 233	
Westminster Abbey	MS 37	

NEW YORK
Pierpont Morgan Library   M. 107

NORWICH
Bridewell Museum   MS 158.926

OXFORD

Bodleian Library	MS Auct. D. 4.4	MS Gough liturg. 8
	MS Barlow 22	MS Lat. liturg. e. 41
	MS Digby 227	MS Laud Misc. 165
	MS Douce 366	MS Rawlinson G. 185

Books

Abelard, Peter. *Petri Abelardi, Opera Theologica.* Edited by Eligii M. Buytaert. Corpus Christianorum, Continuatio Medievalis 11. Turnhout: Brepols, 1969.

Aelred of Rievaulx. *Aelredi Rievallensis Opera Omnia.* Edited by A. Hoste and C. H. Talbot. Corpus Christianorum, Continuatio Medievalis 1. Turnhout: Brepols, 1971.

Beadle, Richard, ed. *The York Plays.* London: E. Arnold, 1982.

Blake, N. F., ed. *Middle English Religious Prose.* Evanston, Ill.: Northwestern University Press, 1972.

Block, K. S., ed. *Ludus Coventriae or The Plaie Called Corpus Christi.* Early English Text Society, vol. 120. London: Oxford University Press, 1922.

Blunt, John Henry, ed. *The Myroure of Oure Ladye.* Early English Text Society, extra series, vol. 19. London: N. Trübner, 1873.

Bokenham, Osbern. *Legendys of Hooly Wummen.* Edited by Mary S. Serjeantson. Early English Text Society, vol. 206. London: Oxford University Press, 1938.

Bonaventura, John. *Meditations on the Supper of Our Lord, and the Hours of the Passion.* Edited by J. Meadows Cowper. Early English Text Society, vol. 60. London: N. Trübner, 1875.

Brooke, Rosalind B., ed. and trans. *Scripta Leonis, Rufini et Angeli, Sociorum S. Fancisci: The Writings of Leo, Rufino and Angelo, Companions of St. Francis.* Oxford: Clarendon Press, 1970.

Butler-Bowden, W., trans. *The Book of Margery Kempe.* New York: Devin-Adair, 1944.

Capgrave, John. *The Life of St. Katherine of Alexandria.* Edited by Carl Horstmann. Early English Text Society, vol. 100. London: Kegan Paul, Trench, Trübner, 1893.

———. *Ye Solace of Pilgrimes.* Edited by C. A. Mills. London: Frowde, 1911.

Catalogus codicum hagiographicorum Latinorum antiquiorum saeculo XVI qui asservantur in Biblioteca Nationali Parisiensi, vol 2. Brussels: Polleunis, Ceuterick et Lefébure, 1889–93.

Clark, Willene B. *The Medieval Book of Birds: Hugh of Fouilloy's Aviarium.* Binghamton, N.Y.: Medieval and Renaissance Texts and Studies, 1992.

Clemence of Barking. *The Life of St. Catherine.* Edited by William MacBain. Oxford: Basil Blackwell, 1964.

Cumming, William P., ed. *The Revelations of Saint Birgitta*. Early English Text Society, o.s., vol. 178. London: Oxford University Press, 1929.

Delany, Sheila, trans. *A Legend of Holy Women: A Translation of Osbern Bokenham's Legends of Holy Women*. Notre Dame, Ind.: University of Notre Dame, 1992.

D'Evelyn, Charlotte, and Anne J. Mill, eds. *The South English Legendary*. 3 vols. Early English Text Society, vols. 235, 236, 244. London: Oxford University Press, 1956, 1959.

De Voragine, Jacobus. *The Golden Legend*. 2 vols. London: Longmans, Green, 1941.

Eccles, Mark, ed. *The Macro Plays*. Early English Text Society, vol. 262. New York: Oxford University Press, 1969.

Foster, Frances A., ed. *The Northern Passion*. 2 vols. Early English Text Society, vols. 145, 147. London: Kegan Paul, Trench, Trübner, 1913, 1916.

———. *A Stanzaic Life of Christ*. Early English Text Society, vol. 166. Oxford: Oxford University Press, 1926.

Furnivall, Frederick J. *Hymns to the Virgin and Christ, The Parliament of Devils and Other Religious Poems*. Early English Text Society, vol. 24. London: N. Trübner, 1867.

Harley, Marta Powell. *A Revelation of Purgatory by an Unknown, Fifteenth-Century Woman Visionary: Introduction, Critical Text, and Translation*. Lewiston, Maine: Edwin Mellen Press, 1985.

Hart, Columba, trans. *Hadewijch: The Complete Works*. New York: Paulist Press, 1980.

Hayes, Zachary, trans. *What Manner of Man?: Sermons on Christ by St. Bonaventure*. Chicago: Franciscan Herald Press, 1974.

Hilton, Walter. *The Scale of Perfection*. Translated by John P. H. Clark and Rosemary Dorward. New York: Paulist Press, 1991.

Hodgson, Phyllis, and Gabriel M. Liegey, eds. *The Orcherd of Syon*. Early English Text Society, vol. 258. New York: Oxford University Press, 1966.

Holmstedt, Gustaf, ed. *Speculum Christiani: A Middle English Religious Treatise of the 14th century*. Early English Text Society, vol. 182. London: Oxford University Press, 1933.

Horstmann, Carl, ed. "Prosalegenden: Die Legenden des ms. Douce 114." *Anglia* 8 (1885): 102–96.

———. *Yorkshire Writers: Richard Rolle of Hampole and His Followers*. London: Swan Sonnenschein, 1895.

Julian of Norwich. *A Book of Showings to the Anchoress Julian of Norwich*. Edited by Edmund Colledge and James Walsh. 2 vols. Toronto: Pontifical Institute of Medieval Studies, 1978.

———. *Showings*. Translated by Edmund Colledge and James Walsh. New York: Paulist Press, 1978.

Kane, Harold, ed., *The Prickynge of Love*. Elizabethan and Renaissance Studies 92:10. Salzburg: Universität Salzburg, 1983.

Lamb, George, trans. *The Life of Catherine of Siena by Blessed Raymond of Capua*. New York: P. J. Kennedy and Sons, 1960.

Legg, J. Wickham, ed. *The Sarum Missal Edited from Three Early Manuscripts*. Oxford: Clarendon Press, 1969.

Littlehales, Henry. *The Primer or Lay Folks Prayer Book*. London: Kegan Paul, Trench, Trübner, 1895.

Love, Nicholas. *Nicholas Love's Mirror of the Blessed Life of Jesus Christ: A Critical Edition*. Edited by Michael G. Sargent. New York: Garland, 1992.

Mack, Frances M., ed. *Seinte Marherete*. Early English Text Society, vol. 193. London: Oxford University Press, 1934.

Mansi, J. D., ed. *Sacrorum Conciliorum: Nova et Amplissima Collecto*. Venice: Antonio Zatta, n.d.

Matthew, F. D., ed. *The English Works of Wyclif*. Early English Text Society, vol. 74. London: Trübner, 1880.

Mechthild of Magdeburg. *The Revelations of Mechthild of Magdeburg*. Edited and translated by Lucy Menzies. New York: Longmans Green, 1953.

Meech, Sanford B., and Hope E. Allen, eds. *The Book of Margery Kempe*. Early English Text Society, vol. 212. New York: Oxford University Press, 1940.

Millet, Bella, ed. *Hali Meidhad*. Early English Text Society, vol. 284. New York: Oxford University Press, 1982.

Millet, Bella, and Jocelyn Wogan-Browne, eds. *Medieval English Prose for Women: Selections from the Katherine Group and Ancrene Wisse*. New York: Oxford University Press, 1990.

Mirk, John. *Instructions for Parish Priests*. Edited by Edward Peacock. Early English Text Society, vol. 37. London: Trübner, 1868.

———. *Mirk's Festial: A Collection of Homilies*. Edited by Theodor Erbe. Early English Text Society, vol. 96. London: Kegan Paul, Trench, Trübner, 1905.

Nolloth, Henry, and T. F. Simmons, eds. *The Layfolk's Catechism, or Archbishop Thoresby's Instructions for the People*. Early English Text Society, vol. 118. London: Kegan Paul, Trench, Trübner, 1901.

Pecock, Reginald. *The Donet*. Edited by Elsie Vaughan Hitchcock. Early English Text Society, vol. 156. London: Oxford University Press, 1921.

———. *The Reule of Crysten Religioun*. Edited by William Cabell Greet. Early English Text Society, vol. 171. London: Oxford University Press, 1927.

Petroff, E., ed. *Medieval Women's Visionary Literature*. New York: Oxford University Press, 1986.

Ragusa, Isa, and Rosalie B. Green, eds. and trans. *Meditations on the Life of Christ: An Illustrated Manuscript of the Fourteenth Century (MS Ital. 115, Paris Bibl. Nat.)*. Princeton: Princeton University Press, 1961.

Richard of St. Victor. *De Quatuor Gradibus Caritatis*. Edited by G. Dumiege. Paris: Vrin, 1967.

———. *Selected Writings on Contemplation*. Translated by Claire Kirchberger. London: Faber & Faber, 1957.

Ross, Woodburn O. *Middle English Sermons*. Early English Text Society, o.s., vol. 209. New York: Oxford University Press, 1960.

Salu, M. B., trans. *The Ancrene Riwle*. London: Burns & Oates, 1955.

Serjeantson, Mary, ed. *Bokenham's Legendys of Hooly Wummen*. Early English Text Society, vol. 206. Oxford: Oxford University Press, 1938.

Simmons, Thomas Frederick, ed. *Lay Folks Mass Book or The Manner of Hearing Mass*. Philadelphia: J. B. Lippincott, 1879.

Talbot, C. H. *The Life of Christina of Markyate: A Twelfth Century Recluse*. Oxford: Clarendon Press, 1959.

Tolkien, J. R. R. *Ancrene Wisse*. Early English Text Society, vol. 249. Oxford: Clarendon Press, 1962.

Weatherly, Edward H., ed. *Speculum Sacerdotale*. Early English Text Society, vol. 200. London: Oxford University Press, 1936.

Secondary Sources

Adair, John. *The Pilgrims' Way: Shrines and Saints in Britain and Ireland*. London: Thames and Hudson, 1978.

Aigrain, René. *L'hagiographie: Ses Sources, ses Méthodes, son Histoire*. Paris: Bloud et Gay, 1953.

Alexander, J. J. G. *Insular Manuscripts: Sixth to Ninth Century*. London: Harvey Miller, 1978.

Anderson, M. D. *Drama and Imagery in English Medieval Churches*. Cambridge: Cambridge University Press, 1963.

Anselm, "Why God Became Man." In *A Scholastic Miscellany: Anselm to Ockham*, edited by Eugene R. Fairweather, 100–183. New York: Macmillan, 1970.

Arbman, Ernst. *Ecstasy or Religious Trance*. 3 vols. Uppsala: Scandinavian University Books, 1963–1970.

Ashley, Kathleen, and Pamela Sheingorn. *Interpreting Cultural Symbols: Saint Anne in Late Medieval Society*. Athens: University of Georgia Press, 1990.

Astill, Grenville, and Annie Grant. *The Countryside of Medieval England*. Oxford: Basil Blackwell, 1988.

Aston, Margaret. "Huizinga's Harvest: England and the Waning of the Middle Ages." *Medievalia et Humanistica*, n. s., 9 (1979): 1–24.

———. *Lollards and Reformers: Images and Literacy in Late Medieval Religion*. London: Hambledon Press, 1984.

Atkinson, Clarissa W. *Mystic and Pilgrim: The Book and World of Margery Kempe*. Ithaca, N.Y.: Cornell University Press, 1983.

———. "'Precious Balsam in a Fragile Glass': The Ideology of Virginity in the Later Middle Ages." *Journal of Family History* 8 (1983): 131–43.

Atwell, R. R. "From Augustine to Gregory the Great: An Evaluation of the Emergence of the Doctrine of Purgatory." *Journal of Ecclesiastical History* 38 (1987): 173–86.

Auerbach, Erich. *Scenes from the Drama of European Literature*. 2d ed. Minneapolis: University of Minnesota Press, 1984.

Aulén, Gustaf. *Christus Victor: An Historical Study of the Three Main Types of the Atonement*. New York: Macmillan, 1969.

Aungier, George. *The History and Antiquities of Syon Monastery of the Parish of Islesworth and the Chapelry of Hounslow*. London: J. B. Nichols and Son, 1840.

Backhouse, Janet. *Books of Hours*. London: The British Library, 1985.

Baker, A. T. "Saints' Lives Written in Anglo-French: Their Historical, Social and Literary Importance." *Transactions of the Royal Society of Literature of the United Kingdoms*, n.s. 4 (1924): 119–56.

Baker, D. C. "'De Arte Lacrimandi': A Supplement and Some Corrections." *Medium Aevum* 52 (1983): 222–26.

Bakhtin, Mikhail. *The Dialogic Imagination*. Translated by Caryl Emerson and Michael Holquist. Austin: University of Texas Press, 1981.

Bal, Mieke. *Death and Dissymmetry*. Chicago: University of Chicago Press, 1988.

Bannister, H. M. "The Introduction of the Cultus of St. Anne in the West." *English Historical Review* 18 (1903): 107–12.

Barasch, Moshe. *Gestures of Despair in Medieval and Early Renaissance Art.* New York: New York University Press, 1976.

———. *Giotto and the Language of Gesture.* New York: Cambridge University Press, 1987.

Barker, Francis. *The Tremulous Private Body: Essays on Subjection.* London: Methuen, 1984.

Bateson, Mary. *Catalogue of the Library of Syon Monastery, Islesworth.* Cambridge: Cambridge University Press, 1898.

Beckwith, Sarah. *Christ's Body: Identity, Culture and Society in Late Medieval Writings.* New York: Routledge, 1993.

Bell, Robert. "Metamorphoses of Spiritual Autobiography." *Journal of English Literary History* 44 (1977): 108–26.

Bellamy, John. *Crime and Public Order in England in the Later Middle Ages.* Toronto: University of Toronto Press, 1973.

Belting, Hans. *The Image and Its Public in the Middle Ages: Form and Function of Early Paintings of the Passion.* Translated by Mark Bartusis and Raymond Meyer. New Rochelle, N.Y.: A. D. Cartazas, 1990.

———. *Likeness and Presence: A History of the Image before the Era of Art.* Translated by Edmund Jephcott. Chicago: University of Chicago Press, 1994.

Bennett, H. S. *Six Medieval Men and Women.* Cambridge: Cambridge University Press, 1955.

Bennett, J. A. W. *Poetry of the Passion: Studies in Twelve Centuries of English Verse.* Oxford: Clarendon Press, 1982.

Bennett, Judith M. *Women in the Medieval English Countryside: Gender and Household in Brigstock before the Plague.* New York: Oxford University Press, 1987.

Berger, David, ed. *History and Hate: The Dimensions of Anti-Semitism.* Philadelphia: Jewish Publications Society, 1986.

Bernstein, Alan E. "Esoteric Theology: William Auvergne on the Fires of Hell and Purgatory." *Speculum* 57 (1982): 509–31.

Bestul, Thomas H. "Chaucer's Parson's Tale and the Late-Medieval Tradition of Religious Meditation." *Speculum* 64 (1989): 600–619.

Bihlmeyer, Karl. "Die Selbstbiographie in der deutschen Mystik des Mittelalters." *Theologische Quartalschrift* 114 (1933): 504–44.

Blench, J. W. *Preaching in England in the Late Fifteenth and Sixteenth Centuries.* New York: Barnes and Noble, 1964.

Blumenfeld-Kosinski, Renate, and Timea Szell, eds. *Images of Sainthood in Medieval Europe.* Ithaca, N.Y.: Cornell University Press, 1991.

Bodenstadt, M. Immaculata, Sister. "The Vita Christi of Ludolphus the Carthusian." *Catholic University of America Studies in Medieval and Renaissance Latin* 16 (1944): 1–160.

Boitani, Piero. *English Medieval Narrative in the Thirteenth and Fourteenth Centuries.* Translated by Joan Krakover Hall. Cambridge: Cambridge University Press, 1982.

Bond, Francis. *Dedications and Patron Saints of English Churches: Ecclesiastical Symbolism: Saints and Their Emblems.* New York: Oxford University Press, 1914.

Bono, James J. "Medical Spirits and the Medieval Language of Life." *Traditio* 40 (1984): 91–130.

Borenius, Tancred, and E. W. Tristram. *English Medieval Painting.* New York: Hacker Art Books, 1976.

Borsook, Eve. *The Mural Painters of Tuscany: From Cimabue to Andrea Del Sarto.* 2d ed. Oxford: Clarendon Press, 1980.

Bossy, John. *Christianity in the West, 1400–1700.* New York: Oxford University Press, 1985.

Braswell, Mary F. *The Medieval Sinner: Characterization and Confession in the Literature of the English Middle Ages.* Toronto: Associated University Press, 1983.

Braun, Barbara. "The Aztecs: Art and Sacrifice." *Art in America* 72 (1984): 126–39.

Brewer, Derek. *English Gothic Literature.* New York: Schocken Books, 1983.

Briscoe, Marianne, and John Coldewey, eds. *Contexts for Early English Drama.* Bloomington: Indiana University Press, 1989.

Brown, D. Catherine. *Pastor and Laity in the Theology of Jean Gerson.* New York: Cambridge University Press, 1987.

Brown, Elizabeth A. R. "Death and the Human Body in the Later Middle Ages and the Legislation of Boniface VIII on the Division of the Corpse." *Viator* 12 (1981): 221–70.

Brown, Peter. *The Body and Society: Men, Women, and Sexual Renunciation in Early Christianity.* New York: Columbia University Press, 1988.

———. *The Cult of the Saints: Its Rise and Function in Latin Christianity.* Chicago: University of Chicago Press, 1981.

Brueggemann, Walter. *The Land: Place as Gift, Promise, and Challenge in Biblical Faith.* Philadelphia: Fortress Press, 1977.

Bugge, John. *Virginitas: An Essay in the History of a Medieval Ideal.* The Hague: Martinus Nijhoff, 1975.

Bullough, Vern L. "Medieval Medical and Scientific Views of Women." *Viator* 4 (1973): 485–501.

Burgess, Clive. "'By Quick and by Dead': Wills and Pious Provision in Late Medieval Bristol." *English Historical Review* 102 (1987): 837–58.

———. "'A Fond Thing Vainly Invented': An Essay on Purgatory and Pious Motive in Late Medieval England." In *Parish, Church and People: Local Studies in Lay Religion, 1350–1750,* edited by S. J. Wright, 56–84. London: Hutchinson, 1988.

Bynum, Caroline Walker. *Fragmentation and Redemption: Essays on Gender and the Human Body in Medieval Religion.* New York: Zone Books, 1991.

———. *Holy Feast and Holy Fast: The Religious Significance of Food to Medieval Women.* Berkeley and Los Angeles: University of California Press, 1987.

———. *Jesus as Mother: Studies in the Spirituality of the High Middle Ages.* Berkeley and Los Angeles: University of California Press, 1982.

Bynum, Caroline Walker, Stevan Harrell, and Paula Richman, eds. *Gender and Religion: On the Complexity of Symbols.* Boston: Beacon Press, 1986.

Byrne, Mary, Sister. *The Tradition of the Nun in Medieval England.* Washington, D.C.: The Catholic University of America, 1932.

Cadden, Joan. "It Takes All Kinds: Sexuality and Gender Differences in Hildegard of Bingen's *Book of Compound Medicine.*" *Traditio* 40 (1984): 149–74.

Caiger-Smith, A. *English Medieval Mural Paintings.* Oxford: Clarendon Press, 1963.

Calkins, Robert G. *Illuminated Books of the Middle Ages.* Ithaca, N.Y.: Cornell University Press, 1983.

Camille, Michael. *Image on the Edge: The Margins of Medieval Art.* Cambridge: Harvard University Press, 1992.

———. "Seeing and Reading: Some Visual Implications of Medieval Literacy and Illiteracy." *Art History* 43 (1985): 26–49.

Camporesi, Piero. *The Incorruptible Flesh: Bodily Mutation and Mortification in Religion and Folklore.* Translated by Tamia Croft-Murray and Helen Elsan. Cambridge: Cambridge University Press, 1988.

Cantarella, Eva. "Dangling Virgins: Myth, Ritual and the Place of Women in Ancient Greece." *Poetics Today* 6 (1985): 91–101.

Carmichael, Ann G. "Past Fasts: Medieval Saints with the Will to Starve." *Journal of Interdisciplinary History* 19 (1989): 635–44.

Carrasco, Magdalena Elizabeth. "An Early Illustrated Manuscript of the Passion of Saint Agatha (Paris, Bibl. Nat., MS lat. 5594)." *Gesta* 24 (1985): 19–32.

———. "Spirituality and Historicity in Pictorial Hagiography: Two Miracles by St. Albinus of Angers." *Art History* 12 (1989): 1–21.

———. "Spirituality in Context: The Romansque Illustrated Life of St. Radegund of Poitiers (Poiters, Bibl. Mun. MS 250)." *Art Bulletin* 72 (1990): 414–35.

Carus, Paul. *The Bride of Christ.* Chicago: Open Court Publishing, 1908.

Case, Sue-Ellen. "Re-Viewing Hrotsvit." *Theater Journal* 35 (1983): 533–42.

Cautley, H. Munro. *Norfolk Churches.* 1949. Reprint. Ipswich: Boydell Press, 1979.

Chazen, Robert. "Medieval Anti-Semitism." In *History and Hate: the Dimensions of Anti-Semitism,* edited by David Berger, 49–65. Philadelphia: Jewish Publications Society, 1986.

Clark, Elizabeth A. "Theory and Practice in Ancient Asceticism: Jerome, Chrysostom, and Augustine." *Journal of Feminist Studies in Religion* 5 (1989): 25–46.

Clemoes, Peter, ed. *Anglo-Saxon England 4.* Cambridge: Cambridge University Press, 1975.

Clopper, Lawrence M. "Florescence in the North's Tradition of Drama and Ceremony." *Fifteenth Century Studies* 9 (1986): 249–55.

Coakley, John. "Gender and the Authority of Friars: The Significance of Holy Women for Thirteenth-Century Franciscans and Dominicans." *Church History* 60 (1991): 445–60.

Cohen, Jeremy. "Robert Chazen's 'Medieval Anti-Semitism': A Note on the Impact of Theology." In *History and Hate: The Dimensions of Anti-Semitism,* edited by David Berger, 67–72. Philadelphia: Jewish Publications Society, 1986.

Coleman, Janet. *Medieval Readers and Writers, 1350–1400.* New York: Columbia University Press, 1981.

Coletti, Theresa. "Sacrament and Sacrifice in the N-Town Passion." *Mediaevalia* 7 (1981): 239–64.

Colledge, Eric. "Epistola Solitarii ad Reges: Alphonse of Pecha as Organizer of Birgittine and Urbanist Propaganda." *Mediaeval Studies* 18 (1956): 19–49.

Constable, Giles. *Attitudes toward Self-Inflicted Suffering in the Middle Ages.* Brookline, Mass.: Hellenic College Press, 1982.

———. "The Popularity of Twelfth Century Spiritual Writers in the Late Middle Ages." In *Renaissance Studies in Honor of Hans Baron,* edited by Anthony Molho and John A. Tedeschi, 3–28. Dekalb: Northern Illinois University Press, 1971.

Conway, Charles Abbott. *The Vita Christi of Ludolph of Saxony and Late Medieval Devotion Centered on the Incarnation: A Descriptive Analysis.* Analecta Cartusiana, vol. 34. Salzburg: Institut für Englische Sprache und Literatur, 1976.

Cooey, Paula M. "Experience, Body, and Authority." *Harvard Theological Review* 82 (1989): 325–42.

Craig, Hardin. *English Religious Drama of the Middle Ages.* Oxford: Clarendon Press, 1960.

Craigie, William A. "The Gospel of Nicodemus and the York Mystery Plays." In *An English Miscellany Presented to Dr. Furnivall,* edited by W. P. Ker, A. S. Napier, and W. W. Skeat, 52–61. Oxford: Clarendon Press, 1901.

Cross, P. R., and S. D. Lloyd. *Thirteenth Century England I: Proceedings of the Newcastle upon Tyne Conference.* Wolfeboro, N.H.: Boydell Press, 1986.

Cunningham, Lawrence S. "Hagiography and Imagination." *Studies in the Literary Imagination* 18 (1985): 79–87.

Davenport, W. A. *Fifteenth-Century English Drama.* Cambridge: D. S. Brewer, 1982.

Davidson, Clifford. "After the Fall: Design in the Old Testament Plays in the York Cycle." *Mediaevalia* 1 (1975): 1–24.

———. *From Creation to Doom: The York Cycle of Mystery Plays.* New York: AMS Press, 1984.

———. "Northern Spirituality and the Late Medieval Drama in York." In *The Spirituality of Western Christendom,* edited by Rozanne Elder, 125–51. Kalamazoo, Mich.: Cistercian Publications, 1976.

———. "The Realism of the York Realist and the York Passion." *Speculum* 50 (1975): 271–83.

———. "Women and the Medieval Stage." *Women's Studies* 11 (1984): 99–113.

———. ed. *A Middle English Treatise on the Playing of Miracles.* Washington, D.C.: University Press of America, 1981.

Davies, R. T. *The Corpus Christi Play of the English Middle Ages.* Totowa, N.J.: Rowman and Littlefield, 1972.

———. ed. *Medieval English Lyrics.* Chicago: Northwestern University Press, 1964.

Davis, Natalie Zemon. "Anthropology and History in the 1980's." *Journal of Interdisciplinary History* 12 (1981): 267–75.

———. "The Reasons for Misrule: Youth Groups and Charivaris in Sixteenth-Century France." *Past and Present* 50 (1971): 41–75.

———. "Some Tasks and Themes in the Study of Popular Religion." In *Pursuit of Holiness in Late Medieval and Renaissance Religion,* edited by Charles Trinkhaus and Heiko A. Oberman, 307–336. Leiden: E. J. Brill, 1974.

D'Avray, D. L. *The Preaching of the Friars: Sermons Diffused from Paris before 1300.* New York: Oxford University Press, 1985.

Debongnie, Pierre. "Essai critique sur l'Histoire des Stigmatisations au Moyen âge." *Etudes Carmelitaines* 21 (1936): 22–59.

De Ganck, Roger. "The Cistercian Nuns of Belgium in the Thirteenth Century." *Cistercian Studies* 5 (1970): 169–87.

Delaisse, L. M. J. "The Importance of Books of Hours for the History of the Medieval Book." In *Gatherings in Honor of Dorothy E. Miner,* edited by Ursula McCracken, Lillian Randall, and Richard Randall, Jr., 203–25. Baltimore: Walters Art Gallery, 1977.

Delehaye, Hippolyte. *The Legends of the Saints: An Introduction to Hagiography.* New York: Fordham University Press, 1962.

Delumeau, Jean. *Sin and Fear: The Emergence of a Western Guilt Culture, 13th–18th Centuries.* Translated by Eric Nicholson. New York: St. Martin's Press, 1990.

DeMause, Lloyd, ed. *The History of Childhood.* New York: Psychohistory Press, 1974.

Denifle, Heinrich. *Die Deutschen Mystiker des 14. Jahrhunderts.* Freiburg: Paulusverlag, 1951.

Dewar, Lindsey. "The Biblical Use of the Term 'Blood.'" *Journal of Theological Studies* 4 (1953): 204–8.

DeWelles, Theodore R. *The Social and Political Context of the Towneley Cycle.* Toronto: University of Toronto Press, 1984.

Dickman, Susan. "Margery Kempe and the Continental Tradition of the Pious Woman." In *The Medieval Mystical Tradition in England: Papers Read at Dartington Hall, July, 1984,* edited by Marion Glasscoe, 150–168. Cambridge: D. S. Brewer, 1984.

Dinzelbacher, Peter. *Vision und Visionsliteratur im Mittelalter.* Stuttgart: Anton Hiersemann, 1981.

Doob, Penelope. *Nebuchadnezzar's Children: Conventions of Madness in Middle English Literature.* New Haven: Yale University Press, 1974.

Droge, Arthur J., and James D. Tabor. *A Noble Death.* New York: Harper SanFrancisco, 1992.

DuBruck, Edelgard E. "The Death of Christ in French Passion Plays of the Late Middle Ages: Its Aspects and Sociological Implications." In *Dies Illa: Death in the Middle Ages,* edited by Jane H. M. Taylor, 81–92. Liverpool: F. Cairns, 1984.

———. ed. *New Images of Medieval Women: Essays toward a Cultural Anthropology.* Lewiston, N.J.: Edwin Mellen Press, 1989.

DuBruck, Edelgard E., and Guy Mermier, eds. *Fifteenth-Century Studies.* Ann Arbor, Mich.: University Microfilms International, 1978.

Duby, Georges. *The Knight, the Lady and the Priest: The Making of Modern Marriage in Medieval France.* Translated by Barbara Bray. New York: Pantheon Books, 1983.

Duffy, Eamon. "Holy Maydens, Holy Wyfes: The Cult of Women Saints in Fifteenth- and Sixteenth-Century England." In *Women in the Church,* edited by W. J. Sheils and Diana Wood, 175–96. Studies in Church History, vol. 27. Oxford: Basil Blackwell, 1990.

———. "Mater Dolorosa, Mater Misericordiae." *New Blackfriars* 69 (1988): 210–27.

———. *The Stripping of the Altars: Traditional Religion in England, 1400–1580.* New Haven: Yale University Press, 1992.

Duggan, Lawrence. "Was Art Really the 'Book of the Illiterate?'" *Word and Image* 5 (1989): 227–51.

Dunbar, Agnes B. C. *A Dictionary of Saintly Women.* 2 vols. London: George Bell and Sons, 1904.

Dunn, E. Catherine. "Popular Devotion in the Vernacular Drama of Medieval England." *Medievalia et Humanistica,* n.s., 4 (1973): 3–76.

Edwards, Graham Robert. "Purgatory: 'Birth' or Evolution." Review of *The Birth of Purgatory,* by Jacques Le Goff. *Journal of Ecclesiastical History* 36 (1985): 634–46.

Elliot, Alison Goddard. *Roads to Paradise: Reading the Lives of the Early Saints.* Hanover, N.H.: University Press of New England, 1988.

Ennen, Edith. *The Medieval Woman.* Translated by Edmund Jephcott. Cambridge: Basil Blackwell, 1989.

Erickson, Carolly. *The Medieval Vision: Essays in History and Perception.* New York: Oxford University Press, 1976.

Erlande-Brandenburg, Alain. *Gothic Art.* New York: Harry N. Abrams, 1983.

Evans, J. *English Art 1307–1461.* Oxford History of English Art, vol. 5. Oxford: Clarendon Press, 1949.

Ferguson, George. *Signs and Symbols in Christian Art.* New York: Oxford University Press, 1954.

Fienberg, Nona. "Thematics of Value in *The Book of Margery Kempe.*" *Modern Philology* 87 (1989): 132–41.

Finke, Laurie. "Mystical Bodies and the Dialogics of Vision." *Philological Quarterly* 67 (1988): 439–50.

Fletcher, Alan J. "The Authorship of the *Fasciculus Morum*: A Review of the Evidence of Bodleian MS Barlow 24." *Notes and Queries* 30 (1983): 205–7.

———. "The Sermon Booklets of Friar Nicholas Philip." *Medium Aevum* 55 (1986): 188–202.

Foster, Frances A. "The Mystery Plays and the Northern Passion." *Modern Language Notes* 26 (1911): 171.

Fouracre, Paul. "Merovingian History and Merovingian Hagiography." *Past and Present* 127 (1990): 3–38.

Fox, Robin Lane. *Pagans and Christians.* New York: Alfred A. Knopf, 1987.

Frame, Robin. *The Political Development of the British Isles, 1100–1400.* Oxford: Oxford University Press, 1990.

Francis, Elizabeth. "A Hitherto Unprinted Version of the *Passio Sanctae Margaritae* with Some Observations on Vernacular Derivatives." *PMLA* 42 (1927): 87–105.

Franklin, Alexander. *Seven Miracle Plays.* New York: Oxford University Press, 1963.

Freedberg, David. *The Power of Images.* Chicago: University of Chicago Press, 1989.

Furst, Lilian R., and Peter W. Graham. *Disorderly Eaters: Texts in Self-Empowerment.* University Park: Pennsylvania State University Press, 1992.

Garrett, Robert M., ed. "De Arte Lacrimandi." *Anglia* 32 (1909): 269–94.

Garth, Helen M. "Saint Mary Magdalene in Medieval Literature." *Johns Hopkins Studies in Historical and Political Science* 67 (1950): 7–114.

Geary, Patrick. "Humiliation of Saints." In *Saints and Their Cults: Studies in Religious Sociology, Folklore, and History*, edited by Stephen Wilson, 123–40. New York: Cambridge University Press, 1990.

Gerould, Gordon H. "A New Text of the *Passio S. Margaritae* with Some Account of Its Latin and English Relations." *PMLA* 39 (1924): 525–56.

———. "The North English Homily Collection: A Study of the Manuscript Relations and the Sources in the Tales." Bachelor of letters diss., Oxford University, 1902.

———. *Saints' Legends.* Boston: Houghton Mifflin Company, 1916.

Gibson, Gail McMurray. "St. Anne and the Religion of Childbed: Some East Anglian Texts and Talismans." In *Interpreting Cultural Symbols: Saint Anne in Late Medieval Society*, edited by Kathleen Ashley and Pamela Sheingorn, 95–110. Athens: University of Georgia Press, 1990.

————. *The Theater of Devotion*. Chicago: University of Chicago Press, 1989.

Girard, René. "The Gospel Passion as Victim's Story." *Cross Currents* 36 (1986): 28–38.

Glasscoe, Marion, ed. *The Medieval Mystical Tradition in England: Papers Read at Dartington Hall, July 1984*. Cambridge: D. S. Brewer, 1984.

Goodich, Michael. "Childhood and Adolescence among the Thirteenth-Century Saints." *History of Childhood Quarterly* 1 (1974): 285–309.

————. "The Contours of Female Piety in Later Medieval Hagiography." *Church History* 50 (1981): 20–32.

————. "A Profile of Thirteenth-Century Sainthood." *Comparative Studies in Society and History* 18 (1976): 429–37.

————. *Vita Perfecta: The Ideal of Sainthood in the Thirteenth Century*. Monographien zur Geschichte des Mittelalters, 25. Stuttgart: Hiesermann, 1982.

Gougaud, Louis. *Devotional and Ascetic Practices in the Middle Ages*. Translated by G. C. Bateman. London: Burns Oates and Washbourne, 1927.

Grabar, André. *Christian Iconography: A Study of Its Origins*. Princeton: Princeton University Press, 1968.

Gransden, Antonia. "A Fourteenth-Century Chronicle from the Grey Friars at Lynn." *English Historical Review* 72 (1957): 270–78.

Gravdal, Kathryn. *Ravishing Maidens: Writing Rape in Medieval French Literature and Law*. Philadelphia: University of Pennsylvania Press, 1991.

Gray, Douglas. *Themes and Images in the Medieval English Religious Lyric*. Boston: Routledge and Kegan Paul, 1972.

Greater Manchester Council, Whitworth Art Gallery. *Medieval and Early Renaissance Treasures in the N.W.* Manchester: Whitworth Art Gallery, n.d.

Gurevich, Aron. *Medieval Popular Culture: Problems of Belief and Perception*. Translated by Janos Bak and Paul Hollingsworth. Cambridge: Cambridge University Press, 1988.

Gwynn, Aubrey, S.J. *The English Austin Friars in the Time of Wyclif*. London: Oxford University Press, 1940.

Hamburger, Jeffrey. *The Rothschild Canticles: Art and Mysticism in Flanders and the Rhineland circa 1300*. New Haven: Yale University Press, 1990.

————. "The Visual and the Visionary: The Image in Late Medieval Monastic Devotions." *Viator* 20 (1989): 161–82.

Hardison, O. B. *Christian Rite and Christian Drama in the Middle Ages: Essays in the Origin and Early History of Modern Drama*. Baltimore: Johns Hopkins University Press, 1965.

Harrison, F. *Treasures of Illumination: English Manuscripts of the Fourteenth Century* (c. 1250–c. 1400). London: The Studio, 1937.

Harthan, John. *The Book of Hours*. New York: Thomas Y. Crowell, 1977.

Hartung, Albert E., ed. *A Manual of the Writings in Middle English, 1050–1500*. 5 vols. New Haven: Connecticut Academy of Arts and Sciences, 1967.

Haskell, Ann S. "The Portrayal of Women by Chaucer and His Age." In *What Manner of Women: Essays in English and American Life and Literature*, edited by Marlene Springer, 1–14. New York: New York University Press, 1977.

Head, Thomas. *Hagiography and the Cult of Saints: The Diocese of Orléans, 800–1200*. New York: Cambridge University Press, 1990.

Heer, Fredrick. *The Medieval World*. New York: New American Library, 1963.

Heffernan, Thomas J. *Sacred Biography: Saints and Their Biographers in the Middle Ages.* New York: Oxford University Press, 1988.

Hentsch, Alice A. *De la littérature didactique du moyen âge s'adressant spécialement aux femmes.* Cahors: Coueslant, 1903. Reprint. Geneva: Slatkine Reprints, 1975.

Herbert, J. A. *Illuminated Manuscripts.* New York: Burt Franklin, 1911.

Herlihy, David. "The Family and Religious Ideologies in Medieval Europe." *Journal of Family History* 12 (1987): 3–17.

Hill, Betty. "The Middle English Prose Version of the Gospel of Nicodemus from Washington, Library of Congress pre-Ac 4." *Notes and Queries* 34 (1987): 156–75.

Hilton, Rodney H. "Women Traders in Medieval England." *Women's Studies* 11 (1984): 139–55.

Hinz, Paulus. *Deus Homo.* Berlin: Evangelische Verlagsanstalt, 1981.

Hirsch, John C. "Author and Scribe in the Book of Margery Kempe." *Medium Aevum* 44 (1975): 145–50.

———. "Prayer and Meditation in Late Medieval England: MS Bodley 789." *Medium Aevum* 48 (1979): 55–66.

———. *The Revelations of Margery Kempe.* Leiden, Netherlands: E. J. Brill, 1989.

Hogg, James, ed. *The "Speculum Devotorum" of an Anonymous Carthusian of Sheen.* Analecta Cartusiana 12, 13. Salzburg: Institut für Englische Sprache und Literatur, 1973.

Holland, Norman N. *The Dynamics of Literary Response.* New York: Oxford University Press, 1968.

Holloway, Julia Bolton, Joan Bechtold, and Constance Wright, eds. *Equally in God's Image.* New York: Peter Lang Publishing, 1990.

Howard, Donald. *Writers and Pilgrims: Medieval Pilgrimage Narratives and Their Posterity.* Berkeley: University of California Press, 1980.

Hudson, Anne. *Lollards and Their Books.* London: Hambledon Press, 1985.

Hudson, Anne, and H. L. Spencer. "Old Author, New Work: The Sermons of MS Longleat 4." *Medium Aevum* 53 (1984): 220–38.

Hughes, Jonathan. *Pastors and Visionaries: Religion and Secular Life in Late Medieval Yorkshire.* Woodbridge, Suffolk: Boydell Press, 1988.

Huizinga, Johan. *The Waning of the Middle Ages: A Study of the Forms of Life, Thought and Art in France in the Netherlands in the XIVth and XVth Centuries.* Translated by F. Hopman. London: E. Arnold, 1924.

James, M. R. "Pictor in Carmine." *Archaeologia* 94 (1951): 141–66.

Jeffrey, David L. *The Early English Lyric and Franciscan Spirituality.* Lincoln: University of Nebraska Press, 1975.

———. "English Saint's Plays." In *Medieval Drama,* edited by Denny Neville, 69–90. London: Edward Arnold, 1973.

Johnson, Phyllis, and Brigitte Cazelles. *Le Vain Siecle Guerpir: A Literary Approach to Sainthood through Old French Hagiography of the Twelfth Century.* Chapel Hill: University of North Carolina Press, 1979.

Johnston, Alexandra F., and Margaret Rogerson. *York: Records of Early English Drama.* Toronto: University of Toronto Press, 1979.

Jolly, Karen Louise. "Magic, Miracle, and Popular Practice in the Early Medieval West: Anglo-Saxon England." In *Religion, Science, and Magic: In Concert and in Conflict,* edited by J. Neusner, E. Frerichs and P.V.M. Flesher, 166–82. New York: Oxford University Press, 1989.

Jones, W. R. "Lollards and Images: The Defense of Religious Art in Later Medieval England." *Journal of the History of Ideas* 34 (1973): 27–50.

Joplin, Patricia K. "The Voice of the Shuttle Is Ours." *Stanford Literary Review* (1984): 25–53.

Jungmann, Josef A. *Public Worship: A Survey*. Collegeville, Minn.: Liturgical Press, 1957.

Kahrl, Stanley J. *Traditions of Medieval English Drama*. London: Hutchinson University Library, 1974.

Kaplan, E. Ann. "Is the Gaze Male?" In *Powers of Desire: The Politics of Sexuality*, edited by Ann Snitow, Christine Stansell, and Sharon Thompson, 309–27. New York: Monthly Review Press, 1983.

Kauffmann, C. M. *Romanesque Manuscripts: 1066–1190*. London: Harvey Miller, 1975.

Kaufman, Michael W. "Spare Ribs: The Conception of Woman in the Middle Ages and the Renaissance." *Soundings* 56 (1973): 139–63.

Kealey, Edward J. *Medieval Medicus: A Social History of Anglo-Norman Medicine*. Baltimore: Johns Hopkins University Press, 1981.

Kelly, J. N. D. *Jerome: His Life, Writings, and Controversies*. London: Duckworth, 1975.

Kendon, Frank. *Mural Paintings in English Churches in the Middle Ages*. London: John Lane, 1923.

Ker, N. R. *Medieval Libraries of Great Britain*. London: Butler and Tanner, 1964.

Kidson, Peter. *The Medieval World*. New York: McGraw-Hill, 1967.

Kieckhefer, Richard. *Unquiet Souls: Fourteenth-Century Saints and Their Religious Milieu*. Chicago: University of Chicago Press, 1984.

Kolve, V. A. *The Play Called Corpus Christi*. Stanford: Stanford University Press, 1966.

Kristeva, Julia. *Tales of Love*. Translated by Leon S. Roudiez. New York: Columbia University Press, 1987.

Kupfer, Marcia. *Romanesque Wall Painting in Central France: The Politics of Narrative*. New Haven: Yale University Press, 1993.

———. "Spiritual Passage and Pictorial Strategy in the Romanesque Frescoes at Vicq." *Art Bulletin* 68 (1986): 35–53.

Lagorio, Valerie M. "Response to Laurie Finke's 'Mystical Bodies and the Dialogics of Vision.'" *Philological Quarterly* 67 (1988): 451–61.

———. "Variations on the Theme of God's Motherhood in Medieval English Mystical and Devotional Writings." *Studia Mystica* 8 (1985): 15–37.

Lane, Barbara. "'The Symbolic Crucifixion' in the Hours of Catherine of Cleves." *Oud-Holland* 86 (1973): 4–26.

Langmuir, Gavin I. "Historiographic Crucifixion." In *Les Juifs au regard de l'histoire*, edited by Gilbert Dahan, 109–27. Paris: Picard, 1985.

———. "Thomas of Monmouth: Detector of Ritual Murder." *Speculum* 59 (1984): 820–46.

———. *Toward a Definition of Antisemitism*. Berkeley and Los Angeles: University of California Press, 1990.

Lasko, P., and N. J. Morgan, eds. *Medieval Art in East Anglia, 1300–1520*. Norwich, Eng.: Jarrold and Sons, 1973.

Lavin, Marilyn Aronberg. *The Place of the Narrative: Mural Decoration in Italian Churches, 431–1600*. Chicago: University of Chicago Press, 1990.

Leach, Arthur F. "Some English Plays and Players." In *An English Miscellany Presented to Dr. Furnivall in Honour of His Seventy-Fifth Birthday*, edited by W. P. Ker, A. S. Napier, and W. W. Skeat, 205–34. Oxford: Clarendon Press, 1901.

Legge, M. D. *Anglo-Norman Literature and Its Background*. Oxford: Clarendon Press, 1963.

Le Goff, Jacques. *The Birth of Purgatory*. Translated by Alfred Goldhammer. Chicago: University of Chicago Press, 1981.

———. *The Medieval Imagination*. Translated by Arthur Goldhammer. Chicago: University of Chicago Press, 1988.

———. *La Naissance du Purgatoire*. Paris: Gallimard, 1981.

Leyerle, John. "Marriage in the Middle Ages: Introduction." *Viator* 4 (1973): 413–18.

Lochrie, Karma. *Margery Kempe and Translations of the Flesh*. Philadelphia: University of Pennsylvania Press, 1991.

Lomperis, Linda, and Sarah Stanbury, eds. *Feminist Approaches to the Body in Medieval Literature*. Philadelphia: University of Pennsylvania Press, 1993.

Louvet, M. *Purgatoire d'après les Révélations des Saints*. Albi: Imprimerie des Apprentis-Orphelins, 1899.

Lovatt, Roger. "The Imitation of Christ in Late Medieval England." *Transactions of the Royal Historical Society*, 5th ser., 18 (1968): 97–122.

Macek, Ellen. "The Emergence of a Feminine Spirituality in *The Book of Martyrs*." *Sixteenth Century Journal* 19 (1988): 63–80.

Macy, Gary. *The Theologies of the Eucharist in the Early Scholastic Period: A Study of the Salvific Function of the Sacrament according to the Theologians, 1080–1220*. New York: Oxford University Press, 1984.

Mâle, Emile. *The Gothic Image: Religious Art in France of the Thirteenth Century*. Translated by Dora Nussey. New York: Harper, 1958.

———. *Religious Art in France: The Late Middle Ages: A Study of Its Iconography and Its Sources*. Translated by Marthiel Matthews. Princeton: Princeton University Press, 1986.

Marks, Richard, and Nigel Morgan. *The Golden Age of English Manuscript Painting, 1200–1500*. New York: George Braziller, 1981.

Marrow, James H. *Passion Iconography in Northern European Art of the Late Middle Ages and Early Renaissance*. Kortrijk, Belg.: Van Ghemmert Publishing, 1979.

———, comp. *Catalogue Essays by Henri L. M. Defoer; Anne S. Korteweg; Wilhelmina C. M. Wüstefeld*. New York: George Braziller, 1990.

McDonnell, Ernest. *The Beguines and Beghards in Medieval Culture*. New Brunswick, N.J.: Rutgers University Press, 1954.

McEniery, Peter. "Pseudo-Gregory and Purgatory." *Pacifica* 1 (1988): 328–34.

McGinn, Bernard. *The Presence of God: A History of Western Christian Mysticism*. 2 vols. New York: Crossroad, 1991, 1993.

———. *Visions of the End: Apocalyptic Traditions in the Middle Ages*. New York: Columbia University Press, 1979.

McKinnon, Effie. "Notes on the Dramatic Structure of the York Cycle." *Studies in Philology* 28 (1931): 438.

McLaughlin, Eleanor C. "Christ My Mother: Feminine Naming and Metaphor in Medieval Spirituality." *Nashotah Review* 15 (1975): 228–48.

———. "Women, Power, and the Pursuit of Holiness." In *Women of Spirit: Female Leader-*

ship in the Jewish and Christian Traditions, edited by Rosemary Ruether and Eleanor McLaughlin, 100–130. New York: Simon and Schuster, 1979.

McNamara, Jo Ann. "Sexual Equality and the Cult of Virginity in Early Christian Thought." *Feminist Studies* 3 (1976): 145–58.

Meade, Dorothy. *The Medieval Church in England*. West Sussex, Eng.: Churchman Publishing, 1988.

Meille, Giovanni. *Christ's Likeness in History and Art*. London: Burns, Oates and Washbourne, 1924.

Michel, A., and M. Jugie. "Purgatoire." In *Dictionnaire de Théologie Catholique*, vol. XIII.i, cols. 1163–1357. Paris: Letouzey et Ané, 1936.

Miles, Margaret. *Image as Insight: Visual Understanding in Western Christianity and Secular Culture*. Boston: Beacon Press, 1985.

Miller, Frances H. "The Northern Passion and the Mysteries." *Modern Language Notes* 34 (1919): 88–92.

Miller, Nancy. *Subject to Change: Reading Feminist Writing*. New York: Columbia University Press, 1988.

Millett, Bella. "The Saints' Lives of the Katherine Group and the Alliterative Tradition." *Journal of English and Germanic Philology* 87 (1988): 16–34.

———. "Some Editorial Problems in the Katherine Group." *English Studies* 71 (1990): 386–94.

———. "The Textual Transmission of Seinte Juliene." *Medium Aevum* 59 (1990): 41–54.

Millett, Bella, and Jocelyn Wogan-Browne. *Medieval English Prose for Women*. Oxford: Clarendon Press, 1990.

Mollat, Michel. *The Poor in the Middle Ages*. New Haven: Yale University Press 1986.

Moorman, John. *A History of the Franciscan Order: From Its Origins to the Year 1517*. Oxford: Clarendon Press, 1968.

Morrin, Margaret J. *John Waldeby, O.S.A., c. 1315–c.1372: English Augustinian Preacher and Writer, with a Critical Edition of His Tract on the "Ave Maria."* Studia Augustiniana Historica, 2. Rome: Ed. Analecta Augustiniana, 1975.

Morris, Leon L. "The Biblical Use of the Term 'Blood.'" *Journal of Theological Studies* 3 (1952): 216–27.

Mosher, Joseph Albert. *The Exemplum in the Early Religious and Didactic Literature of England*. New York: AMS Press, 1966.

Mueller, Janel. *The Native Tongue and the Word: Developments in English Prose Style, 1380–1580*. Chicago: University of Chicago Press, 1984.

Mulvey, Laura. *Visual and Other Pleasures*. Bloomington: University of Indiana Press, 1989.

Murray, Jacqueline. "Sexuality and Spirituality: The Intersection of Medieval Theology and Medicine." *Fides et Historia* 23 (1991): 20–36.

Nabofa, M. Y. "Blood Symbolism in African Religion." *Religious Studies* 21 (1985): 389–405.

Neuss, Paula, ed. *Aspects of Early English Drama*. Cambridge: D. S. Brewer, 1983.

Newman, Barbara. *From Virile Woman to WomanChrist: Studies in Medieval Religion and Literature*. Philadelphia: University of Pennsylvania Press, 1995.

Nicholson, R. H. "The Trial of Christ the Sorcerer in the York Cycle." *Journal of Medieval and Renaissance Studies* 16 (1986): 125–69.

Nilgen, Ursula. "The Epiphany and the Eucharist: On the Interpretation of Eucharistic Motifs in Medieval Epiphany Scenes." *Art Bulletin* 49 (1967): 311–14.

Norton, Christopher, and David Park, eds. *Cistercian Art and Architecture in the British Isles.* Cambridge: Cambridge University Press, 1986.

O'Connor, Edward, ed. *Dogma of the Immaculate Conception.* Notre Dame, Ind.: Notre Dame University Press, 1958.

Ohly, Friedrich. *The Damned and the Elect: Guilt in Western Culture.* Translated by Linda Archibald. Cambridge: Cambridge University Press, 1992.

Ombres, Robert. "Latins and Greeks in Debate over Purgatory, 1230–1439." *Journal of Ecclesiastical History* 35 (1984): 1–14.

Owst, G. R. *Literature and Pulpit in Medieval England: A Neglected Chapter in the History of English Letters and of the English People.* Cambridge: Cambridge University Press, 1933.

———. *Preaching in Medieval England: An Introduction to Sermon Manuscripts of the Period c. 1350–1450.* New York: Russell and Russell, 1965.

Pächt, Otto. *The Rise of Pictorial Narrative in Twelfth-Century England.* Oxford: Clarendon Press, 1962.

Pantin, W. A. *The English Church in the Fourteenth Century.* Cambridge: Cambridge University Press, 1955.

———. "Instructions for a Devout and Literate Layman." In *Medieval Learning and Literature: Essays Presented to Richard William Hunt,* edited by J. J. G. Alexander and M. T. Gibson, 398–422. Oxford: Clarendon Press, 1976.

———. "The Monk-Solitary of Farne: A Fourteenth-Century English Mystic." *English Historical Review* 59 (1944): 162–86.

Parker, Elizabeth C. *The Descent from the Cross: Its Relation to Extra-Liturgical "Depositio" Drama.* New York: Garland, 1978.

Partner, Nancy F. "Making Up Lost Time: Writing on the Writing of History." *Speculum* 61 (1986): 90–117.

———. "'And Most of All for Inordinate Love': Desire and Denial in *The Book of Margery Kempe.*" *Thought* 64 (1989): 254–67.

Patch, Howard Rollin. *The Other World according to Descriptions in Medieval Literature.* Smith College Studies in Modern Languages, n.s. 1. Cambridge, Mass.: Harvard University Press, 1950.

Peacock, James L. "Mystics and Merchants in Fourteenth-Century Germany." *Journal for the Scientific Study of Religion* 8 (1969): 47–59.

Pelikan, Jaroslav. *The Christian Tradition: A History of the Development of Doctrine.* 4 vols. Chicago: University of Chicago Press, 1978–1984.

———. *Jesus through the Centuries.* New York: Harper and Row, 1985.

Perrin, Norman. *The New Testament.* 2d ed. New York: Harcourt Brace Jovanovich, 1982.

Petroff, E. A., ed. *Medieval Women's Visionary Literature.* New York: Oxford University Press, 1986.

Pfaff, R. W. *New Liturgical Feasts in Later Medieval England.* Oxford: Clarendon Press, 1970.

Phillips, John. *The Reformation of Images: Destruction of Art in England, 1535–1660.* Berkeley: University of California Press, 1973.

Porter, Roy. "Margery Kempe and the Meaning of Madness." *History Today* 38 (1988): 39–44.

Potter, Robert. "Divine and Human Justice." In *Aspects of Early English Drama*, edited by Paula Neuss, 129–41. Cambridge: D. S. Brewer, 1983.

———. *The English Morality Play: Origins, History and Influence of a Dramatic Tradition*. London: Routledge and Kegan Paul, 1975.

———. "The Unity of Medieval Drama: European Contexts for Early English Dramatic Traditions." In *Contexts for Early English Drama*, edited by Marianne Briscoe and John C. Coldewey, 41–55. Bloomington.: Indiana University Press, 1989.

Power, Eileen. *Medieval English Nunneries c. 1275–1535*. Cambridge: Cambridge University Press, 1922.

Price, Jocelyn. "The Liflade of Seinte Juliene and Hagiographic Convention." *Medievalia et Humanistica* 14 (1986): 37–58.

———. "La Vie de Sainte Modwenne: A Neglected Anglo-Norman Hagiographic Text, and Some Implications for English Secular Literature." *Medium Aevum* 57 (1988): 172–89.

———. "The Virgin and the Dragon: The Demonology of 'Seinte Margarete.'" *Leeds Studies in English* 16 (1985): 337–57.

Prosser, Eleanor. *Drama and Religion in the English Mystery Plays*. Stanford: Stanford University Press, 1966.

Purvis, J. S. *The York Cycle of Mystery Plays*. London: SPCK, 1957.

Raw, Barbara C. *Anglo-Saxon Crucifixion Iconography and the Art of the Monastic Revival*. New York: Cambridge University Press, 1990.

Rawlinson, Mary C. "The Sense of Suffering." *Journal of Medicine and Philosophy* 11 (1986): 39–62.

Reiss, Edmund. "The Tradition of Moses in the Underworld and the York Plays of the Transfiguration and Harrowing." *Mediaevalia* 5 (1979): 141–64.

Rickert, Margaret. *Painting in Britain: The Middle Ages*. London: Penguin Books, 1954.

Ringbom, Sixten. "Devotional Images and Imaginative Devotions: Notes on the Place of Art in Late Medieval Private Piety." *Gazette des Beaux Arts*, 6th ser., 73 (1969): 159–70.

Ringler, Siegfried. "Die Rezeption Mittelalterlicher Frauenmystik als Wissenschaftliches Problem, Dargestellt am Werk der Christine Ebner." In *Frauenmystik im Mittelalter*, edited by Peter Dinzelbacher and Dieter R. Bauer, 178–200. Ostfildern bei Stuttgart: Schwabenverlag, 1985.

Robb, David M. "The Iconography of the Annunciation in the Fourteenth and Fifteenth Centuries." *Art Bulletin* 18 (1936): 480–526.

Robertson, Elizabeth. *Early English Devotional Prose and the Female Audience*. Knoxville: University of Tennessee Press, 1990.

Rollins, Hyder E. "Notes on Some English Accounts of Miraculous Fasts." *Journal of American Folklore* 34 (1921): 357–76.

Rosenthal, Joel T. *The Purchase of Paradise*. Toronto: University of Toronto Press, 1972.

Ross, Ellen M. "Spiritual Experience and Women's Autobiography: The Rhetoric of Selfhood in 'The Book of Margery Kempe.'" *Journal of the American Academy of Religion* 59 (1991): 527–44.

———. "Suffering, the Spiritual Journey, and Women's Experience in Late Medieval Mysticism." In *Maps of Flesh and Light: Aspects of the Religious Experience of Medieval Women Mystics*, edited by Ulrike Wiethaus, 45–59. Syracuse, N.Y.: Syracuse University Press, 1993.

Ross, Susan A. "'Then Honor God in Your Body' (1 Corinthians 6:20): Feminist and Sacramental Theology of the Body." *Horizons: The Journal of the College Theology Society* 16 (1989): 7–27.

Rowland, Beryl. *Medieval Women's Guide to Health*. Kent, Ohio: Kent State University Press, 1981.

Rubin, Miri. *Charity and Community in Medieval Cambridge*. Cambridge: Cambridge University Press, 1987.

———. *Corpus Christi: The Eucharist in Late Medieval Culture*. New York: Cambridge University Press, 1992.

———. "Corpus Christi: Inventing a Feast." *History Today* 40 (1990): 15–21.

Ruether, Rosemary, and Eleanor McLaughlin, eds. *Women of Spirit: Female Leadership in the Jewish and Christian Traditions*. New York: Simon and Schuster, 1979.

Salter, Elizabeth. *English and International: Studies in the Literature, Art, and Patronage of Medieval England*. Edited by Derek Pearsall and Nicoletta Zeeman. Cambridge: Cambridge University Press, 1988.

Sanday, Peggy Reeves. *Divine Hunger: Cannibalism as a Cultural System*. Cambridge: Cambridge University Press: 1986.

Sandler, Lucy Freeman. *Gothic Manuscripts: 1285–1385*. Vol. 5 of *A Survey of Manuscripts Illuminated in the British Isles*. Oxford: Harvey Miller, 1986.

Saunders, O. Elfrida. *A History of English Art in the Middle Ages*. Oxford: Clarendon Press, 1932.

Scarry, Elaine. *The Body in Pain: The Making and Unmaking of the World*. New York: Oxford University Press, 1985.

Schapiro, Meyer. "The Image of the Disappearing Christ: The Ascension in English Art around the Year 1000." *Gazette des Beaux Arts*, 6th ser., 23 (1943): 135–52.

Schiller, Gertrud. *Iconography of Christian Art*. Translated by Janet Seligman. Greenwich, Conn.: New York Graphic Society, 1971.

———. *Ikonographie der christlichen Kunst*. 4 vols. Gütersloh: Humphries, 1971–1972.

Schirmer, Walter F. *John Lydgate: A Study in the Culture of the Fifteenth Century*. Translated by Ann E. Kelp. London: Methuen, 1961.

Schneider, Robert A. "Mortification on Parade: Penitential Processions in Sixteenth- and Seventeenth-Century France." *Renaissance and Reformation* 10 (1985): 123–46.

Schrader, J. L. *The Waning Middle Ages: An Exhibition: The University of Kansas Museum of Art, Nov.–Dec. 1969*. New York: French, 1969.

Scott, Joan W. "Gender: A Useful Category of Historical Analysis." *American Historical Review* 91 (1986): 1053–75.

Shaw, Graham. *The Cost of Authority: Manipulation and Freedom in the New Testament*. Philadelphia: Fortress Press, 1983.

Sheils, W. J., ed. *The Church and Healing: Papers Read at the XXth Summer Meeting and the XXIst Winter Meeting of the Ecclesiastical History Society*. Oxford: Basil Blackwell, 1982.

Sheingorn, Pamela. *The Easter Sepulchre in England*. Early Drama, Art and Music Reference Series, no. 5. Kalamazoo: Medieval Institute Publications, 1987.

———. "The Moment of Resurrection in the Corpus Christi Plays." *Medievalia et Humanistica*, n.s., 11 (1982): 111–29.

———. "The Visual Language of Drama: Principles of Composition." In *Contexts for*

Early English Drama, edited by Marianne Briscoe and John C. Coldewey, 173–91. Bloomington: Indiana University Press, 1989.

Shorr, Dorothy C. *The Christ Child in Devotional Images in Italy during the XIV Century.* New York: George Wittenborn, 1954.

Simons, W., and J. E. Ziegler. "Phenomenal Religion in the Thirteenth Century and Its Image: Elisabeth of Spalbeeck and the Passion Cult." In *Women in the Church*, edited by W. J. Sheils and Diana Wood, 117–26. Oxford: Basil Blackwell, 1990.

Siraisi, Nancy G. *Medieval and Early Renaissance Medicine.* Chicago: University of Chicago Press, 1990.

Smith, David. "Aspects of the Interrelationship of Divine and Human Bodies in Hinduism." *Religion* 19 (1989): 211–19.

Smith, Julia M. H. "Oral and Written: Saints, Miracles, and Relics in Brittany, c. 850–1250." *Speculum* 65 (1990): 309–43.

Snyder, James. *Medieval Art: Painting, Sculpture, Architecture: 4th–14th Centuries.* Englewood Cliffs, N.J.: Prentice-Hall, 1989.

Southern, Richard. *Western Views of Islam in the Middle Ages.* Cambridge: Harvard University Press, 1962.

Spencer, H. Leith. *English Preaching in the Late Middle Ages.* Oxford: Clarendon Press, 1993.

Spiegel, Shalom. *The Last Trial.* New York: Behrman House, 1967.

Steele, Francesca M. *The Life of St. Walburga.* St. Louis, Mo.: B. Herder, 1921.

Stemmler, Theo. *Liturgische Feiern und geistliche Spiele.* Tübingen: Max Niemeyer Verlag, 1970.

Stevens, Martin. *Four Middle English Mystery Cycles: Textual, Contextual and Critical Interpretations.* Princeton: Princeton University Press, 1987.

———. "The Intertextuality of Late Medieval Art and Drama." *New Literary History* 22 (1991): 317–37.

Stroumsa, Gedaliahu G. "*Caro salutis cardo*: Shaping the Person in Early Christian Thought." *History of Religions* 30 (1990): 25–50.

Sullivan, Lawrence E. "Body Works: Knowledge of the Body in the Study of Religion." *History of Religions* 30 (1990): 86–99.

Swanson, R. W. *Church and Society in Late Medieval England.* New York: Basil Blackwell, 1989.

Swarzenski, Hanns. *Monuments of Romanesque Art: The Art of Church Treasures in North-Western Europe.* Chicago: University of Chicago Press, 1974.

Tammi, D. Guido. *Due Versioni della Leggenda di Santa Margherita d'Antiocha.* Piacenza: Scuola Aritigiana dal Libro, 1958.

Tanner, Norman P. *The Church in Late Medieval Norwich, 1370–1532.* Toronto: Pontifical Institute of Medieval Studies, 1984.

———. ed. *Heresy Trials in the Diocese of Norwich, 1428–1431.* London: Butler and Tanner, 1977.

Taylor, Henry Osborn. *The Medieval Mind: A History of the Development of Thought and Emotion in the Middle Ages.* 2 vols., 4th ed. Cambridge, Mass.: Harvard University Press, 1962.

Tentler, Thomas N. *Sin and Confession on the Eve of the Reformation.* Princeton: Princeton University Press, 1977.

Thomas, Marcel. *The Golden Age: Manuscript Painting at the Time of Jean, Duke of Berry.* New York: George Braziller, 1979.

Thompson, A. Hamilton. *The English Clergy and Their Organization in the Later Middle Ages.* Oxford: Clarendon Press, 1947.

Thompson, E. Margaret. *The Carthusian Order in England.* New York: Macmillan, 1930.

Thurston, Herbert. *The Physical Phenomena of Mysticism.* Chicago: Regnery, 1952.

Tristram, Ernest William. *English Wall Painting of the Fourteenth Century.* Edited by Eileen Tristram. London: Routledge and Kegan Paul, 1955.

Trotzig, Brigitta. "The Crucified, He Whom I Saw: Brigid of Sweden." *Cross Currents* 35 (1985): 294–305.

Tubach, Frederic C. *Index Exemplorum: A Handbook of Medieval Religious Tales.* Helsinki: Finnish Academy of Sciences and Letters, 1969.

Tydeman, William. *The Theatre in the Middle Ages.* New York: Cambridge University Press, 1978.

Vauchez, André. *The Laity in the Middle Ages: Religious Beliefs and Devotional Practices.* Edited by Daniel E. Bornstein. Notre Dame, Ind.: University of Notre Dame Press, 1993.

———. *La Sainteté en Occident aux Derniers Siècles du Moyen Age: d'après les Procès de Canonisation et les Documents Hagiographiques.* Rome: École Française de Rome, 1988.

Vloberg, Maurice. "The Iconography of the Immaculate Conception." In *The Dogma of the Immaculate Conception: History and Significance,* edited by Edward Dennis O'Connor, 463–50. Notre Dame, Ind.: University of Notre Dame Press, 1958.

Vriend, J. *The Blessed Virgin Mary in the Medieval Drama of England.* Purmerend, Holl.: J. Muusses, 1928.

Wakelin, M. F. "A New Vernacular Version of a Nun's Profession." *Notes and Queries* 31 (1984): 459–61.

Wallace, Mark I. *Fragments of the Spirit: Nature, Violence, and the Renewal of Creation.* New York: Continuum, 1996.

Ward, Benedicta. *Miracles and the Medieval Mind: Theory, Record and Event, 1000–1215.* Philadelphia: University of Pennsylvania Press, 1982.

Warren, Ann K. *Anchorites and Their Patrons in Medieval England.* Berkeley: University of California Press, 1985.

Watkins, Renée. "Two Women Visionaries and Death: Catherine of Siena and Julian of Norwich." *Numen* 30 (1983): 174–98.

Watson, Andrew G., ed. *Medieval Libraries of Great Britain: Supplement to the Second Edition.* London: Offices of the Royal Historical Society, 1987.

Watson, Nicholas. "The Composition of Julian of Norwich's *Revelation of Love.*" *Speculum* 68 (1993): 637–83.

Wenzel, Siegfried. *Verses in Sermons: Fasciculus Morum and Its Middle English Poems.* Cambridge, Mass.: Mediaeval Academy of America, 1978.

———, ed. and trans. *Fasciculus Morum: A Fourteenth-Century Preacher's Handbook.* University Park: Pennsylvania State University Press, 1989.

Wickham, Glynne. *The Medieval Theatre.* New York: St. Martin's Press, 1974.

Wieck, Roger S. *Time Sanctified: The Book of Hours in Medieval Art and Life.* New York: George Braziller, 1988.

Wiethaus, Ulrike. "Suffering, Love, and Transformation in Mechthild of Magdeburg." *Listening* 22 (1987): 139–50.

———, ed. *Maps of Flesh and Light: The Religious Experience of Medieval Women Mystics.* New York: Syracuse University Press, 1993.

Wittig, Joseph. "Figural Narrative in Cynewulf's *Juliana.*" In *Anglo Saxon England 4*, edited by Peter Clemoes, 37–55. Cambridge: Cambridge University Press, 1975.

Wolpers, Theodor. *Die Englische Heiligenlegende des Mittelalters.* Tübingen: Max Niemeyer Verlag, 1964.

Wood, Charles T. "The Doctor's Dilemma: Sin, Salvation and the Menstrual Cycle in Medieval Thought." *Speculum* 56 (1981): 710–27.

Woolf, Rosemary. *The English Mystery Plays.* London: Routledge and Kegan Paul, 1972.

———. *The English Religious Lyric in the Middle Ages.* Oxford: Clarendon Press, 1968.

———. "Saints' Lives." In *Continuations and Beginnings: Studies in Old English Literature*, edited by E. G. Stanley, 37–66. London: Nelson, 1966.

Wrider, Anne J. "Water, Fire, and Blood: Defilement and Purification from a Ricoeurian Perspective." *Anglican Theological Review* 67 (1985): 137–48.

Wyschogrod, Edith. *Saints and Postmodernism: Revisioning Moral Philosophy.* Chicago: University of Chicago Press, 1990.

Zaleski, Carol G. "St. Patrick's Purgatory: Pilgrimage Motifs in a Medieval Otherworld Vision." *Journal of the History of Ideas* 46 (1985): 467–85.

Zeeman, Elizabeth. "Nicholas Love: A Fifteenth-Century Translator." *Review of English Studies*, n.s., 6 (1955): 113–27.

Ziegler, Johanna. *Sculpture of Compassion: The Pietà and the Beguines in the Southern Low Countries, c. 1300–c. 1600.* Rome: Academia Belgica, 1992.

Zika, Charles. "Hosts, Processions and Pilgrimages: Controlling the Sacred in Fifteenth-Century Germany." *Past and Present* 118 (1988): 25–64.

Index